I0812748

The Campus History Series

NORTHERN KENTUCKY UNIVERSITY

On The Cover: This photograph was taken from the balcony of the Pompilio House showing the crowds gathered for the groundbreaking ceremony at the new Highland Heights campus. Classes at the Covington campus were cancelled so that students could attend the ceremony. Standing room was allotted to 10 area high school bands, several of which can be seen in the background. This location is now the beginning of Nunn Drive and the front entrance of the university.

The Campus History Series

NORTHERN KENTUCKY UNIVERSITY

JENNIFER GREGORY

ARCADIA PUBLISHING

Copyright © 2006 by Jennifer Gregory
ISBN 0-7385-4316-0

Published by Arcadia Publishing
Charleston SC, Chicago IL, Portsmouth NH, San Francisco CA

Printed in the United States of America

Library of Congress Catalog Card Number: 2006926327

For all general information contact Arcadia Publishing at:
Telephone 843-853-2070
Fax 843-853-0044
E-mail sales@arcadiapublishing.com
For customer service and orders:
Toll-Free 1-888-313-2665

Visit us on the Internet at www.arcadiapublishing.com

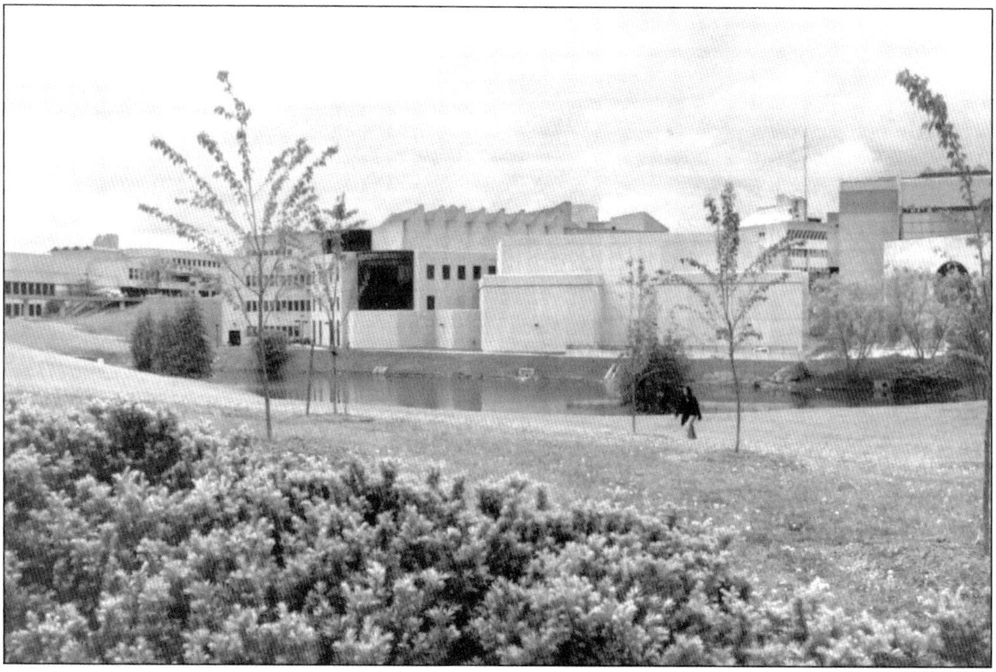

This is a view of the campus across Lake Inferior. The name of the campus lake was chosen by students in a contest run by the student newspaper, *The Northerner*. In 2006, renovation work was completed that expanded the size of the lake and added waterfalls and a bridge. Another contest was held to rename the lake. This time, submissions were narrowed to a list of six possibilities for voting, and the winner, Loch Norse, was announced at the lake dedication ceremony on September 6, 2006.

Contents

ACKNOWLEDGMENTS

I would like to offer my deepest gratitude to all of the faculty and staff at Northern Kentucky University who assisted me in locating and identifying photographs or otherwise contributed to the successful completion of this book. I want to convey special thanks to NKU's campus photographer, Joe Ruh, and his colleagues for their patient and helpful assistance in making sense of the university's photograph collections.

Projects of this sort are extremely time consuming and somewhat stressful, and I want to thank my husband, Michael, for helping minimize both the time and stress. It is often handy to have another librarian in the family, and his help sped things up greatly. Bringing me dinner at work and constantly telling me "it will all be okay" were also greater contributions than one might think.

Finally, no acknowledgement of those who helped make this book possible would be complete without recognizing the founders of Northern Kentucky University and the ensuing administrators, professors, and staff who maintain NKU as a vital and respected part of the community. In short, my thanks to everyone who has made the university a place worth writing about.

INTRODUCTION

Northern Kentucky University's roots are tied in with two other organizations—the University of Kentucky and the YMCA's nighttime law school. In the 1940s, there were no schools of higher education in the fast-growing region of Northern Kentucky. Residents had to attend classes in Cincinnati, Ohio, on the other side of the river and pay out-of-state tuition, or they had to move elsewhere in the state. While local residents may commute to Lexington or Louisville for graduate-level night courses now, this simply wasn't even a possibility before the development of the interstate highway system.

In 1948, the University of Kentucky announced its plan to change the woeful state of affairs in the northernmost region of the commonwealth. Until recently, the University of Kentucky headed the community college system in Kentucky, spawning new campuses as needed. On April 1, 1948, the officers made it clear that another branch campus was in the offing in Covington. For the first time, higher education would be available to northern residents. That fall, the plan became a reality, and the new Northern Extension Center of the University of Kentucky, often known simply as "the Northern Center," opened its doors to students. The school became a feeder for the main campus in Lexington, funneling students south to complete the final two years of a bachelor's degree.

The other school that would eventually become pivotal to the founding of Northern Kentucky University was the night law school at the YMCA across the river in Cincinnati. Forced by the necessity of accreditation to merge with a four-year college, the newly named Salmon P. Chase College of Law brought the first graduate-level program to Northern, smoothing the rough road of accreditation for the new campus and paving the way for future graduate programs at NKU.

One

The University of Kentucky, Northern Center

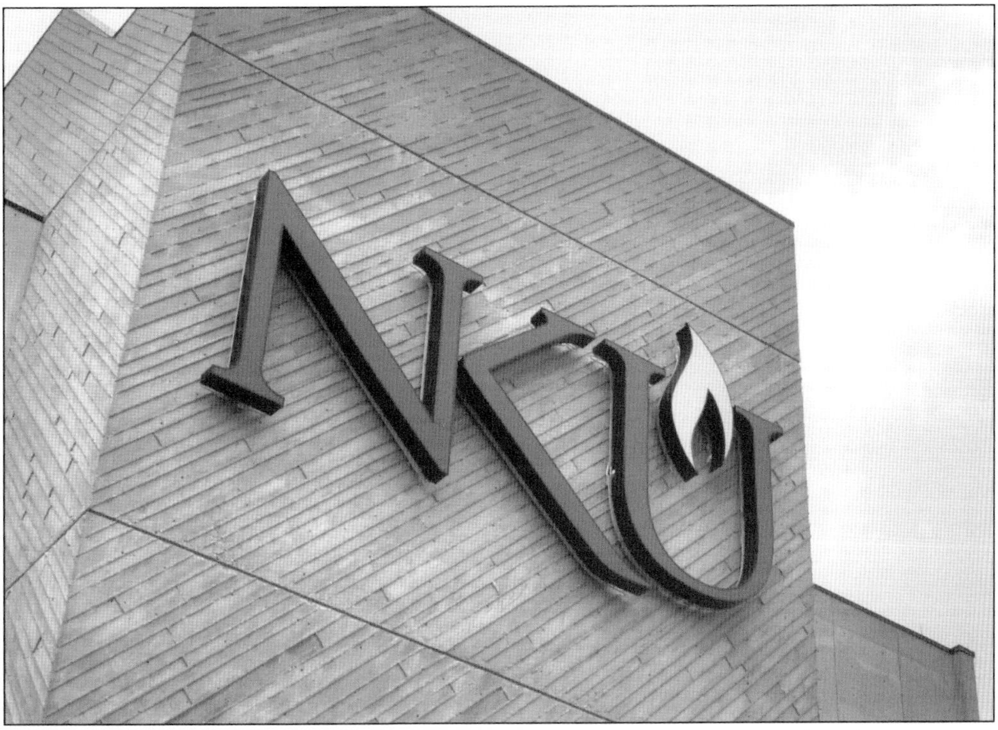

Building the current Northern Kentucky University was a long road not only for administrators, faculty, and staff, but also for local residents who had a dream for higher education in the rapidly growing Northern Kentucky region. The university actually has its origins in another institution: the feeder campus built by the University of Kentucky, the Northern Center.

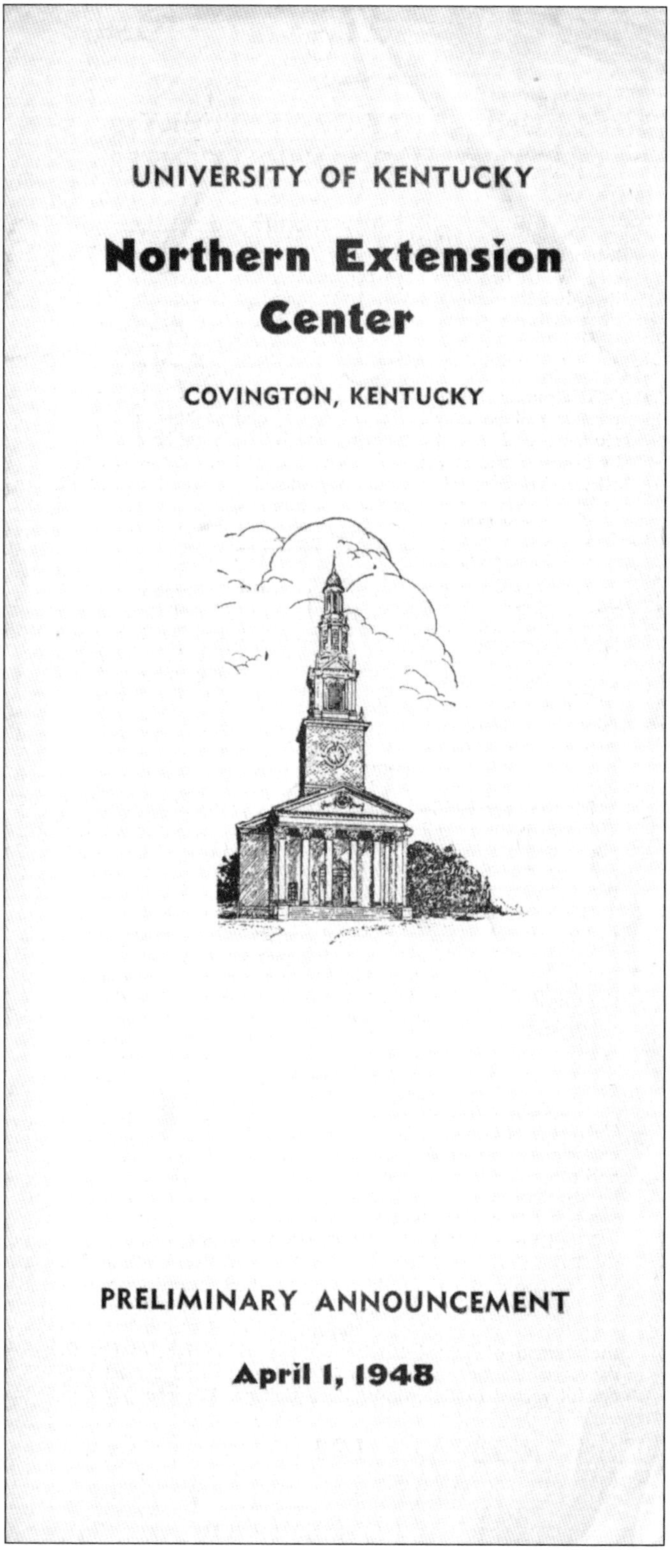
UNIVERSITY OF KENTUCKY

Northern Extension Center

COVINGTON, KENTUCKY

PRELIMINARY ANNOUNCEMENT

April 1, 1948

This is the pamphlet announcing the new branch campus in Northern Kentucky. Under the leadership of university president H. L. Donovan, the University of Kentucky would now offer northern residents the full freshman-year class load, including courses in history, math, science, English, and a foreign language. Full-time, in-state tuition was $57 a semester, while part-time students paid $5 for each credit hour. The pamphlets were distributed with an attached reply card, as it was necessary to make immediate arrangements to start in the fall. For the next few months, questions had to be directed to Lexington, but potential students were promised that an administrator, Dr. W. C. Wesley, the newly named director of the center, would be in an office at the local elementary school by the first of July and available to assist them in getting registered. (Courtesy of Publishing Department, University of Kentucky.)

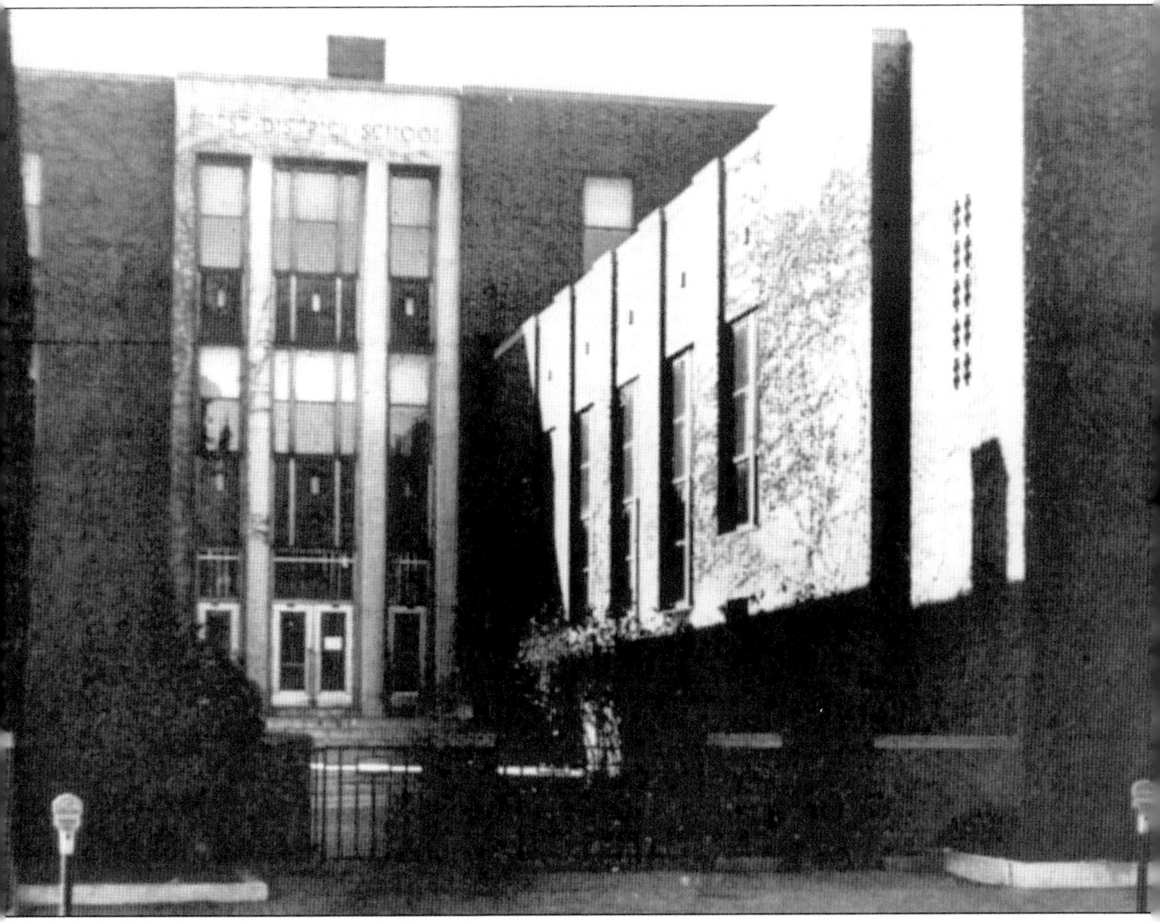

Through arrangements with the Covington Board of Education, the new community college branch of the University of Kentucky, the Northern Extension Center, opened for classes on the top floor of the First District Elementary School on the corner of Sixth and Scott Streets in downtown Covington. The school also housed the student organizations, which quickly sprang up, and the faculty and staff offices. As there were no proper science classrooms in an elementary school, science classes were held at Covington's Holmes High School, which was located across town. The center also utilized facilities at the local YMCA, as well as hosting student activities in Devou Park and other nearby locations. (Courtesy of Publishing Department, University of Kentucky.)

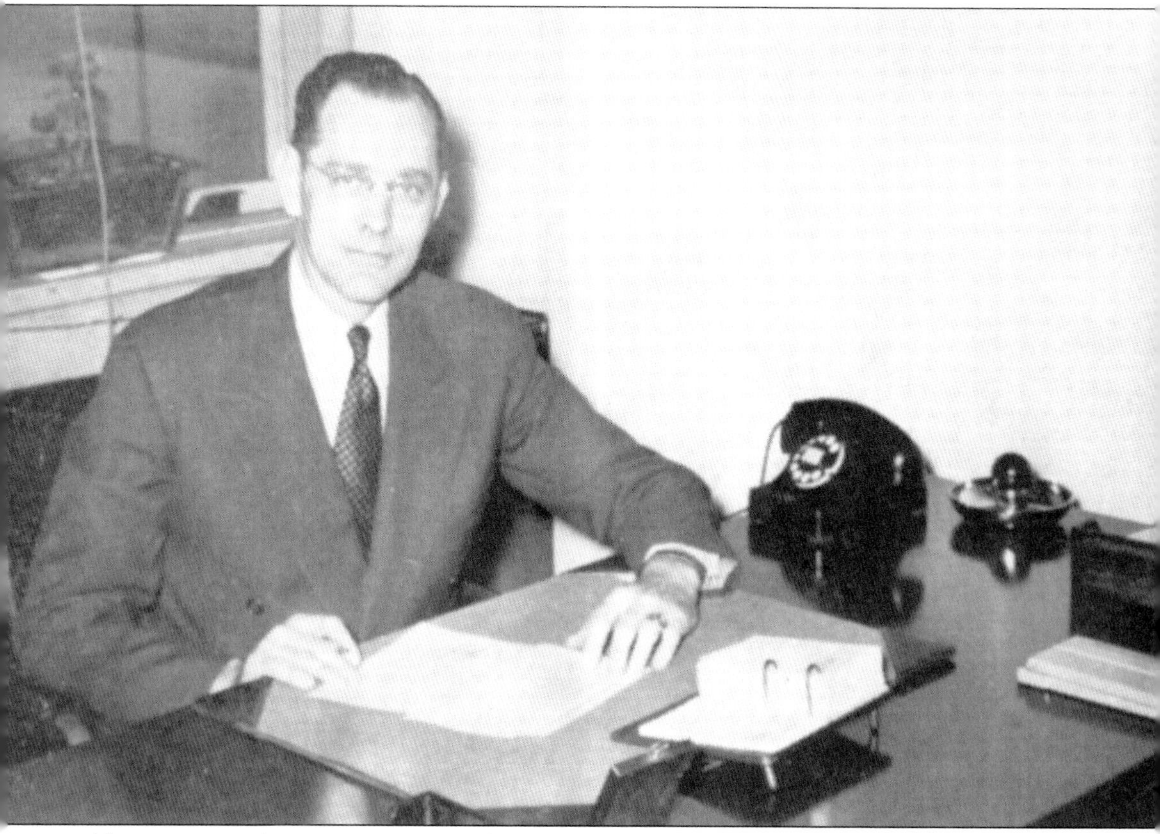

Thomas L. Hankins soon took over from Dr. W. C. Wesley at the end of the first year as the director of the Northern Extension Center, later Northern Community College. He remained in this position until shortly before the college was merged into the new Northern Kentucky State College. While Wesley had gotten things off the ground, Hankins had the unenviable task of building up an entirely new branch campus scattered across three different facilities located in different parts of Covington, Kentucky. In 1974, the one permanent building built for the Northern Center was named Hankins Hall in his honor. (Courtesy of Publishing Department, University of Kentucky.)

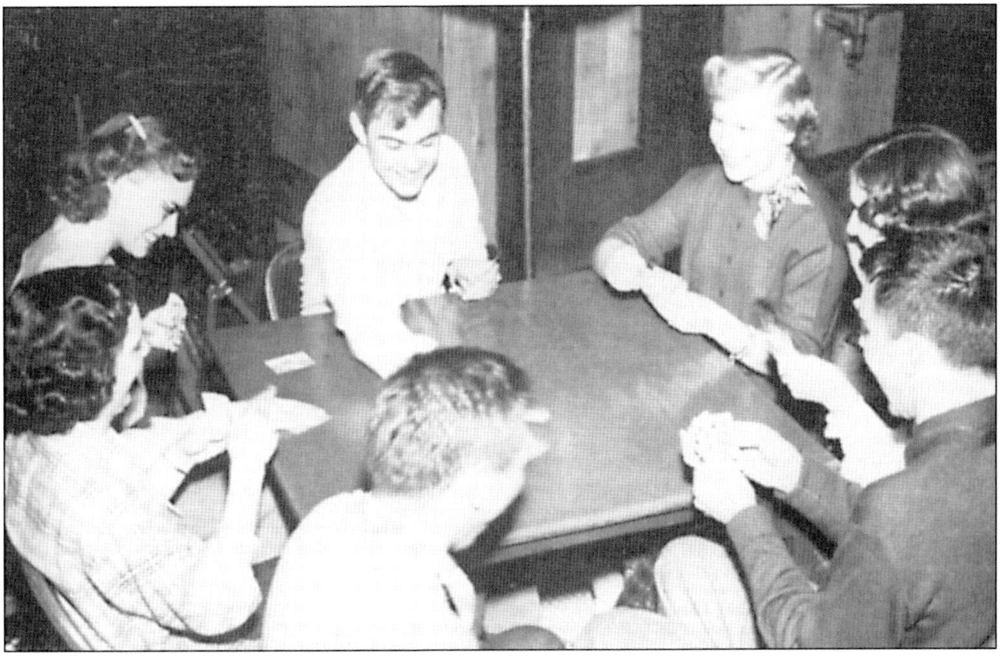

The average elementary school building falls well short of the recreational facilities of the average college campus. The First District School building was no different. The University of Kentucky made agreements with the Covington YMCA in order to make the facilities at the YMCA available to their Northern Center students. The students took full advantage of this option, using the YMCA as a kind of student center as well as recreational and athletic center. The students above are playing cards around a table at the YMCA. Those in the photograph below enjoy the YMCA's swimming pool, the site of a number of student swim parties. (Courtesy of Publishing Department, University of Kentucky.)

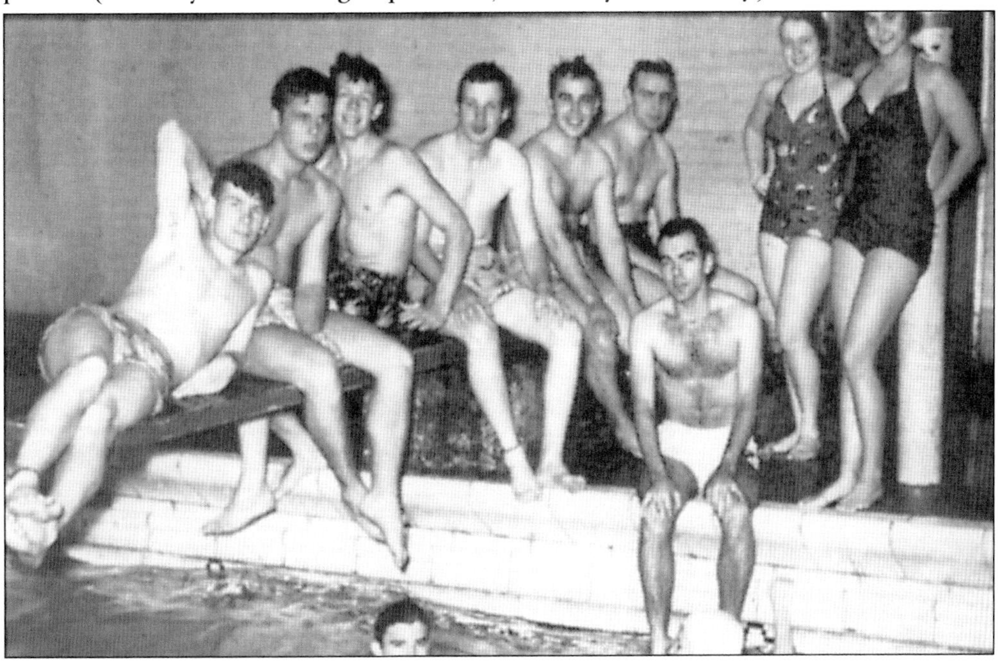

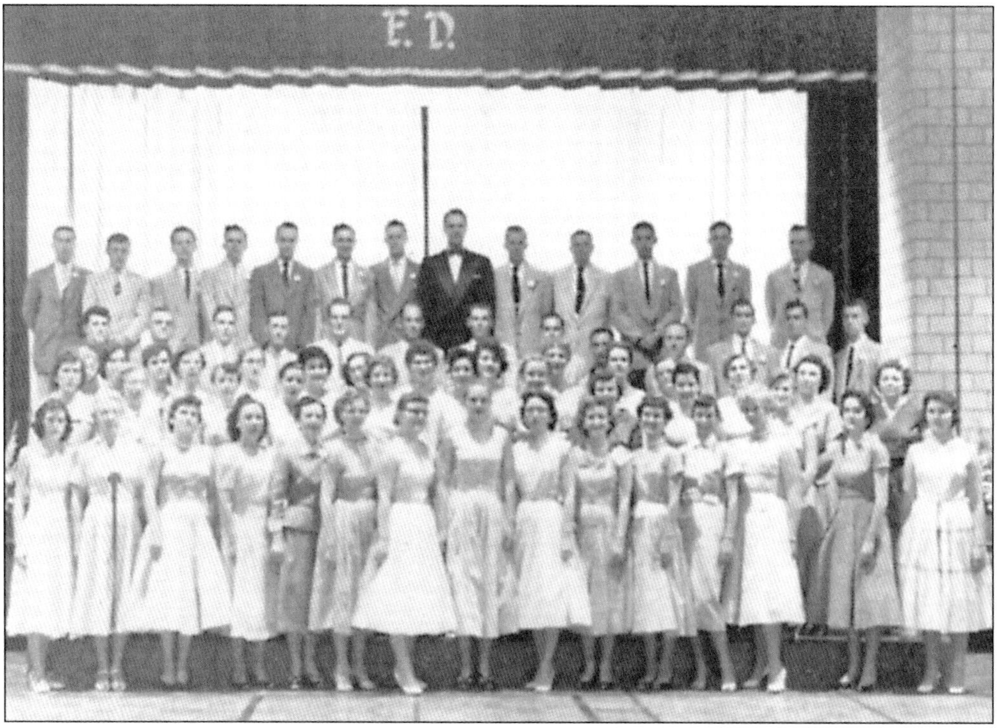

The Northern Center's Mixed Chorus is shown on the stage at the First District Elementary School. While some recreational and student activities took place in the elementary school building, the community college contracted with the nearby YMCA to provide students with facilities such as a swimming pool. Student organizations also used other nearby recreational locations such as Devou Park for events such as class picnics. (Courtesy of Publishing Department, University of Kentucky.)

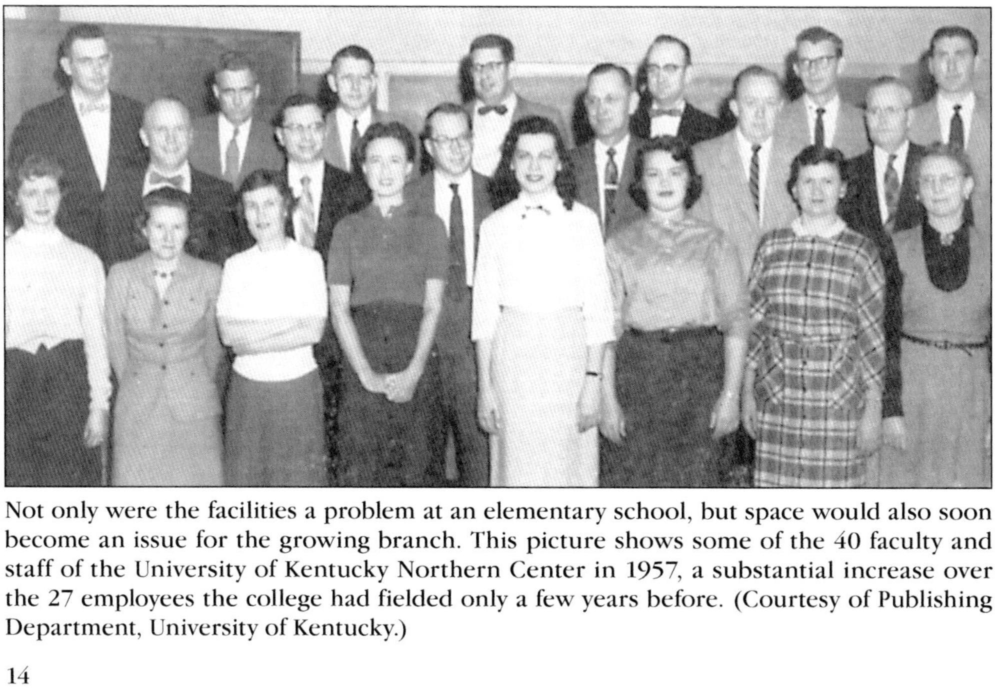

Not only were the facilities a problem at an elementary school, but space would also soon become an issue for the growing branch. This picture shows some of the 40 faculty and staff of the University of Kentucky Northern Center in 1957, a substantial increase over the 27 employees the college had fielded only a few years before. (Courtesy of Publishing Department, University of Kentucky.)

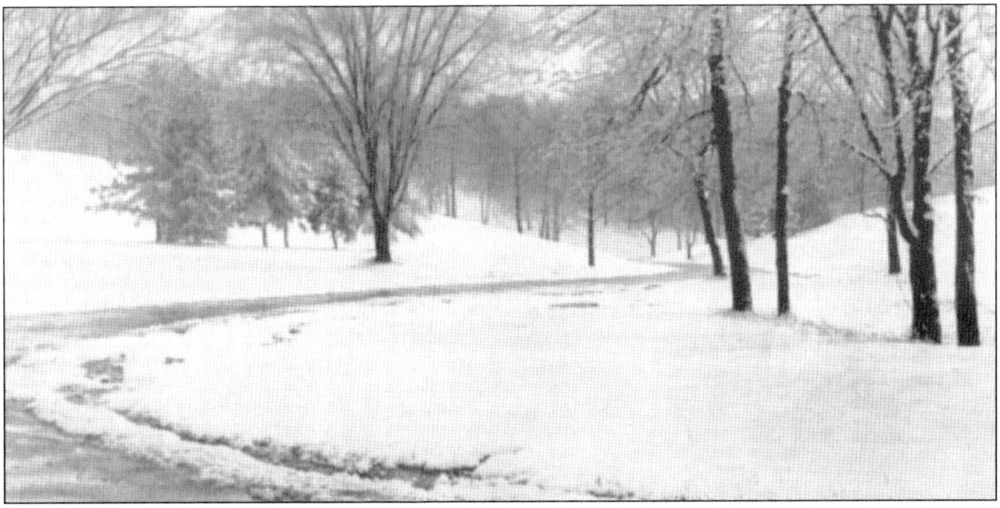

This pleasant winter landscape shows part of the 44-acre tract attached to Covington's Devou Park, where the University of Kentucky would build its new campus. The building that became the permanent home of the Northern Center was later named for the center's director, Thomas L. Hankins. (Courtesy of Publishing Department, University of Kentucky.)

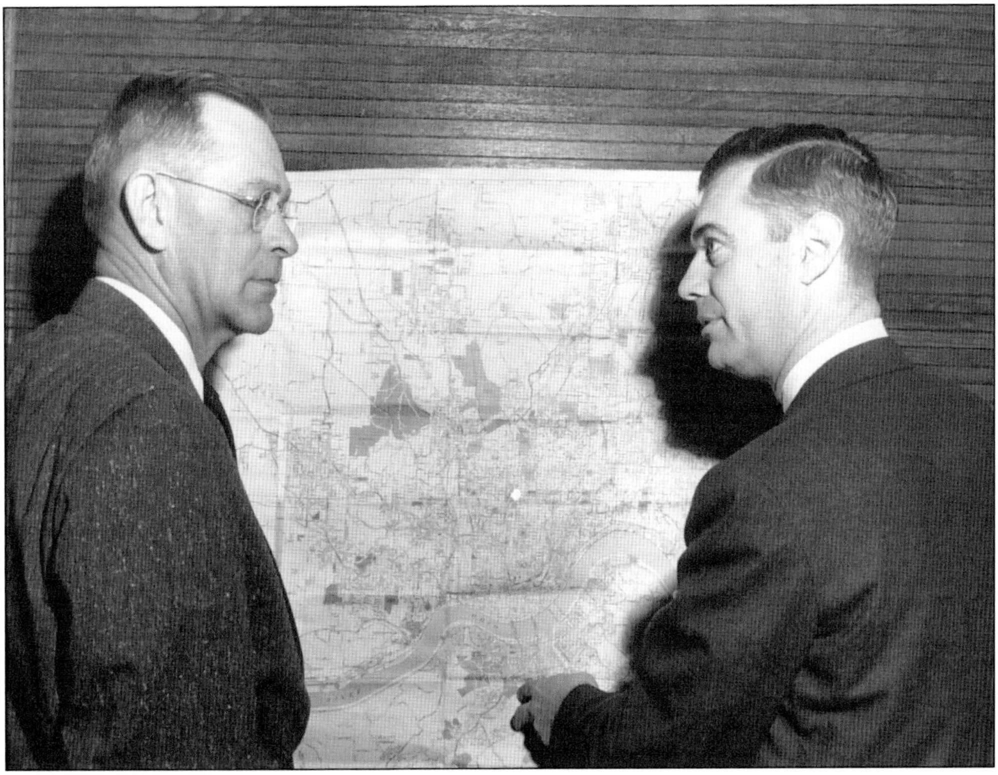

Northern Center director Thomas L. Hankins (left) and University of Kentucky president Frank G. Dickey discuss the proposed Covington site for the community college campus. The site was located on a hilltop near Dixie Highway, a major local thoroughfare. Heavily wooded, the winding drive to the top ends at the parking lot and a stunning view of the Ohio River and the Cincinnati skyline. (Courtesy of Publishing Department, University of Kentucky.)

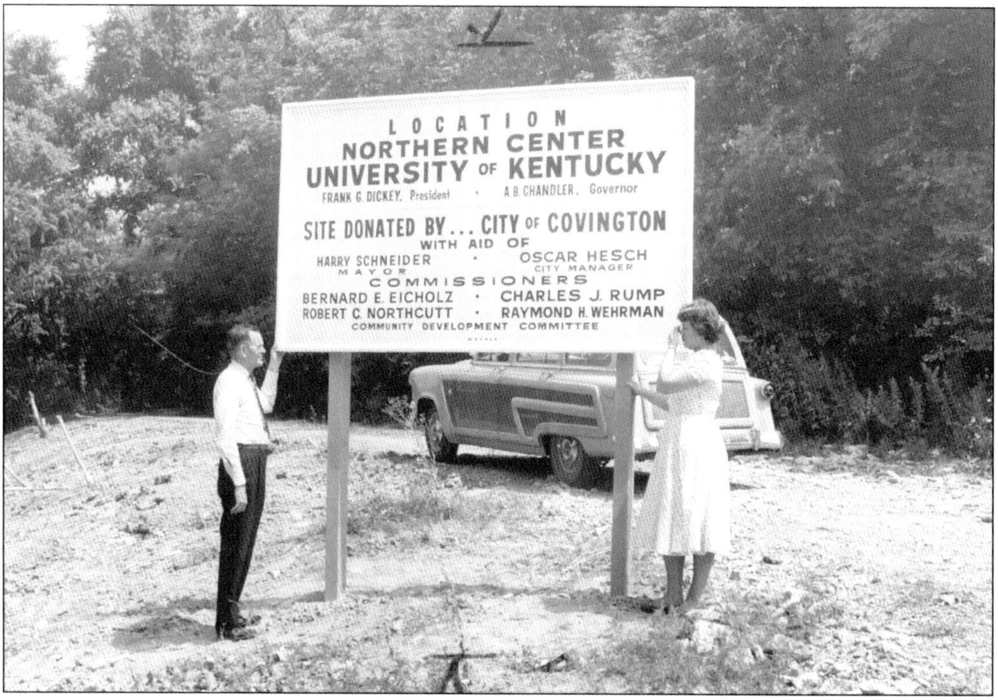

As work is ready to begin on the new campus in Covington, Thomas L. Hankins, director of the Northern Center, and Ruth Webb, the center's librarian, are pictured next to the large announcement sign at the construction site. (Courtesy of Publishing Department, University of Kentucky.)

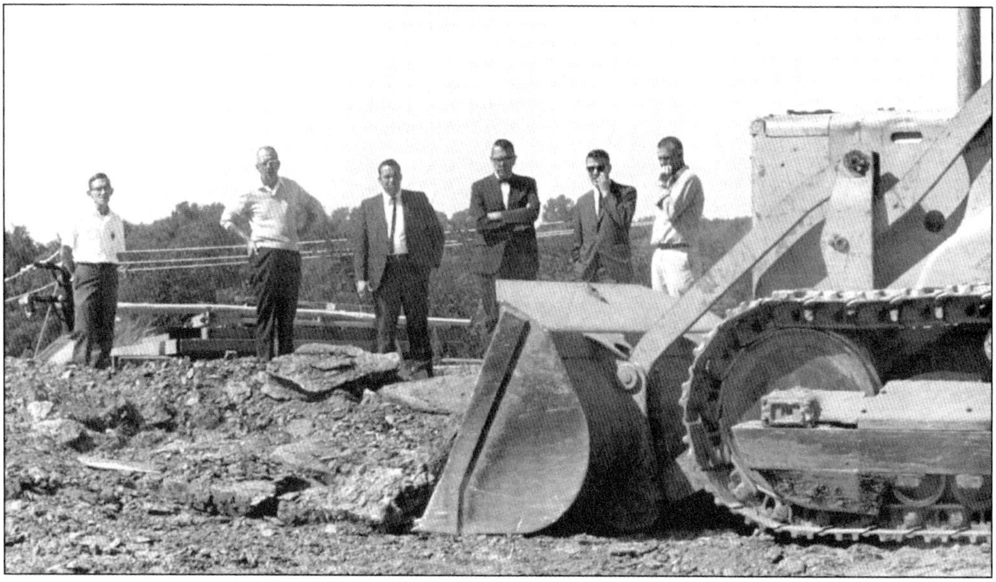

While groundbreakings are common at NKU, this rarely seen photograph shows the groundbreaking for the Northern Center's first (and only) permanent building at the new Covington campus. The center would be merged into Northern Kentucky State College before any other buildings could be added. (Courtesy of Publishing Department, University of Kentucky.)

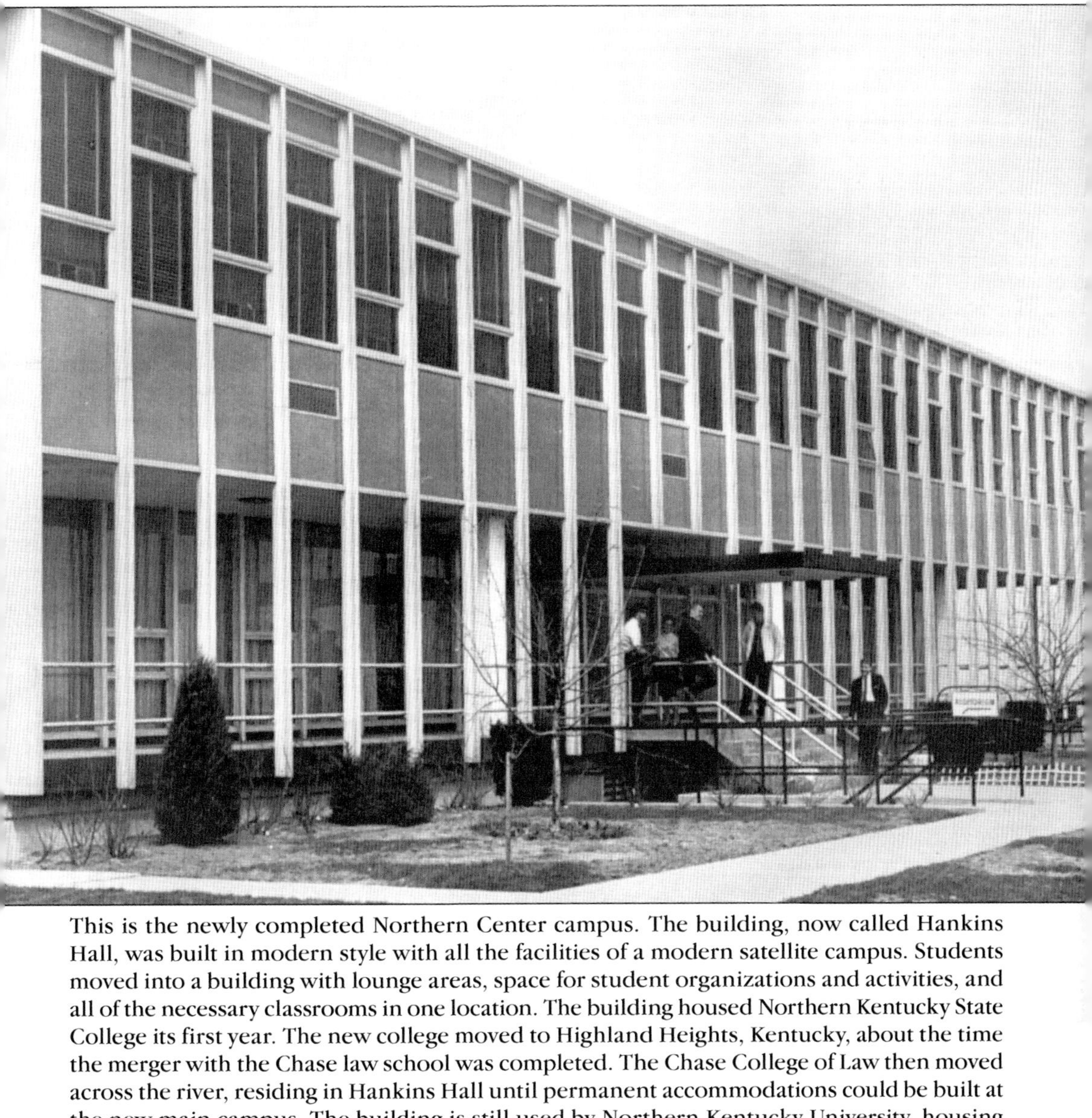

This is the newly completed Northern Center campus. The building, now called Hankins Hall, was built in modern style with all the facilities of a modern satellite campus. Students moved into a building with lounge areas, space for student organizations and activities, and all of the necessary classrooms in one location. The building housed Northern Kentucky State College its first year. The new college moved to Highland Heights, Kentucky, about the time the merger with the Chase law school was completed. The Chase College of Law then moved across the river, residing in Hankins Hall until permanent accommodations could be built at the new main campus. The building is still used by Northern Kentucky University, housing many distance- and community-education programs. (Courtesy of Publishing Department, University of Kentucky.)

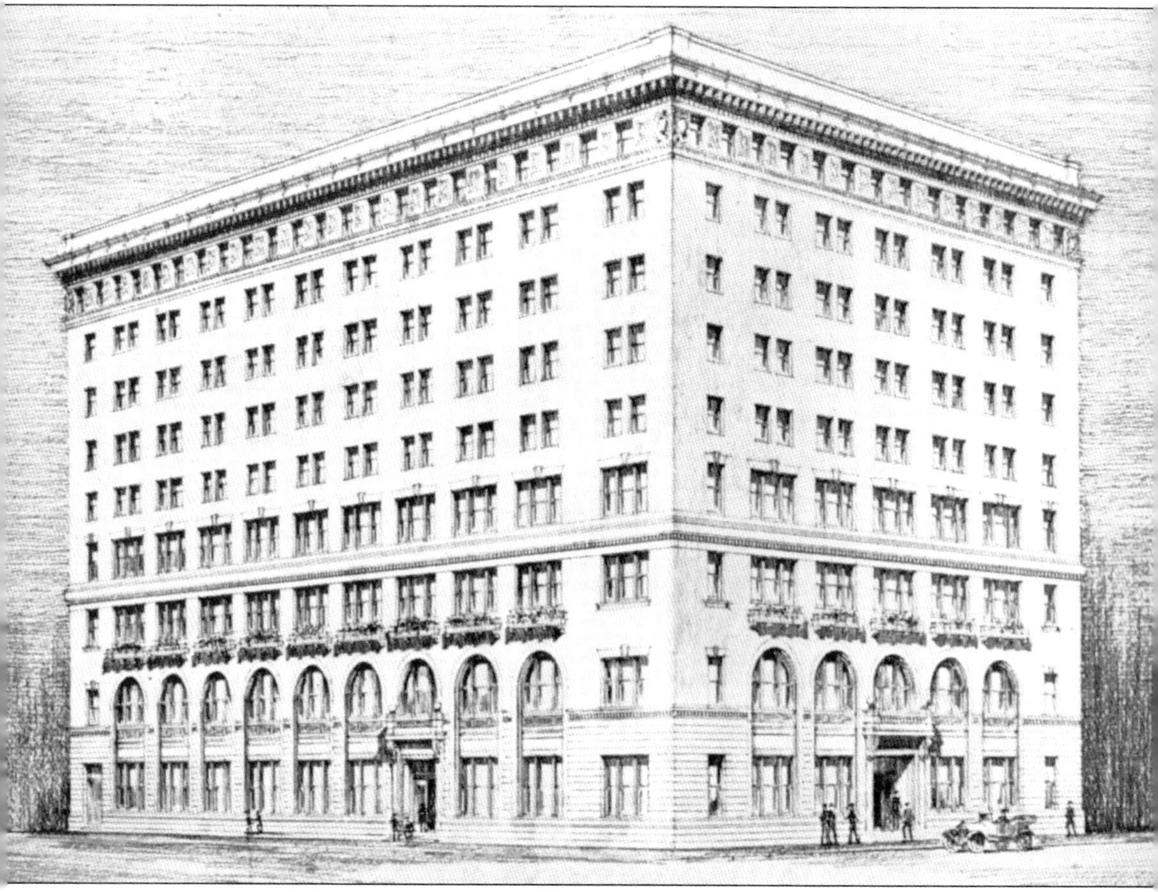

The Chase College of Law began as an affiliate of the YMCA, at one time operating under the name Young Men's Christian Association Night Law School. From its inception, the law school was housed on the top floors of the YMCA building in downtown Cincinnati, with the pool and gyms on the lower floors. In the 1960s, the law accreditation organization ordered the school to affiliate with a four-year college. This order led to the eventual merger of Chase with the new Northern Kentucky State College and the law school's move across the Ohio River.

Two

The Steely Era and the Birth of Northern Kentucky State College

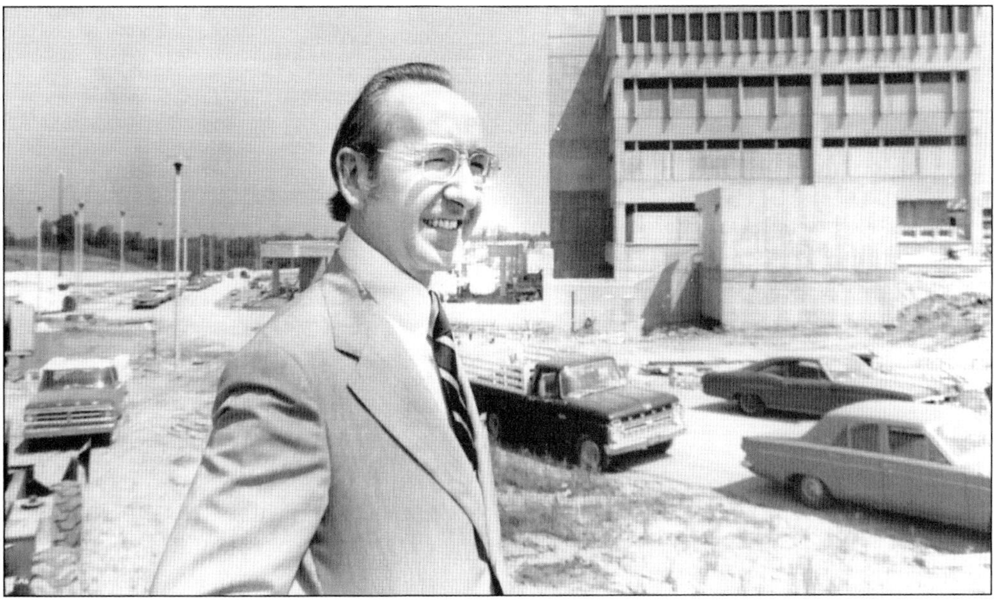

Dr. W. Frank Steely, first president of Northern Kentucky State College (NKSC), walks about campus in 1972. He surveys the campus he has built from scratch and appears pleased with the progress. Though at this time the campus was still too small for the needs of the college, Steely had every right to be proud of what had been accomplished. Just a few short years before, the thriving college had existed in name only.

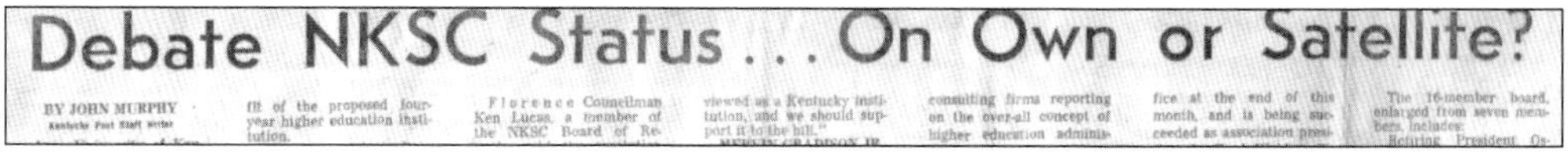

Debate NKSC Status . . . On Own or Satellite?

BY JOHN MURPHY

The Northern Kentucky Chamber of Commerce pushed a merger of NKSC, which at that time existed only on paper, with the thriving University of Kentucky Northern Center. They argued that the region did not need both and that the need for a four-year college was much greater than a two-year college. Current students agreed, and the sentiment of local residents was in favor of the plan. The only parties opposed to the idea were the University of Kentucky (UK) and the local UK alumni who worried that educational quality would go down if UK left the area. As can be seen in the above headline, alumni even proposed the idea of NKSC becoming a satellite campus of UK, a four-year college within the UK system. After months of wrangling, the NKSC Board of Regents made its unanimous decision in favor of acquiring the Northern Center in a whirlwind 20-minute meeting. The plan moved forward and met with final approval by both the Council on Higher Education, a state-wide body that governs all universities in Kentucky, and the Kentucky General Assembly.

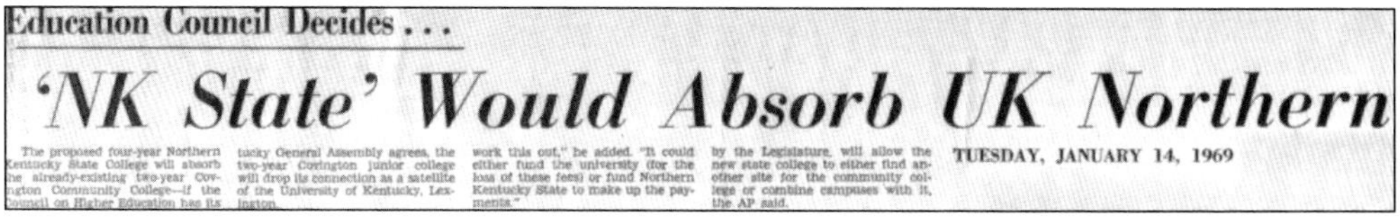

Education Council Decides . . .

'NK State' Would Absorb UK Northern

TUESDAY, JANUARY 14, 1969

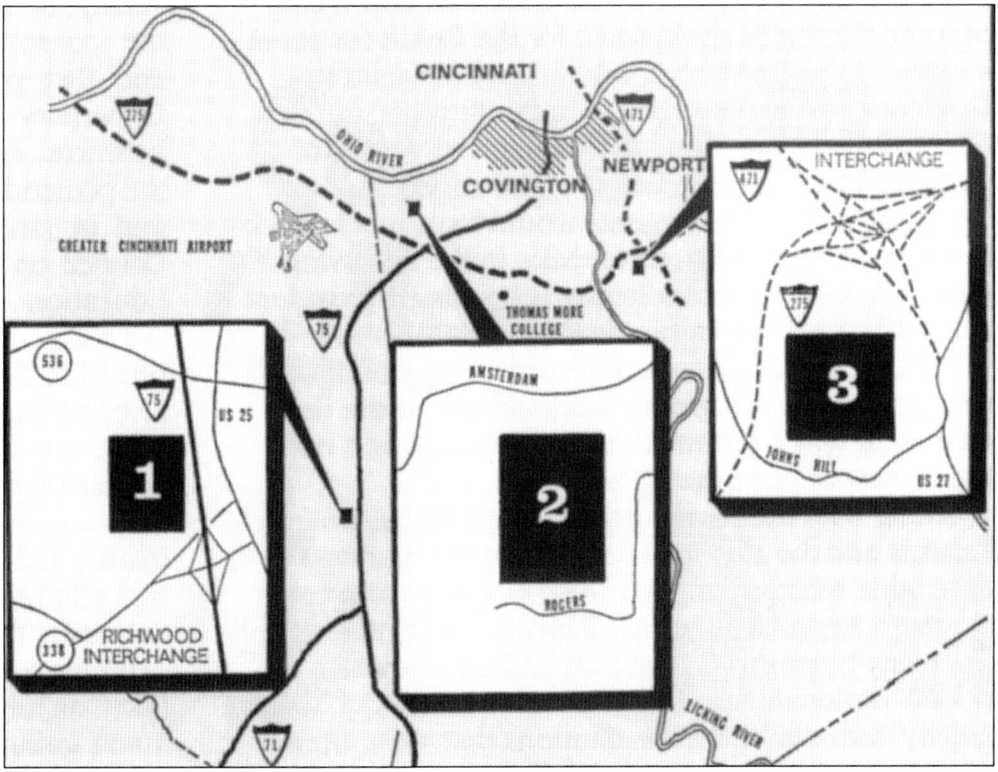

It was obvious that a four-year college could not continue at the Covington campus for very long. The building was overcrowded, and there was little room to expand on the small hilltop. The NKSC Board of Regents began looking for a site to build a new campus. All three Northern Kentucky counties submitted proposals as part of the fierce competition for the coveted campus. The Campbell County location was chosen due to the interstates that were soon to be built nearby. This was expected to make the campus easy to reach, drawing more students who would have to commute each day. Unfortunately the new campus was open before the interstates, leading to heavy traffic and continuous traffic jams in the beginning.

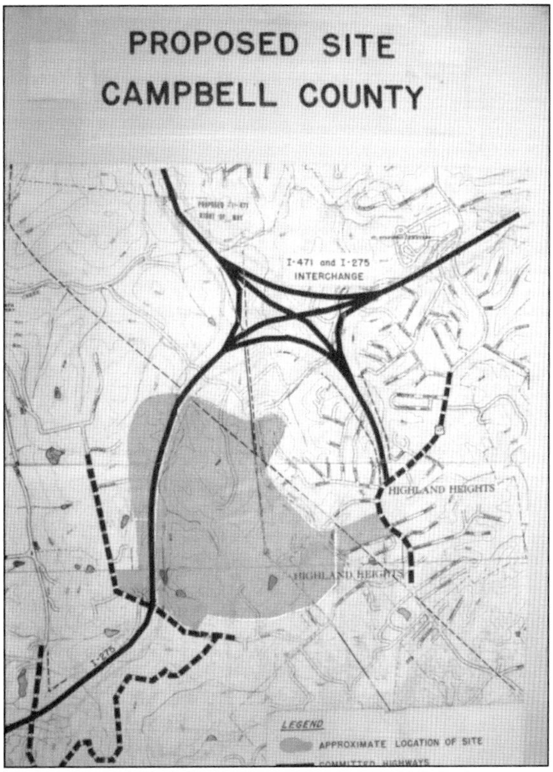

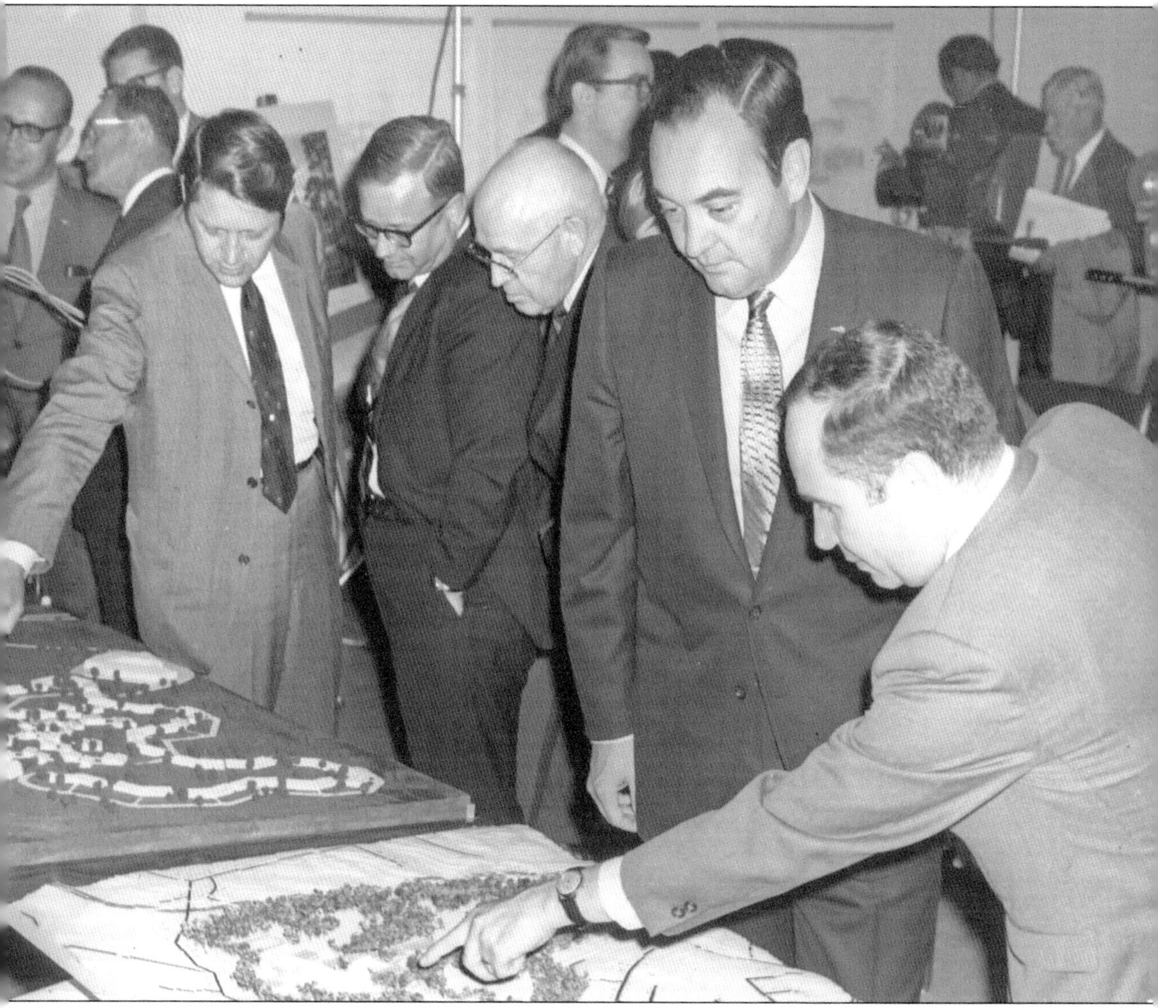

Kentucky governor Louie B. Nunn was a staunch supporter of a four-year college in Northern Kentucky. Without his tireless advocacy before the state legislature, it's doubtful the dream of Northern Kentucky State College would have become a fully funded reality. Here Nunn looks on as NKSC regent Charles Wiley points out a feature on one of three proposed plans for building a new NKSC campus. One plan had been proposed by each the three northernmost counties in Kentucky, with Campbell County as the eventual winner. The first building built on the new campus and the entrance drive were named in honor of Nunn. Newspaper cartoonists lampooned this decision by depicting the campus with Nunn's name on every signpost and tree, asking, "It's whose college?"

The new site of the NKSC campus was a farm in Highland Heights. At that point, little existed on the land aside from the lake, a few farm buildings, and nearby residential homes. Several NKSC students sit under the sign announcing the forthcoming campus. As can be seen, NKSC, and later NKU, students have always been a mix of different age groups.

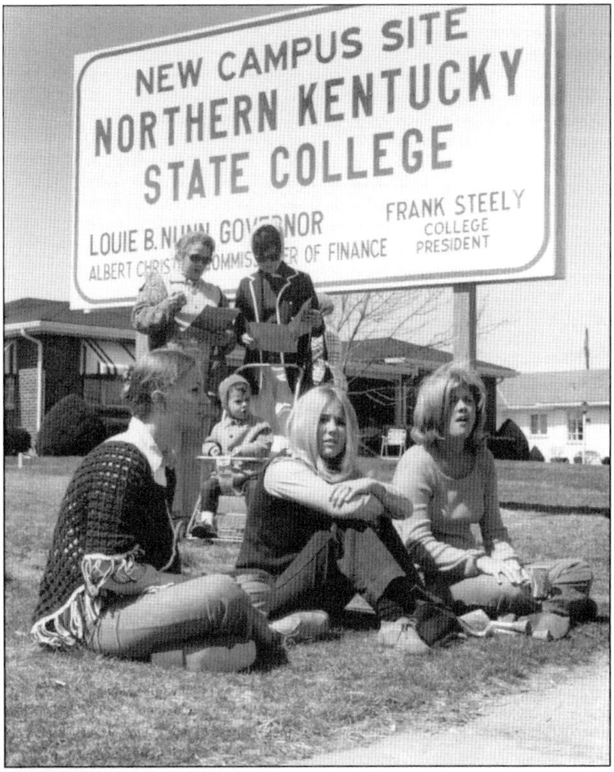

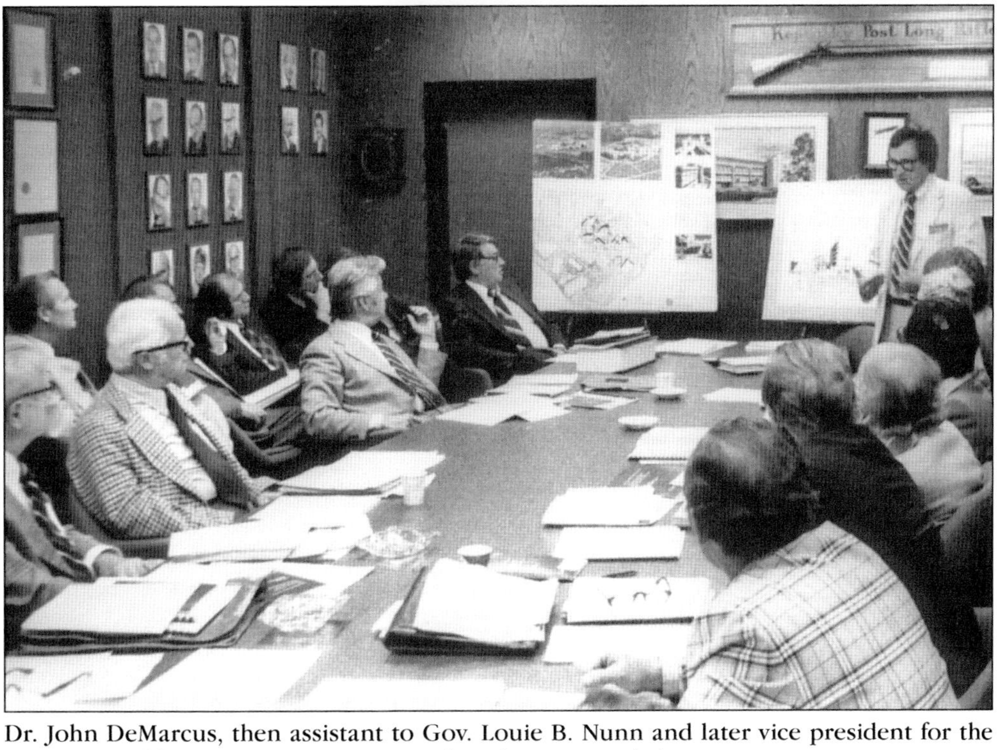

Dr. John DeMarcus, then assistant to Gov. Louie B. Nunn and later vice president for the university, addresses a committee regarding the proposed site.

Creating a new college from scratch requires the creation of a number of items that established universities take for granted. Many of these are created in a hurry by whomever is available at the time, undergoing revision in the future. The logo above is one of the earliest versions used by the Northern Kentucky State College. The later version below is the one most frequently associated with the early state college years. The NKSC logo actually went through at least three versions. The later logo for NKU also changed several times, most recently in 2004.

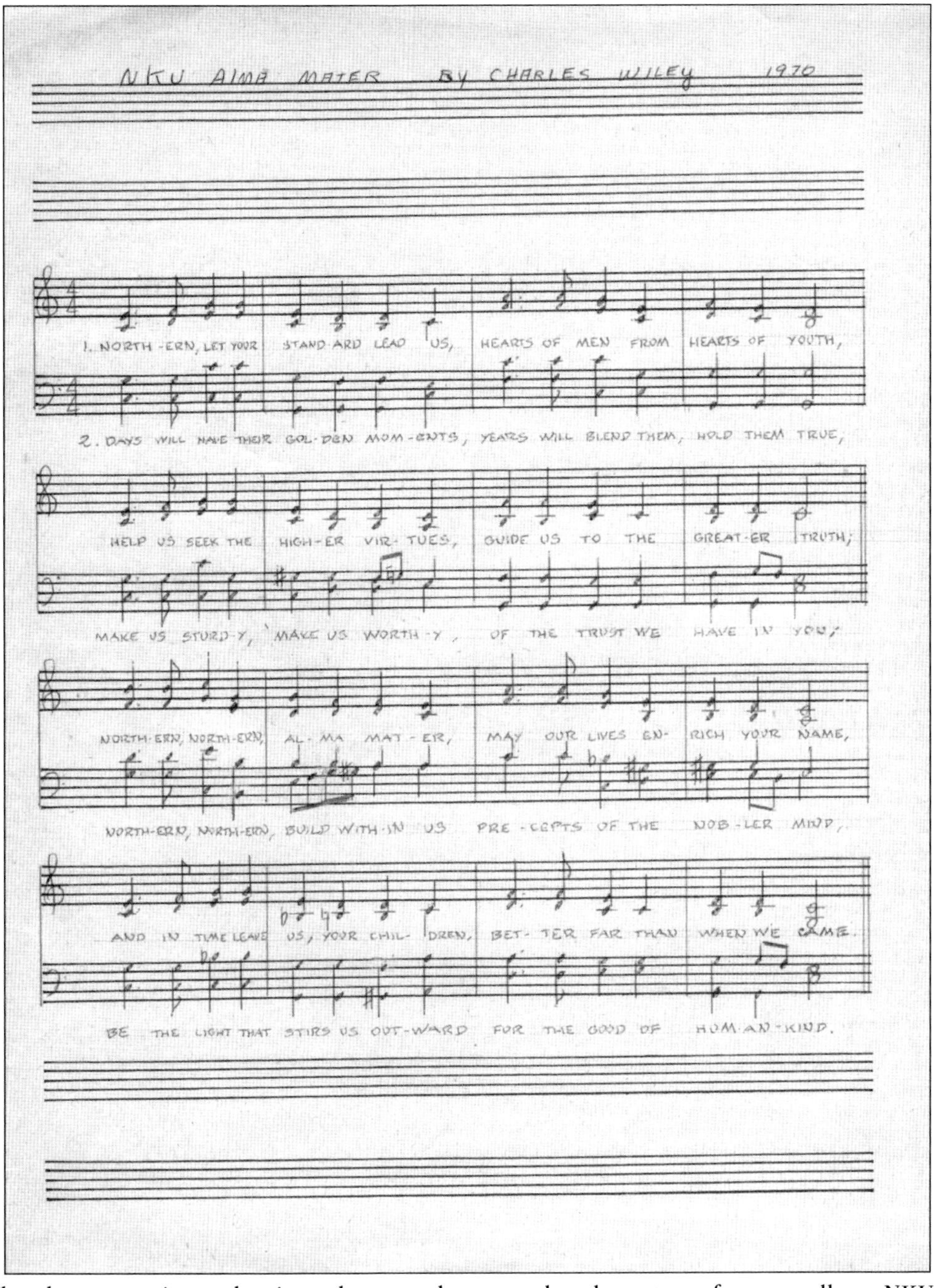

The alma mater is another item that must be created at the outset of a new college. NKU's alma mater was written by one of the founding members of the Board of Regents, Charles Wiley. He submitted the song for board approval before the college had students to sing it. The alma mater as it is now sung has been altered by various music professors over the years, often to allow different accompanying instruments. The original handwritten score above is still available in the University Archives. This copy has been consulted by more current music professors with an interest in performing the alma mater in a form closer to the way it was originally written.

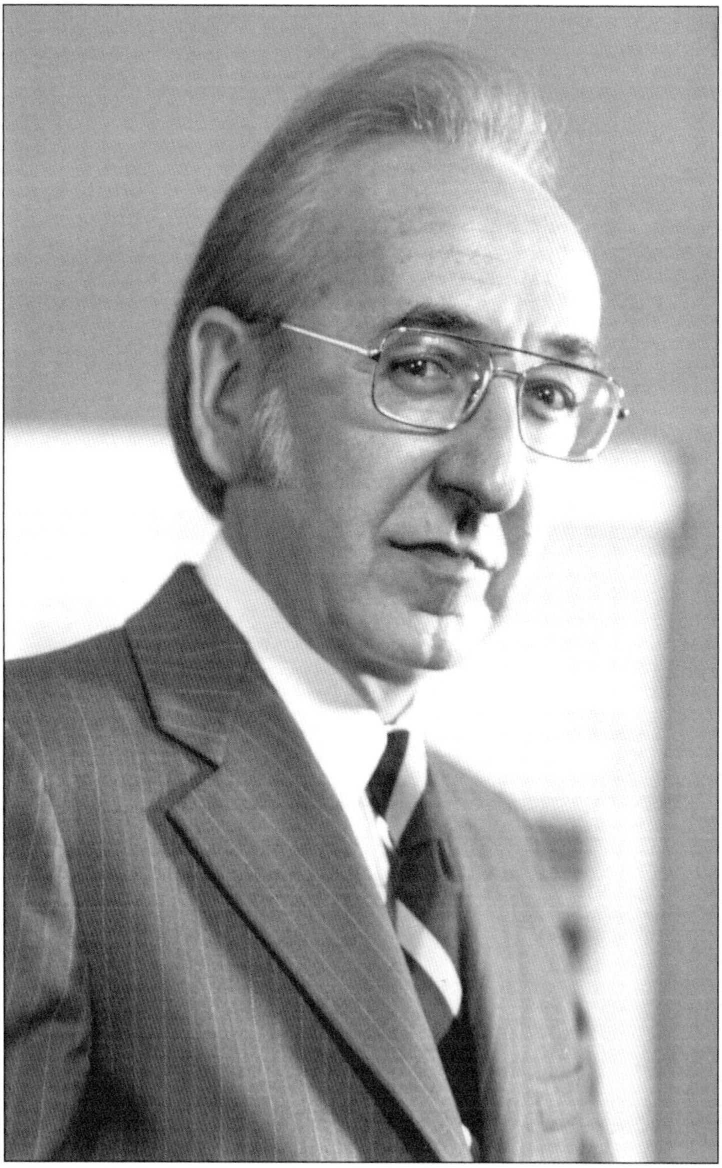

Pictured is Dr. W. Frank Steely, founding president of Northern Kentucky University. In 1969, NKSC was moving ahead rapidly, but the new college still lacked a major component—faculty and staff. The Board of Regents began its search for a university president. The leading candidate was Dr. A. D. Albright, the executive vice president for the University of Kentucky. Ironically, a few years earlier, his position had required him to fight against NKSC in order to retain the UK Northern Center. That summer all indications were that Albright would be chosen, but he declined the position to accept a Fulbright Fellowship overseas. When no president had been chosen by November, the Council on Higher Education began to show signs of anxiety. The Board of Regents sent reassurances that an end to the search was in sight. Soon after, they recommended Kentucky native Dr. W. Frank Steely for the position, Steely hit the ground running. Knowing that university funding was to be debated at a meeting of the Kentucky General Assembly that January, Steely rented a jeep near his Virginia home to make the trip through the snow-covered mountains.

NORTHERN KENTUCKY STATE COLLEGE
Class Schedule Summer Session - 1970
(Revised: April 21,1970)

CALL NO.	DEPT.	COURSE NO.	SUBJECT	CREDIT	HOUR	INSTRUCTOR	ROOM
002	A-S	180	BASIC DESIGN	2	6:55-9:35	Weiner	WB-12
004	BIO	101	BIOLOGY	3	8:20-10:00	Beach	Aud.
006	CHEM	100	INTRO CHEMISTRY	4	6:55-8:10	Weil	Aud.
008	CHEM	101	CHEM 100 LAB	0	8:20-10:00	Weil	11
010	*ECON	260	PRIN OF ECONOMICS	3	8:20-9:35	Owings	D-1
012	ENG	005	BASIC PRIN OF ENGLISH	3	5:30-6:45	Lasater	D-3
014	ENG	101-1	FRESHMAN COMPOSITION	3	5:30-6:45	Lindsey	A-1
016	ENG	101-2	FRESHMAN COMPOSITION	3	6:55-8:10	Dickson	B-3
018	ENG	101-3	FRESHMAN COMPOSITION	3	8:20-9:35	Lasater	D-3
020	ENG	102	FRESHMAN COMPOSITION (Prereq: ENG 101)	3	5:30-6:45	Robbins	C-3
022	ENG	161	INTRO TO LITERATURE	3	6:55-8:10	Robbins	A-1
024	*ENG	262	WEST.WORLD LITERATURE 1660 TO PRESENT	3	6:55-8:10	Lindsey	C-3
026	*ENG	264	MAJOR BLACK WRITERS	3	8:20-9:35	Dickson	B-3
028	GEO	152	REG GEO OF WORLD	3	5:30-6:45	Williams	Aud.
030	HIS	104	HIS OF EUROPE TO 1713	3	5:30-6:45	Nickell	D-1
032	HIS	108	HIS US THRU 1865	3	8:20-9:35	Thomas	19
034	HIS	109	HIS US SINCE 1865	3	6:55-8:10	Nickell	D-1
036	MA	111	COLLEGE ALGEBRA	3	6:55-8:10	Brown	B-1
038	MA	113	ANALYTICS & CALCULUS I (Prereq:Consent of Instr)	4	8:20-10:10	Brown	B-1
040	MA	122	FUND CONCEPTS OF MA I (Prereq:Consent of Instr)	3	5:30-6:45	McKenney	A-3
042	MA	123	FUND CONCEPTS OF MA II (Prereq:Consent of Instr)	3	6:55-8:10	McKenney	A-3
044	*MUS	200	MUSIC IN WESTERN CIV	3	6:55-8:10	Thomas	19
046	PS	151	AMERICAN GOVERMENT	3	5:30-6:45	Henry	19
048	SOC	101	INTRO SOCIOLOGY (Formerly SOC 151)	3	5:30-6:45	Peterson	C-1
050	SOC	152	MODERN SOC PROBLEMS (Prereq:SOC 151 or Consent)	3	6:55-8:10	Peterson	C-1
052	SP	181-1	BASIC PUBLIC SPEAKING	3	5:30-6:45	Hellwig	B-1
054	SP	181-2	BASIC PUBLIC SPEAKING	3	8:20-9:35	Hellwig	C-1

*Not open to Freshman
Any course not having sufficient enrollment will be cancelled.
ALL classes meet Monday thru Thursday. All times are p.m.

Registration Date June 15, 1-5 and 7-8:30 p.m.
Classwork begins June 16 Classwork ends August 6

FEES	Resident	Out-of-State
FULL-TIME	$80.00	$260.00
PART-TIME	$14.00 (credit hour)	$ 44.00 (credit hour)

FEES ARE PAYABLE ON REGISTRATION DAY

The first classes at the new NKSC were taught during the summer session of 1970. A broad range of courses were taught, including chemistry, English, history, and math. A few of the courses were geared toward upperclassmen, specifically the students who were enrolled at the Northern Center during the merger. The new college did not want these students to be lost in the shuffle. Given the number of courses that had been offered by UK at the center, it is easy to see why some prospective students were worried that merging the two schools was a step backward. Today's summer class schedule is printed in newspaper format on several sheets of small, crowded text. The 1970 schedule doesn't even fill the page, the last fourth being a listing of dates and costs. In an era of rising tuition, most current students are extremely amused by the costs listed. Full-time, in-state tuition was $80 for the semester. Part-time students only paid $14 per credit hour.

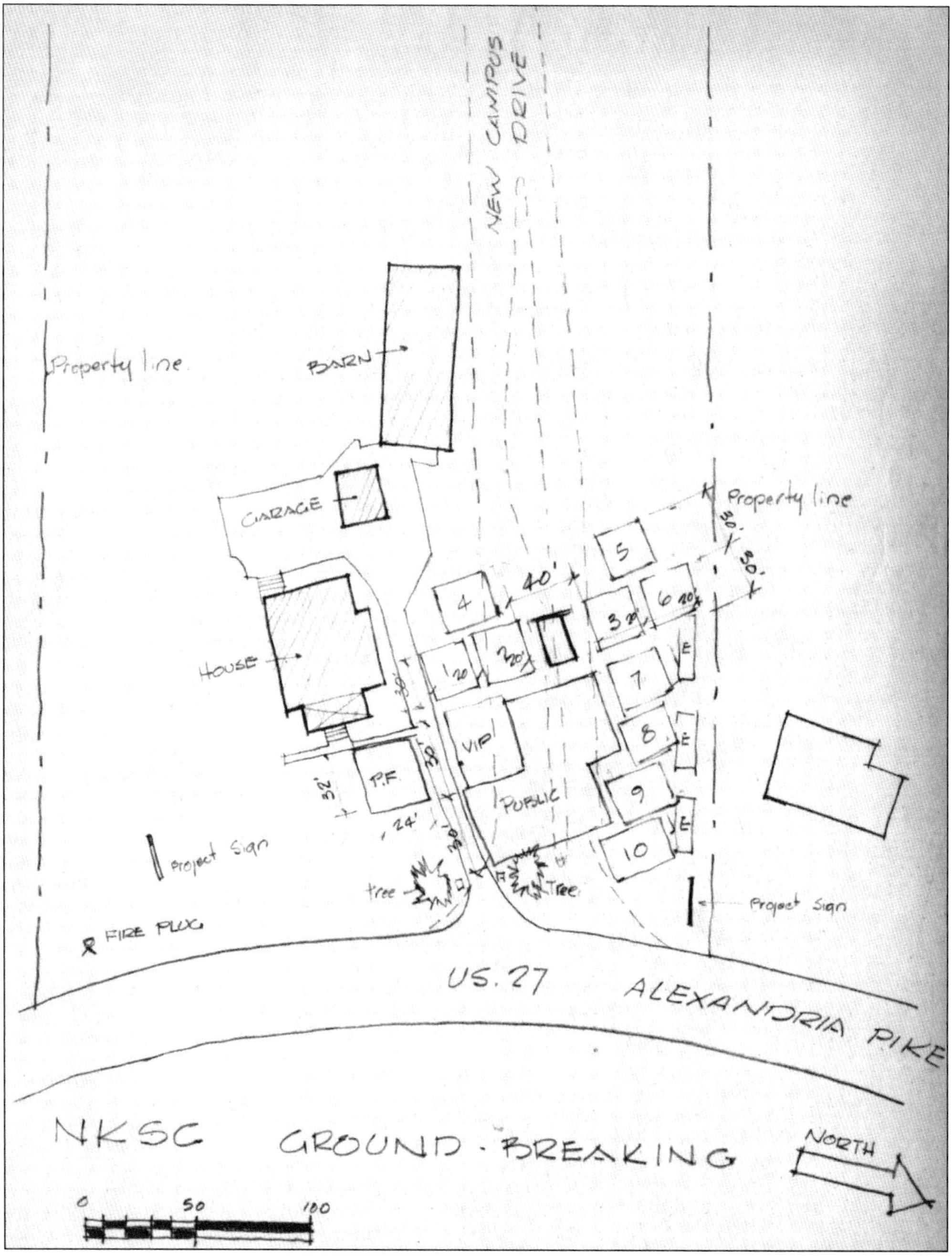

The groundbreaking for the campus of a new college is a once-in-a-lifetime event. The groundbreaking for the Highland Heights campus was carefully orchestrated. The diagram shows the careful placing of more than a dozen local marching bands, the stage for the speakers, the VIP seating, and the areas set aside for students and members of the public to stand. Classes at the Covington campus were cancelled for the event, and faculty members were strongly urged to bring their students to the groundbreaking ceremony.

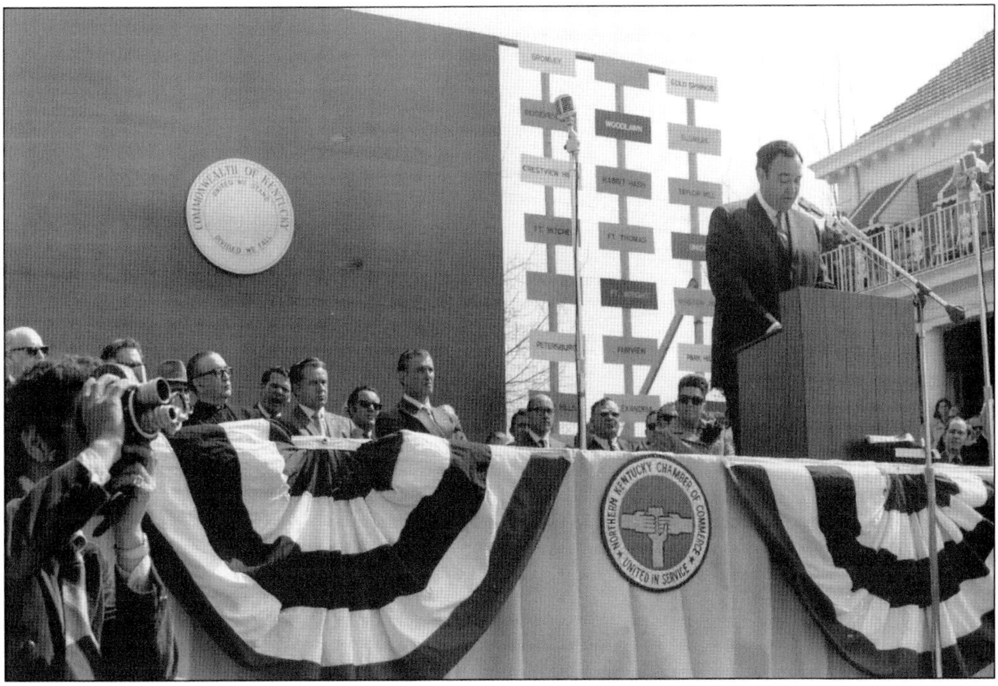

Gov. Louie B. Nunn delivers the keynote address at the groundbreaking for the new campus in Highland Heights. The rows of small signs behind him list the numerous Northern Kentucky communities that would be supported by the new college.

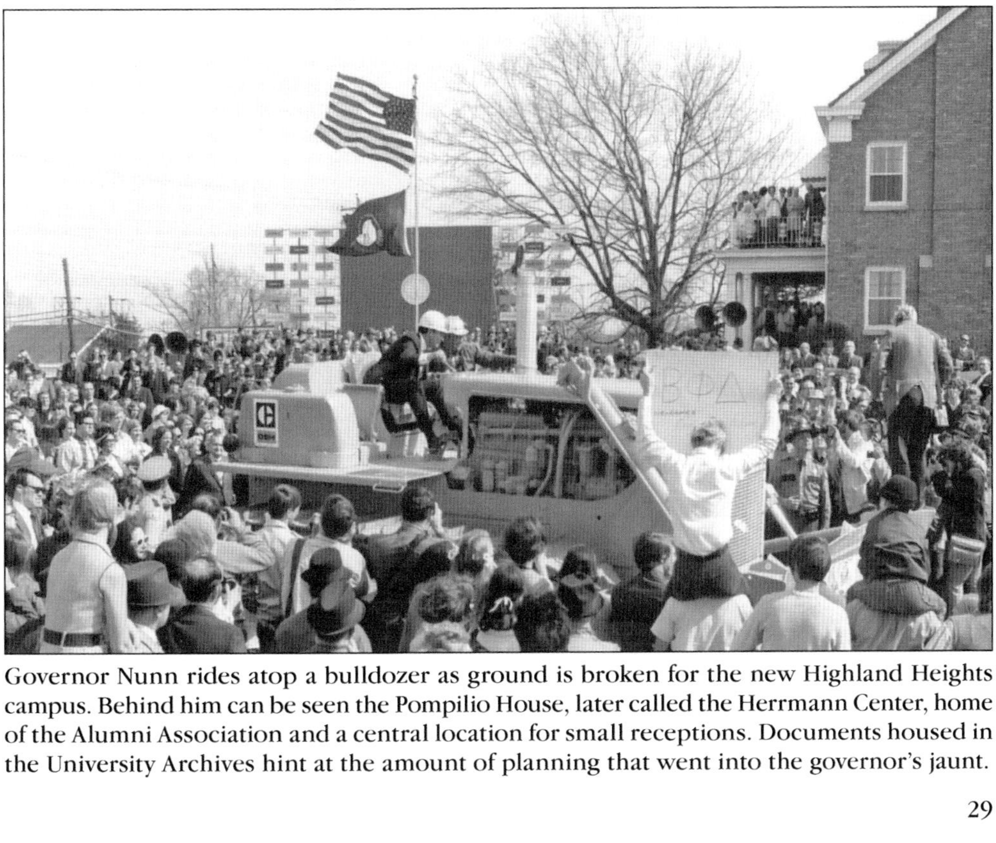

Governor Nunn rides atop a bulldozer as ground is broken for the new Highland Heights campus. Behind him can be seen the Pompilio House, later called the Herrmann Center, home of the Alumni Association and a central location for small receptions. Documents housed in the University Archives hint at the amount of planning that went into the governor's jaunt.

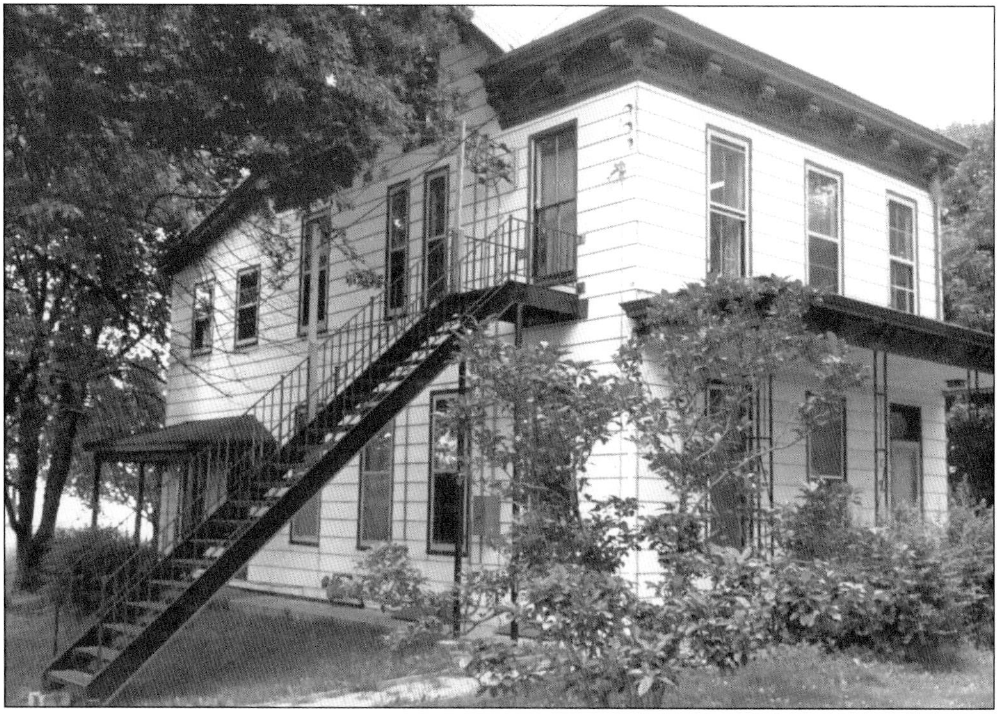

The Keene Complex housed the offices, classrooms, and workrooms for the art and music departments. The complex consisted of the farmhouse above, the barn below, and a number of outbuildings. The barn housed the kilns for the art department as well as the theater scene shop. Faculty offices were in the farmhouse, as were the graphic arts and photography labs, which occupied the attic and basement spaces. The location on Johns Hill Road was used for several years. Continued building opened up space for these departments elsewhere, allowing all but the pottery and ceramics classes to move out completely. These classes required the kilns near the barn until a new ceramics building was built in 1997.

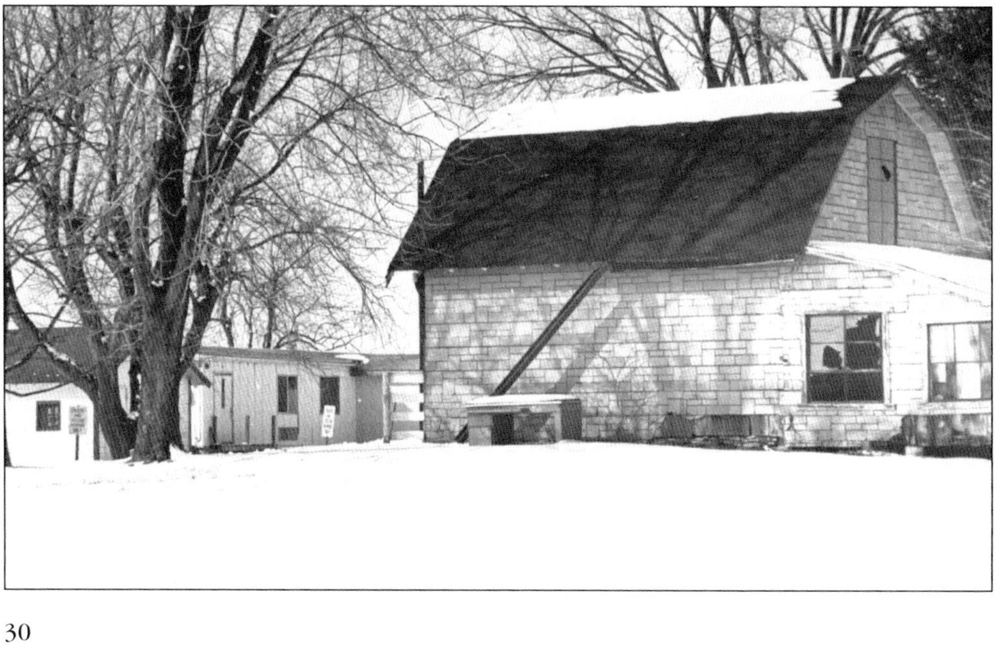

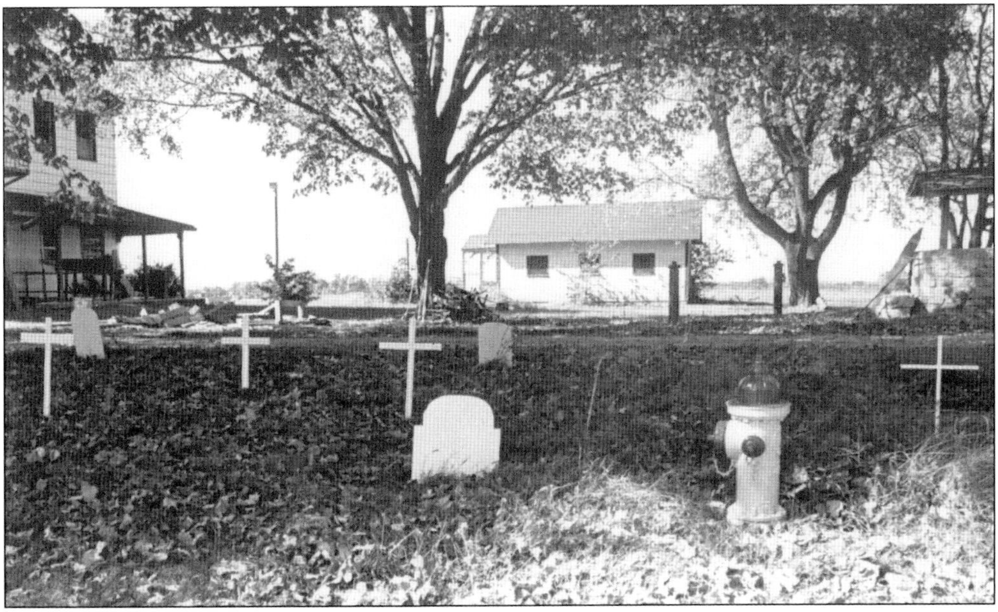

An old farm can be a spooky place at Halloween. Students took advantage of the ambiance at the Keene Complex to host a haunted house. The graveyard in this picture is located at the front of the farmhouse with the old stone well to the right.

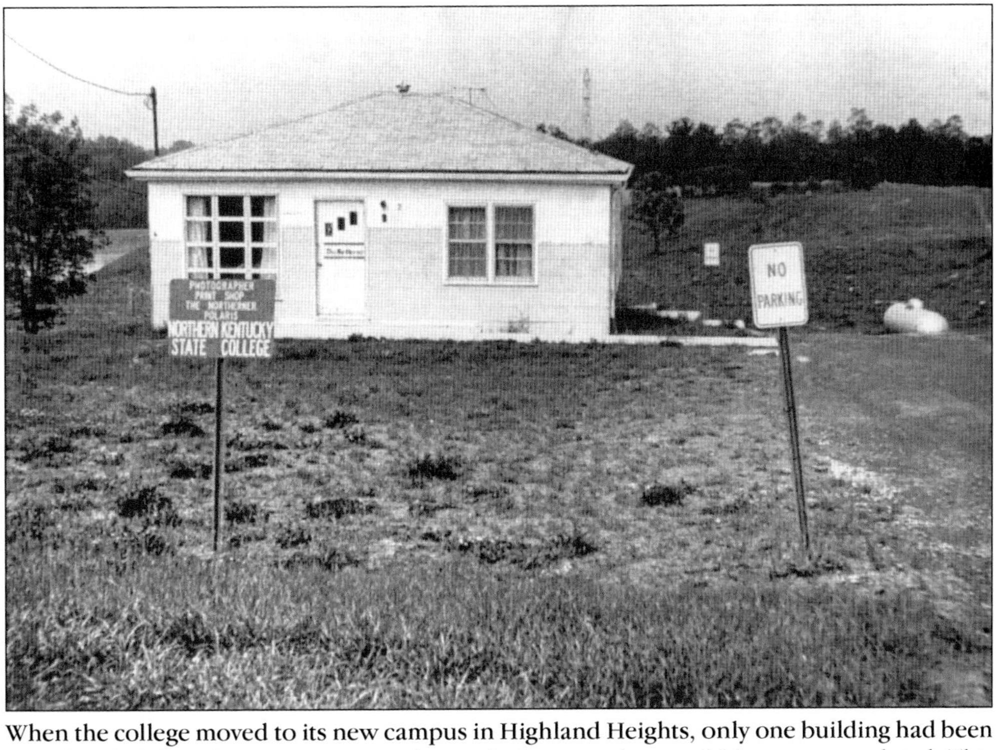

When the college moved to its new campus in Highland Heights, only one building had been completed. Other departments were housed wherever they could be accommodated. This is the first home of the *Northerner*, the student newspaper, and the *Polaris*, the short-lived annual. The campus print shop was located in the basement of the building.

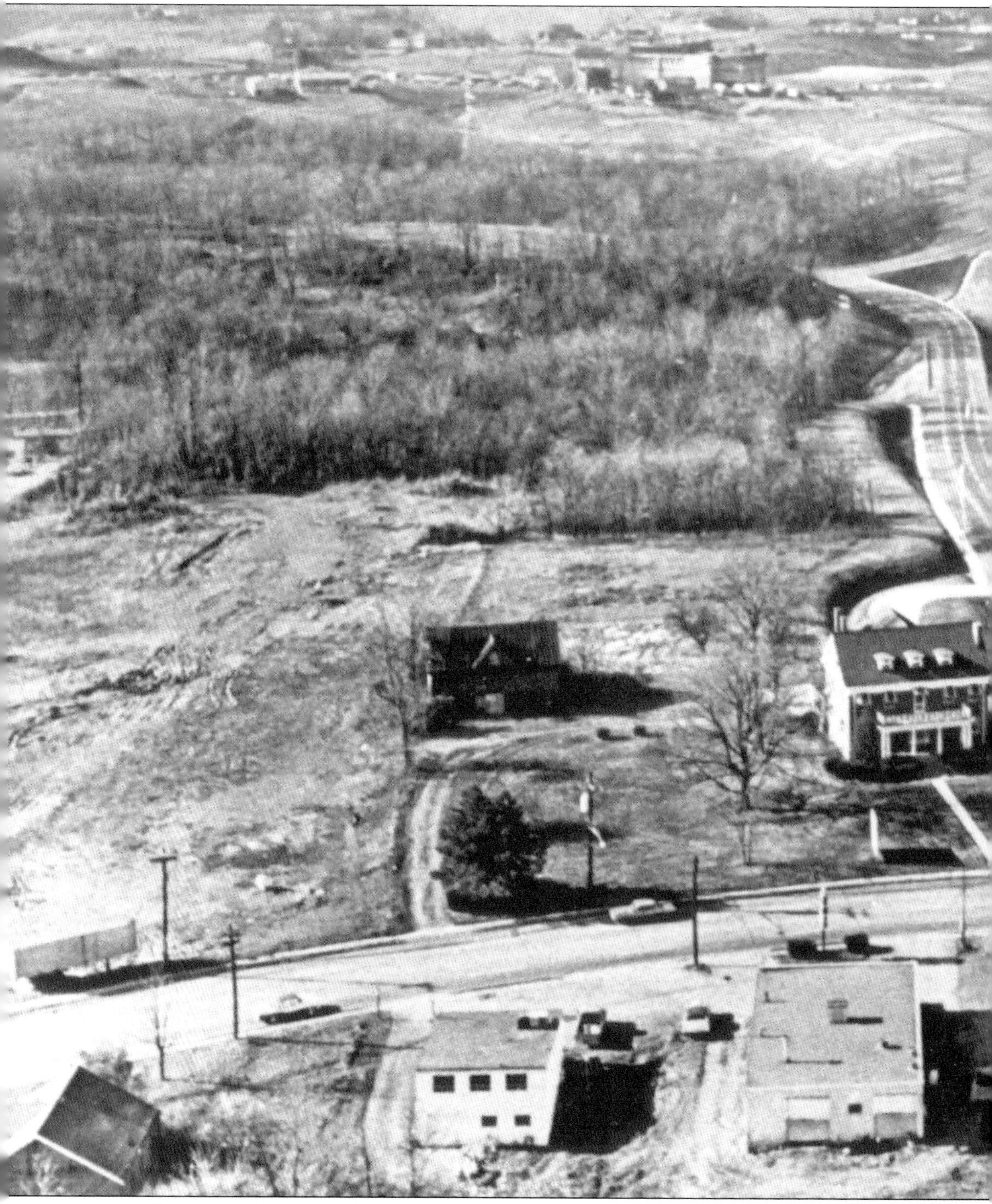

Pictured is an aerial view of the NKSC campus taken in the spring of 1972. Nunn Drive is nearing completion, and a cluster of buildings can be seen in the background. At this time, the only new building completed for the campus was Nunn Hall. The administration and campus-wide facilities such as the bookstore and the university library were housed there, as were a number of classrooms and offices. Many of the academic departments were housed

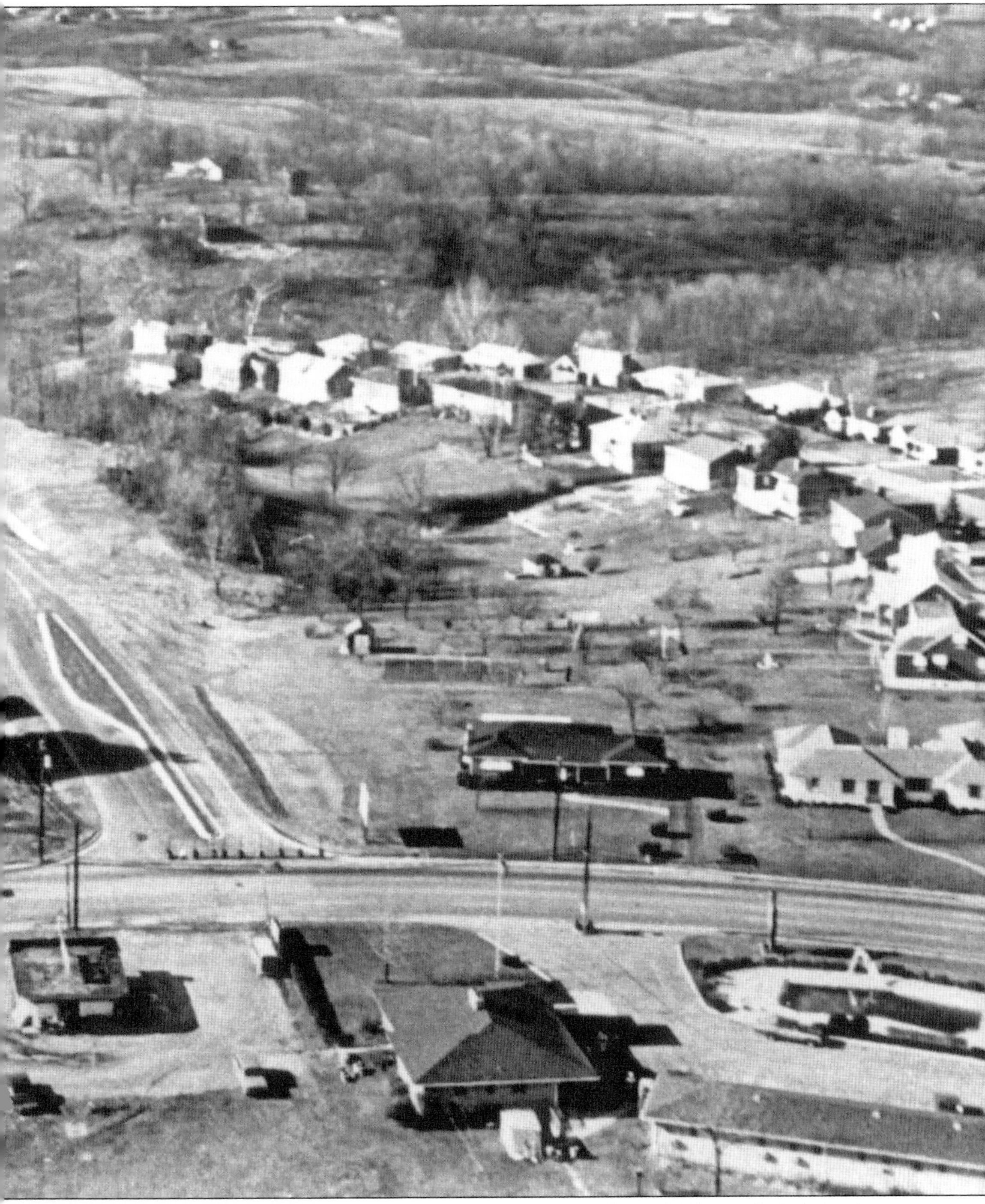

in pre-existing residential and farm buildings on Johns Hill Road. This included the theater scene shop located in a barn loft, the photography studio in a farmhouse cellar, and the music practice room in a renovated kennel. University faculty, staff, and students pulled together. University president W. Frank Steely summed up the situation by stating, "Never before did so many do so much with so little."

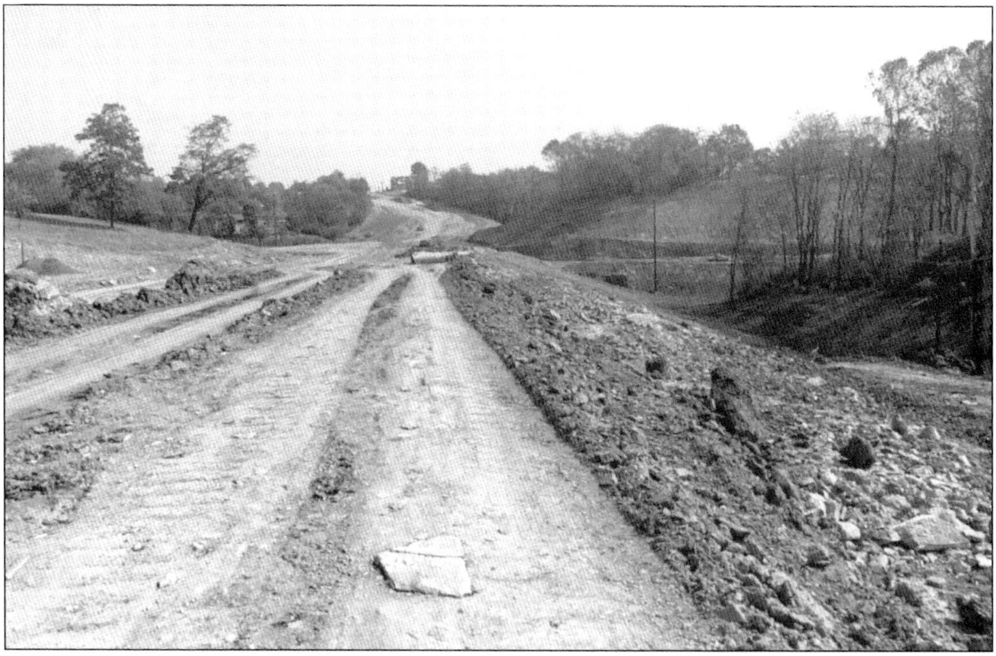

This photograph shows the beginnings of construction of Nunn Drive. The Pompilio House can be seen in the distance on U.S. Highway 27 in Highland Heights. This intersection would eventually become the main entrance for the campus.

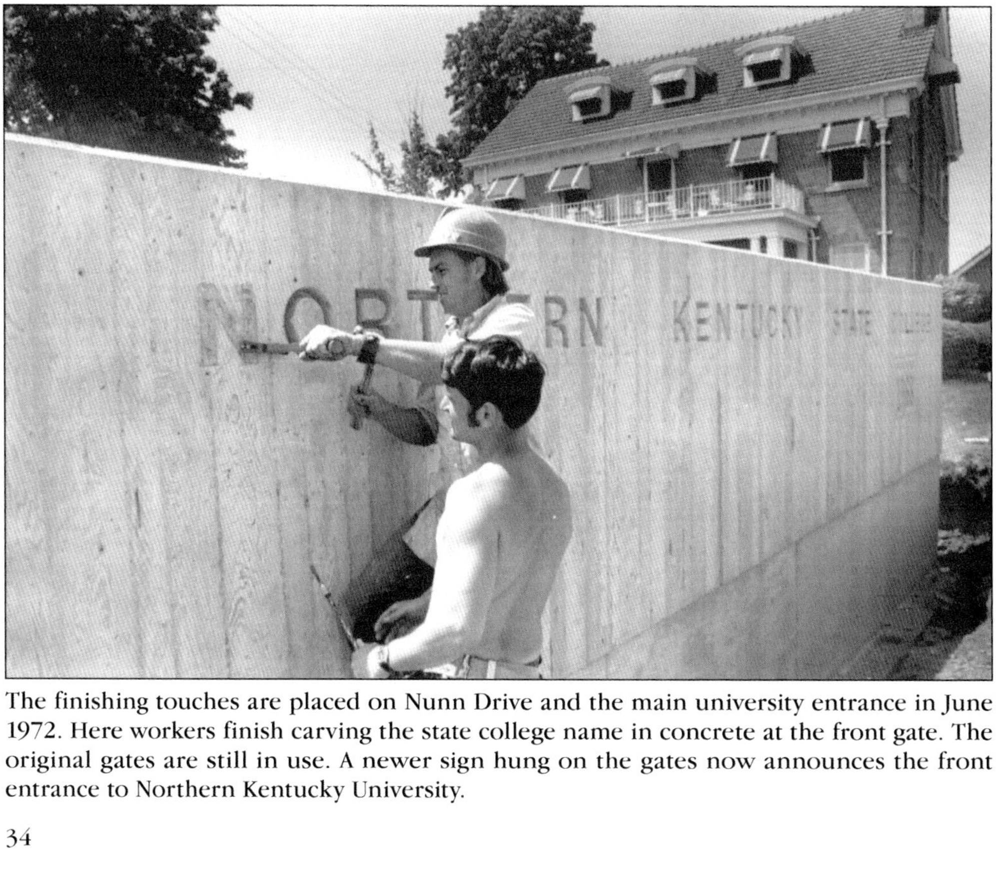

The finishing touches are placed on Nunn Drive and the main university entrance in June 1972. Here workers finish carving the state college name in concrete at the front gate. The original gates are still in use. A newer sign hung on the gates now announces the front entrance to Northern Kentucky University.

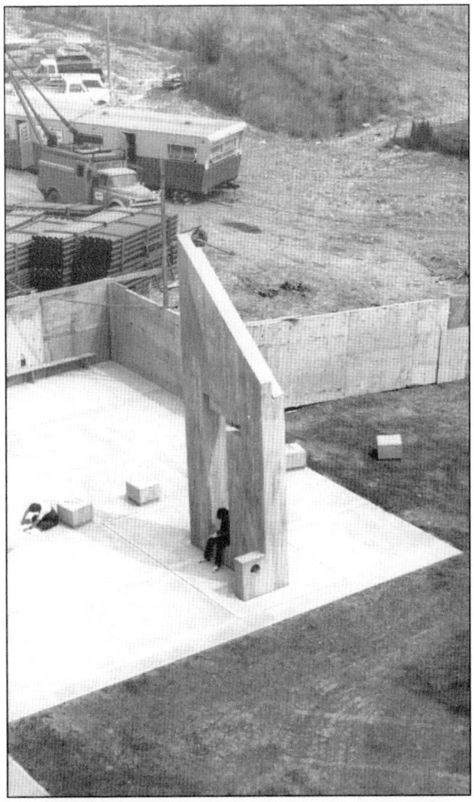

The university's original central plaza was built with an integrated sundial. At right, the pieces of the sundial can be clearly seen not long after they were erected. The sighting groove points to the North Star, hence the official name Gnomonium Polaris Nordum. As can be seen in the later picture below, the sundial is located in the middle of campus near the student center. Because of its convenient location, it has always been a popular destination for students, who can often be found between classes sitting on the concrete blocks that mark the hours.

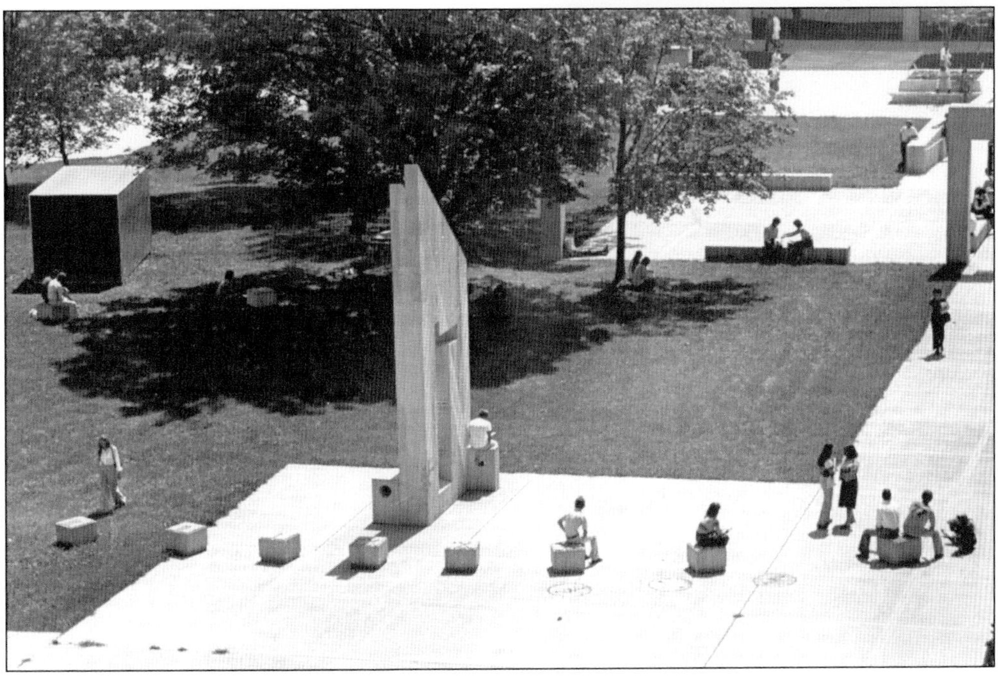

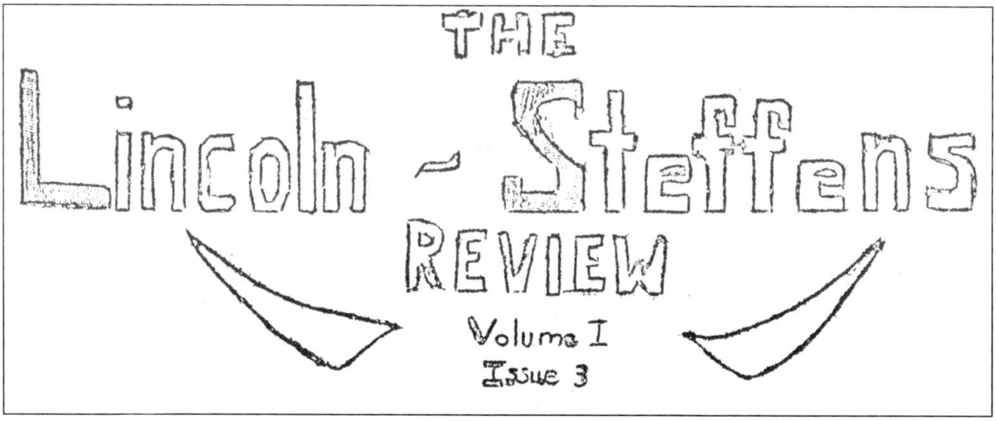

With the move to the new campus, student activities were in full swing, including the student newspaper, *The Northerner*. Of course, no campus is without its problems. Amid complaints of censorship at the student paper, several short-lived "underground" newspapers appeared, including the *Lincoln-Steffens Review*.

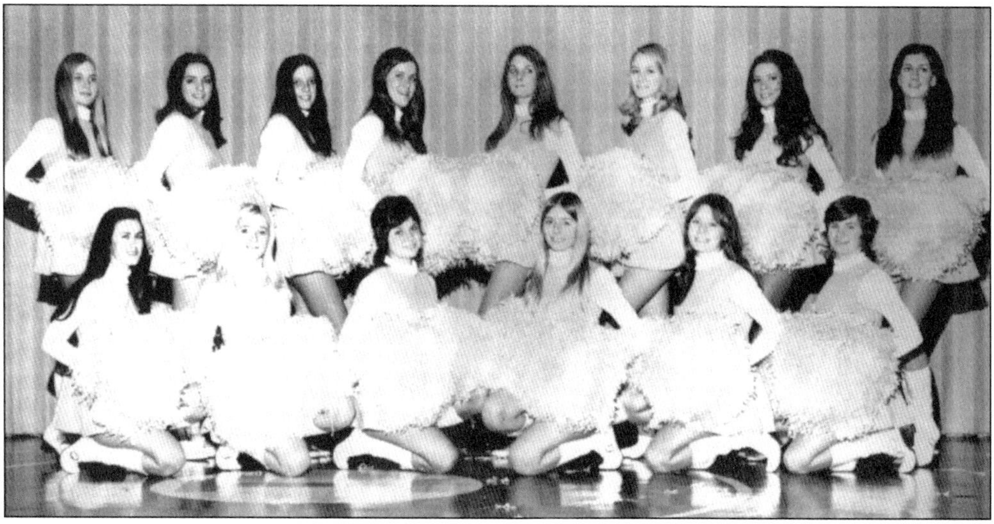

The NKSC Golden Girls drill team produced a calendar for 1972 featuring all 14 members of the squad. This group photograph appeared on the cover. The team members are, from left to right, (first row) Holly Boswell (cocaptain), Tracy Lovelace, Pam Applegarth, Jackie DeHart (captain), Carla Hardebeck, Aprille Zeigler; (second row) Linda Larkin, Shirley Belcher, Karen Fisk, Sharon Martin, Lois Herrmann, Cindy McMillian, Debe Chapman, and Gayle Herrmann.

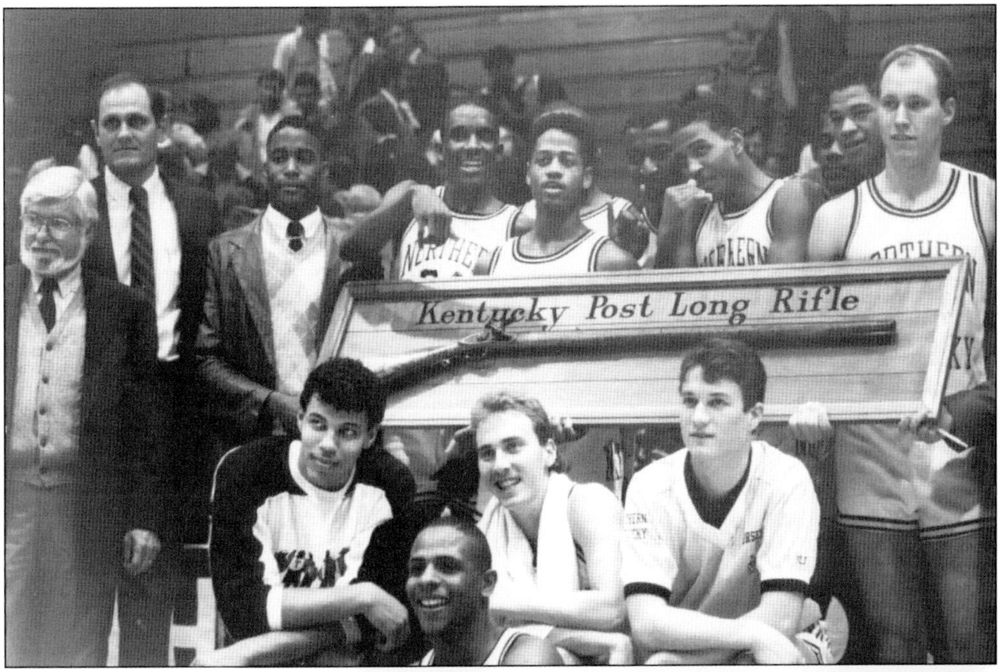

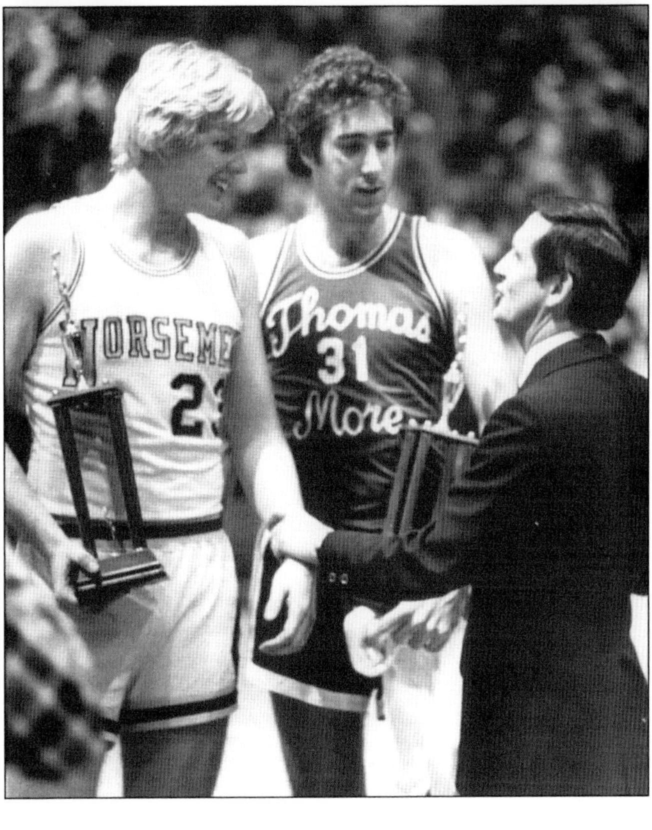

Before enrollment growth forced NKU into a different conference, there had been a long-standing rivalry with nearby private school Thomas More College. The *Kentucky Post* newspaper donated a rebuilt Kentucky long rifle as a trophy for the annual grudge match between the two schools. The rifle hung in the office of the president of the winning school until the following year. Above, the winning NKU basketball team is shown holding the rifle. Two MVPs were also chosen every year, one from each team. The two MVPs from one of the games are shown at right, holding the trophies they were awarded at the end of the game. They are Dan Doellman (NKU 23) and Todd Bender (Thomas More 31).

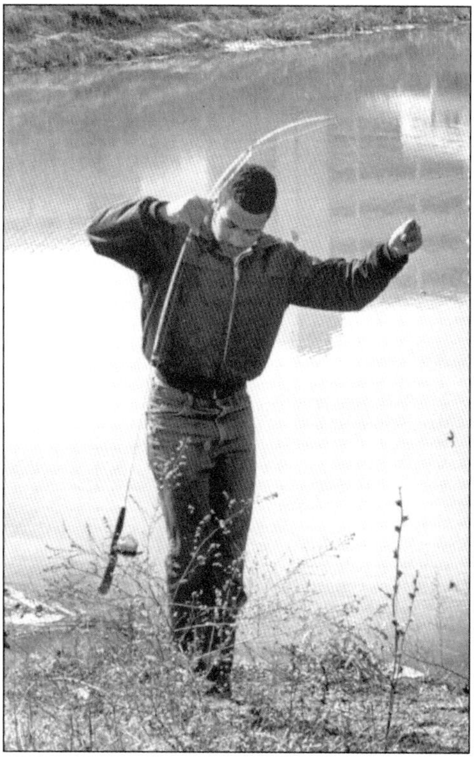

Terrell Winfrey enjoys the fishing on Lake Inferior. Fishing in the campus lake was a common activity in NKU's early days, attracting faculty, staff, and students to the lake shore.

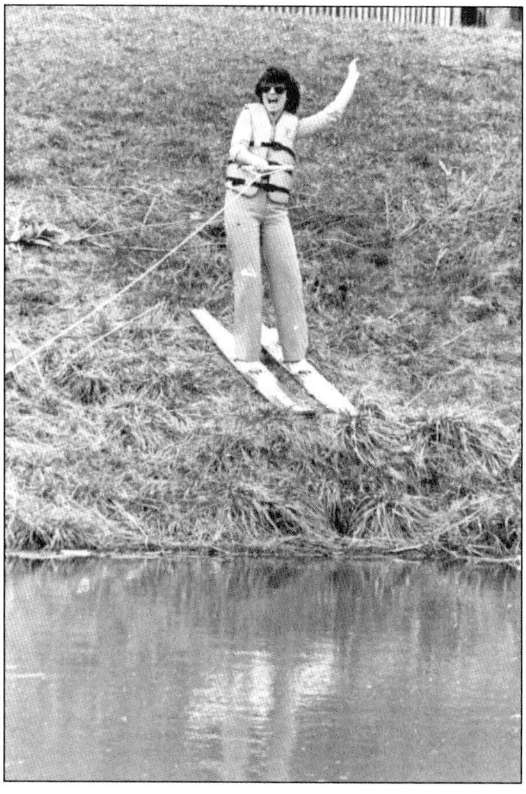

Goofiness reigns at the Rites of Spring, where one woman pretends to water ski on the edge of Lake Inferior. Inaugurated in 1973, the Rites of Spring is an annual event that allows the denizens of the campus to relieve their cabin fever at the end of winter.

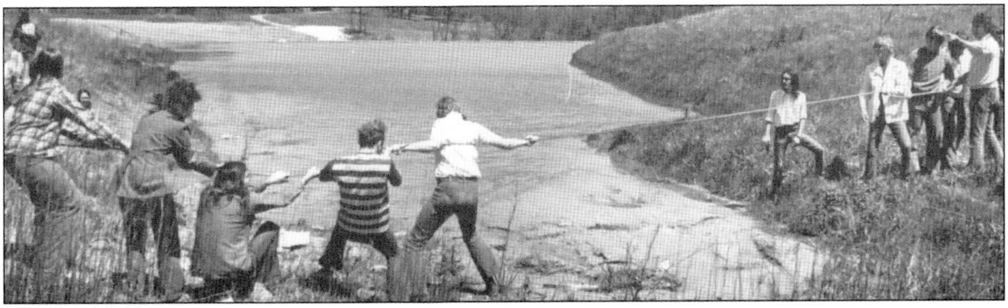

Each year the Rites of Spring featured a tug-of-war across a narrow finger of the campus lake. This narrow channel was normally filled with algae, making it the murkiest corner of the lake. The prospect of a dunking in the green water provided the students with extra incentive to win the annual competition.

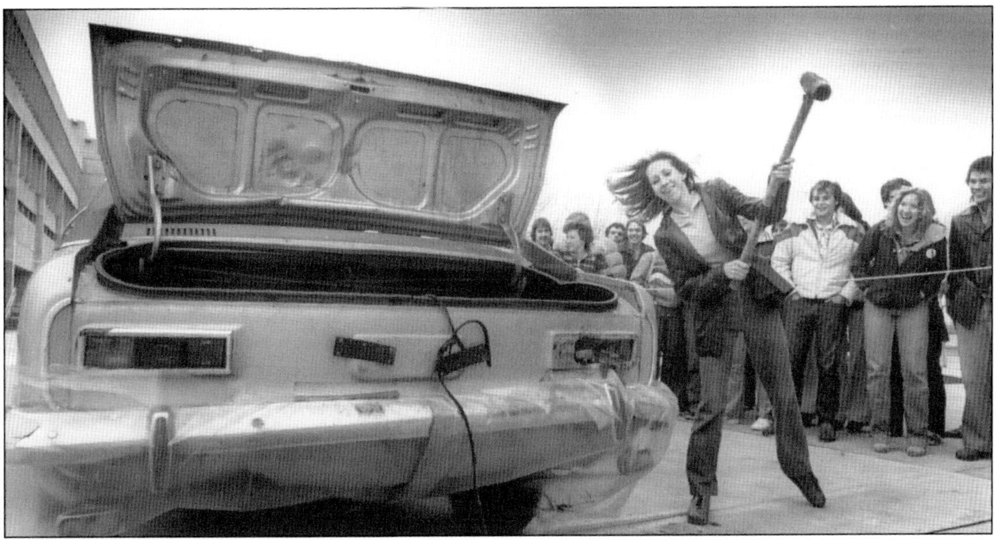

The Rites of Spring was often scheduled just before spring semester finals to give the campus community a chance to let off a little steam before entering the most stressful time of the academic year. This photograph displays 1970s-style stress management. In the annual car bash, the campus community is invited to wield a sledgehammer against an old car, as this student does with great joy.

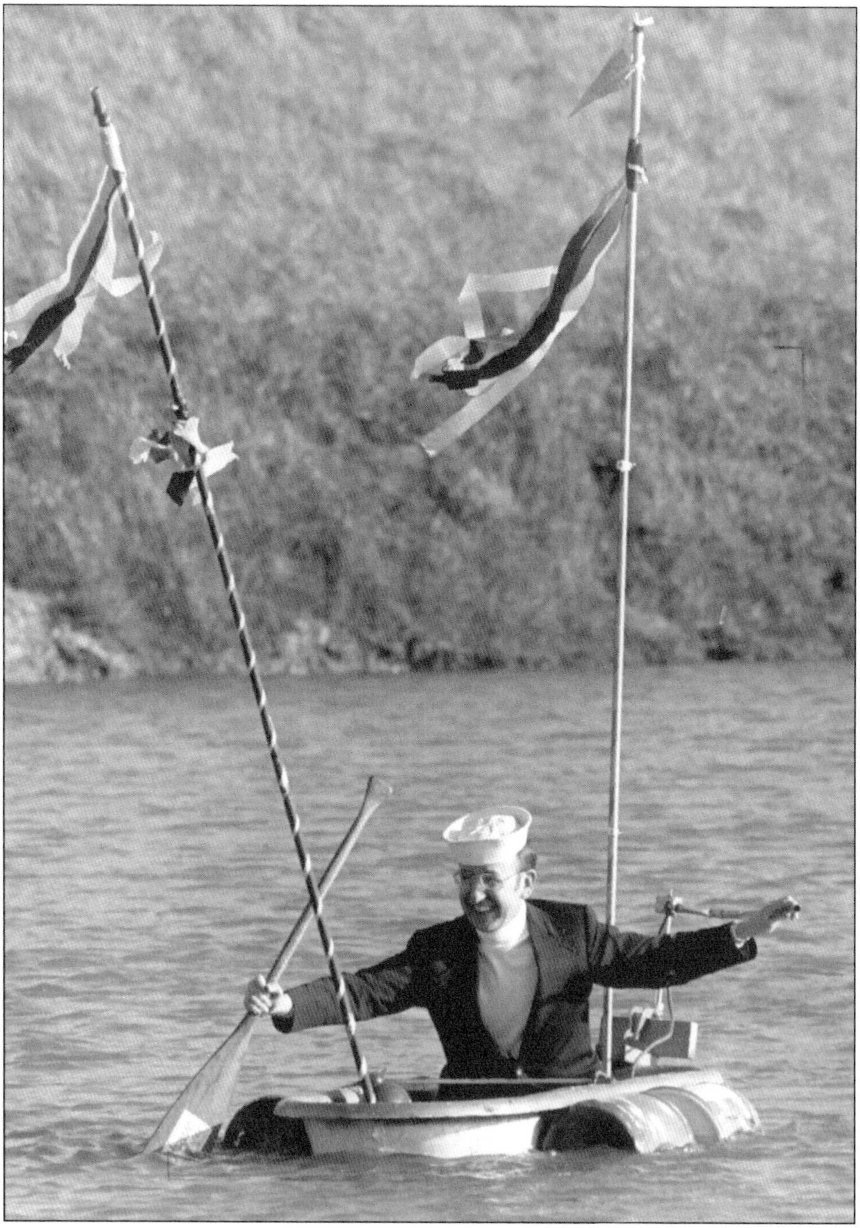

University president Dr. Frank Steely jauntily pilots his bathtub across Lake Inferior, opening the first Bathtub Regatta in 1973. Steely admitted he was allowed a motor for the occasion. The motor handle can just be seen under his left hand. The oar he holds was purely for show, but actual competitors had to row their way across the lake. The rules on this point were quite strict, and competitors could be disqualified for not rowing all the way onto the shore. The claw-footed bathtubs were held up by rigged pontoons of various designs. The annual event was a campus favorite, drawing crowds to the lake shore to watch. Rumor had it that numerous sunken bathtubs were quietly rusting away on the lake bottom. When the lake was temporarily drained for a renovation project in 2005, there was even talk of whether any discovered tubs would be placed in the University Archives. Much to the disappointment of some on campus, no bathtubs were found.

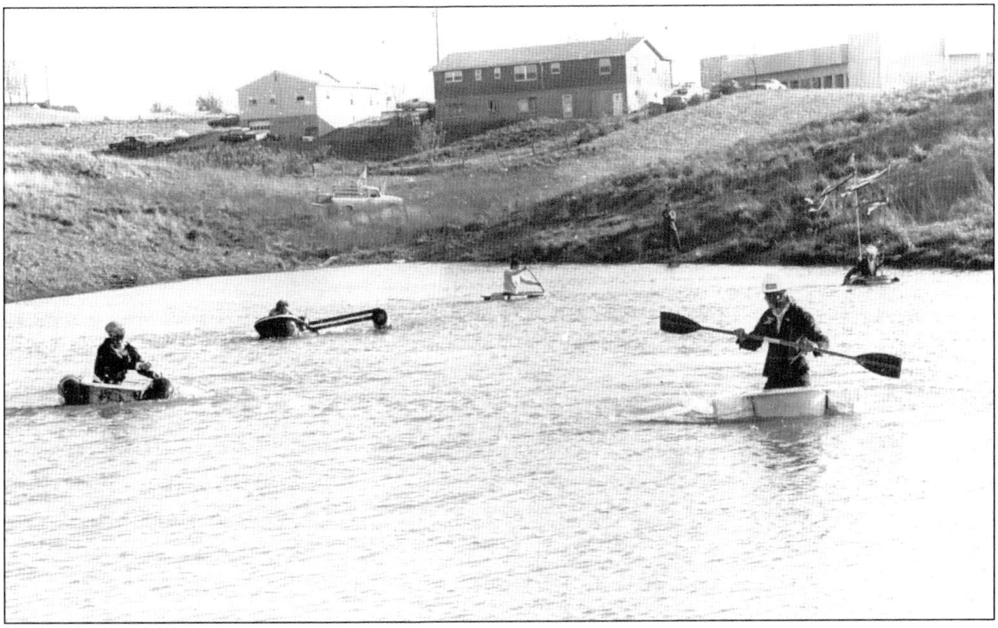

The first Bathtub Regatta is in full swing. Pictured are Tim Weber in the lead and Charles Gilbert in second place, followed by Jerry Helm with the pontoon outrigger on his bathtub. In the distance, John DeMarcus and Frank Steely can be seen in their tubs. Jerry Helm was later disqualified for pushing his bathtub onto the shore of the lake.

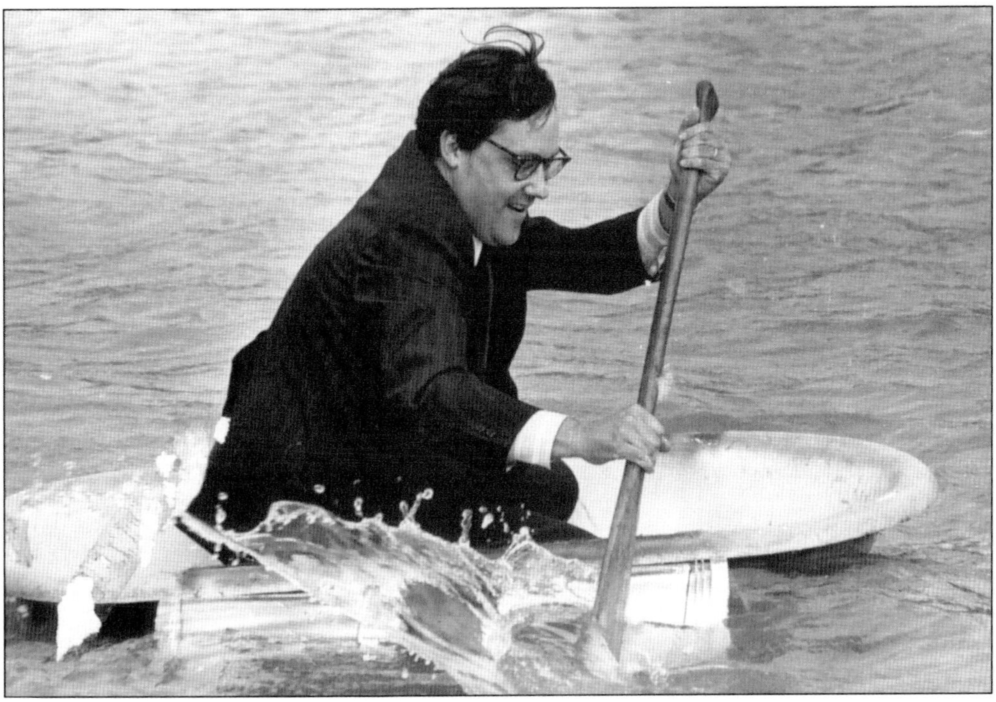

Dr. John DeMarcus, then vice president for administration, paddled furiously in the inaugural Bathtub Regatta, part of the 1973 Rites of Spring celebration.

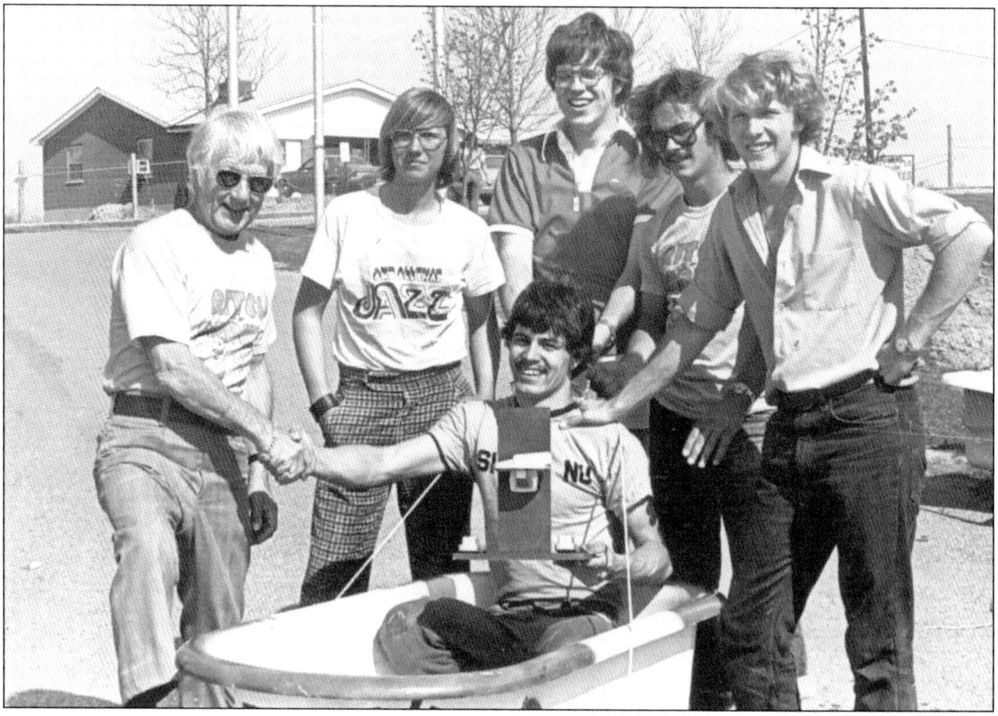

Local television personality Bob Shreve, host of many Saturday morning programs, congratulates the crew of the winning bathtub in the annual regatta. The student who piloted the tub to victory holds the trophy.

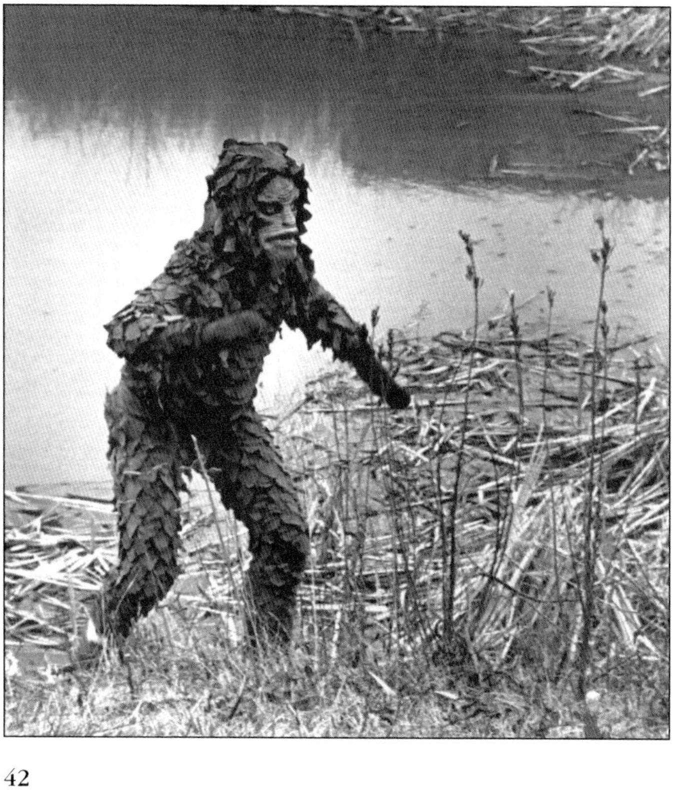

The Rites of Spring featured other events, such as tricycle and office chair races, a watermelon toss, and eating competitions. The eating competitions often featured the local favorite Skyline chili, practically an icon in the greater Cincinnati region. Many students also turned up in strange hats or even stranger costumes. This photograph shows the Creature from Lake Inferior attending the annual festivities.

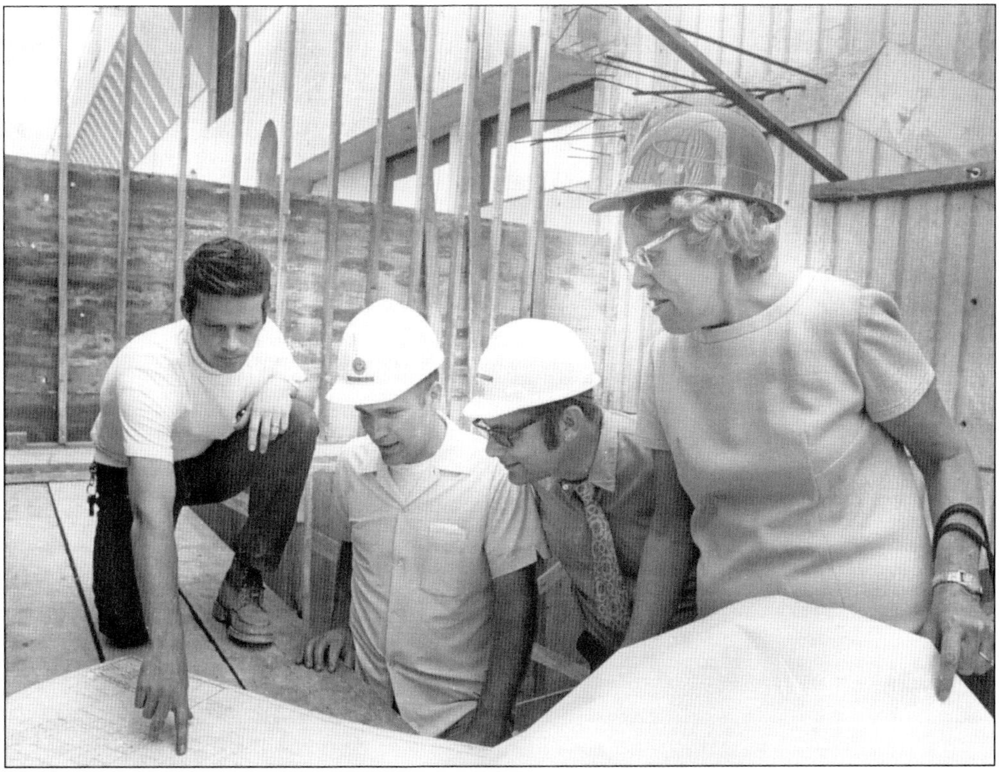

Several academic administrators get their first look at the plans for the science building. Completed in 1974, the new building housed the physical and life science departments as well as providing temporary quarters to the music and psychology departments, who were awaiting their own buildings. Pictured from left to right are Terry Selby, field engineer with Fisk-Rinehart, an architectural firm; Dr. Bart Braden, professor of math and physical sciences; Dr. Ron Singer, professor of psychology; and Dr. Clara Richards, professor of biology.

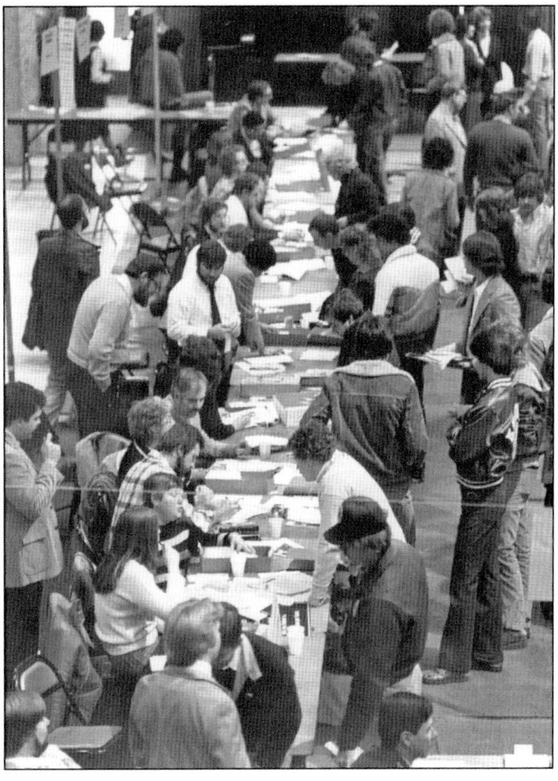

In the crowded conditions prevailing on the new campus, walk-in registration could be a madhouse. Students plunged into the structured chaos with the goal of a full schedule.

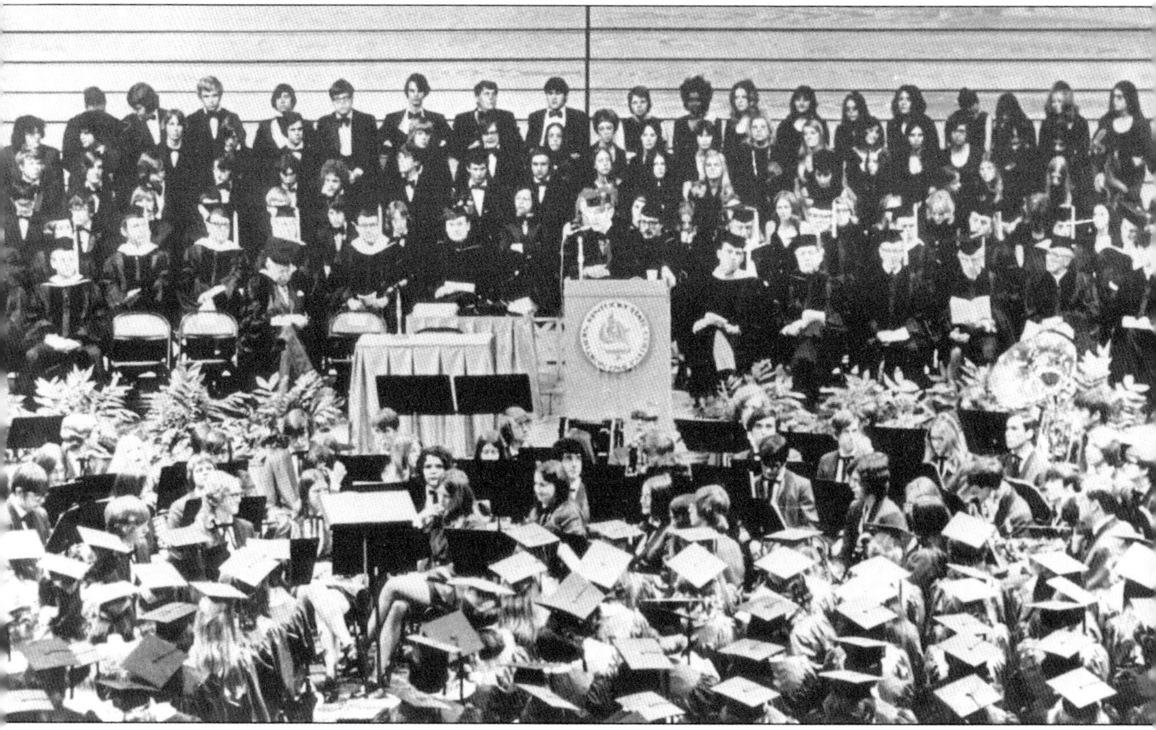

The ultimate goal was graduation. Northern Kentucky State College graduated its first class of 611 students in May 1973 in the newly completed Regents Hall. The college's rapid growth eventually made it impossible to continue to hold commencement in Regents, and the ceremonies were moved to an arena in Cincinnati, Ohio. In 2006, ground was broken for a new arena at Northern that will allow commencement to return to campus.

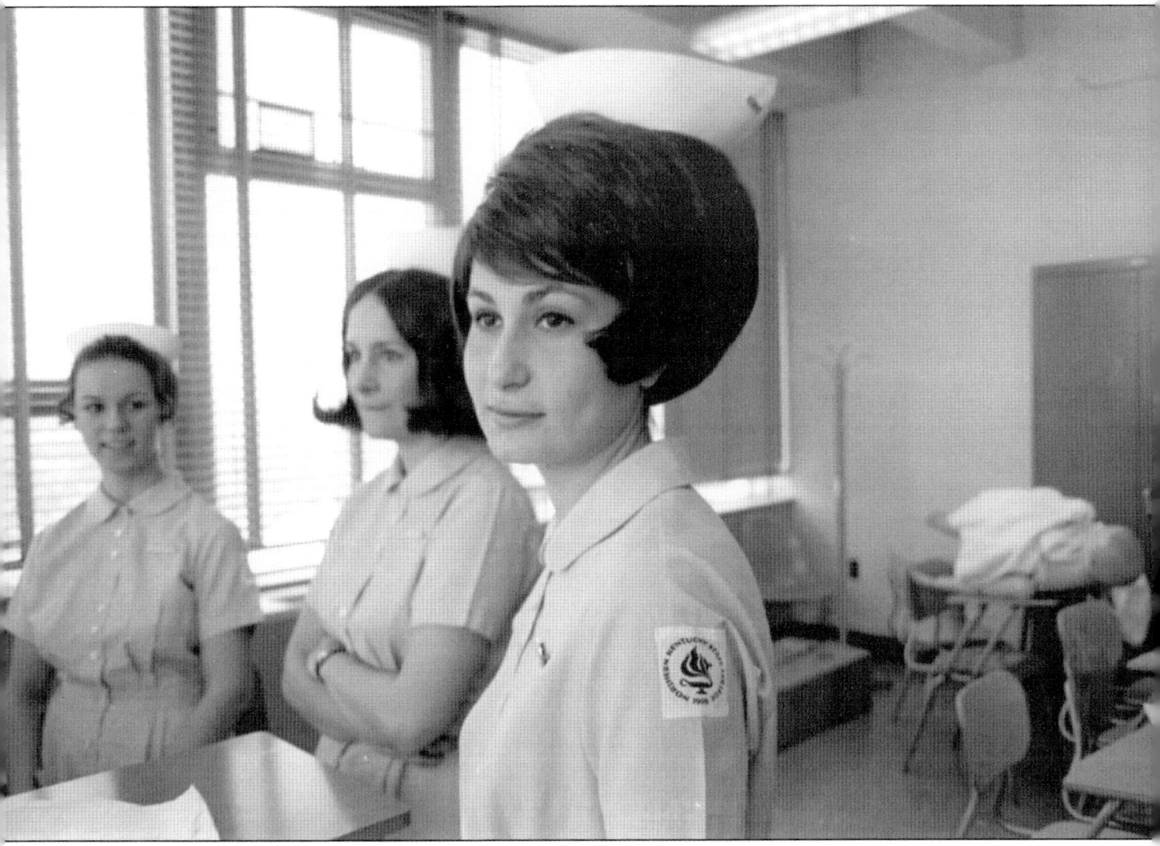

While taking part in the main commencement in Regents Hall, some of the departments also had their own special ceremonies. Here the first graduating class of student nurses awaits its capping ceremony in the nursing school in May 1973.

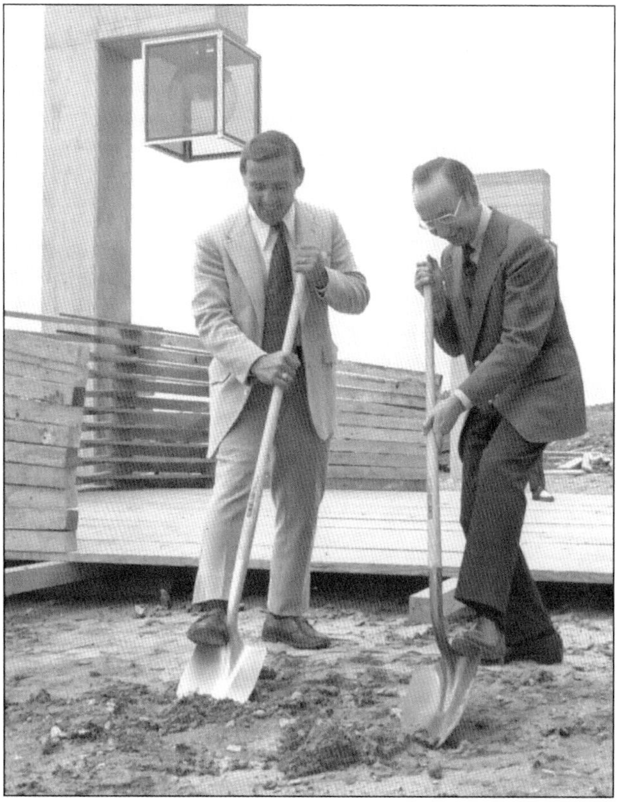

Groundbreakings were a common site on NKSC's campus as the college grew faster than even the most optimistic predictions. Scenes like the one below were, and still are, commonplace. Construction equipment abounds, and hard hats are as prevalent as backpacks. From the beginning, it has been a race to build classrooms fast enough to accommodate the ever-increasing numbers of students applying to fill the seats. The photograph at left shows part of the groundbreaking for the W. Frank Steely Library in October 1973. Pictured are Regent Ken Lucas (left) and President Steely, for whom the new building is to be named.

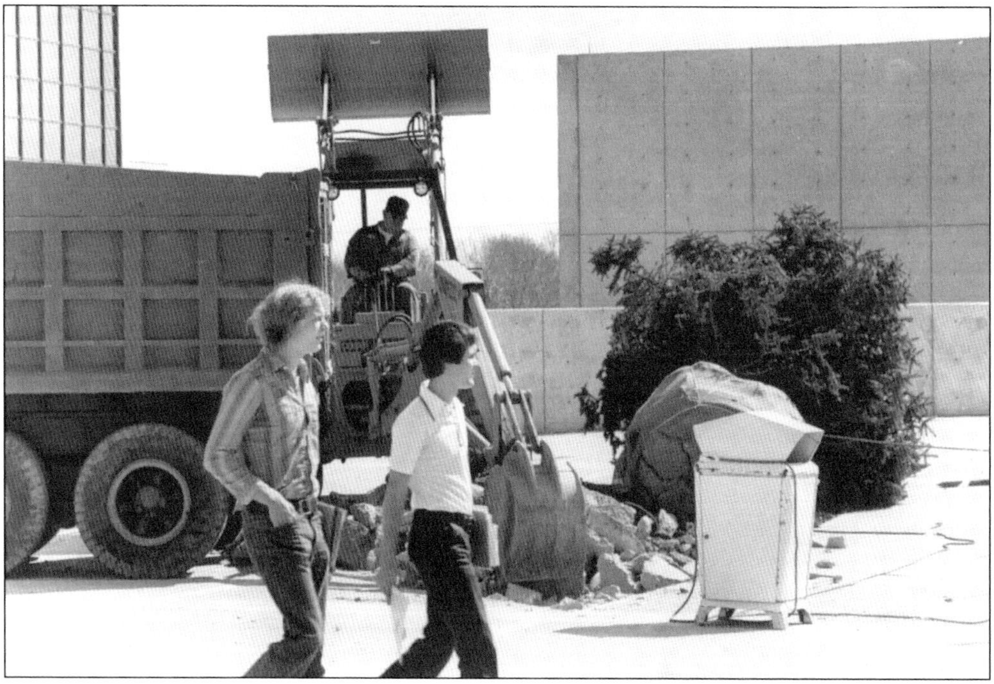

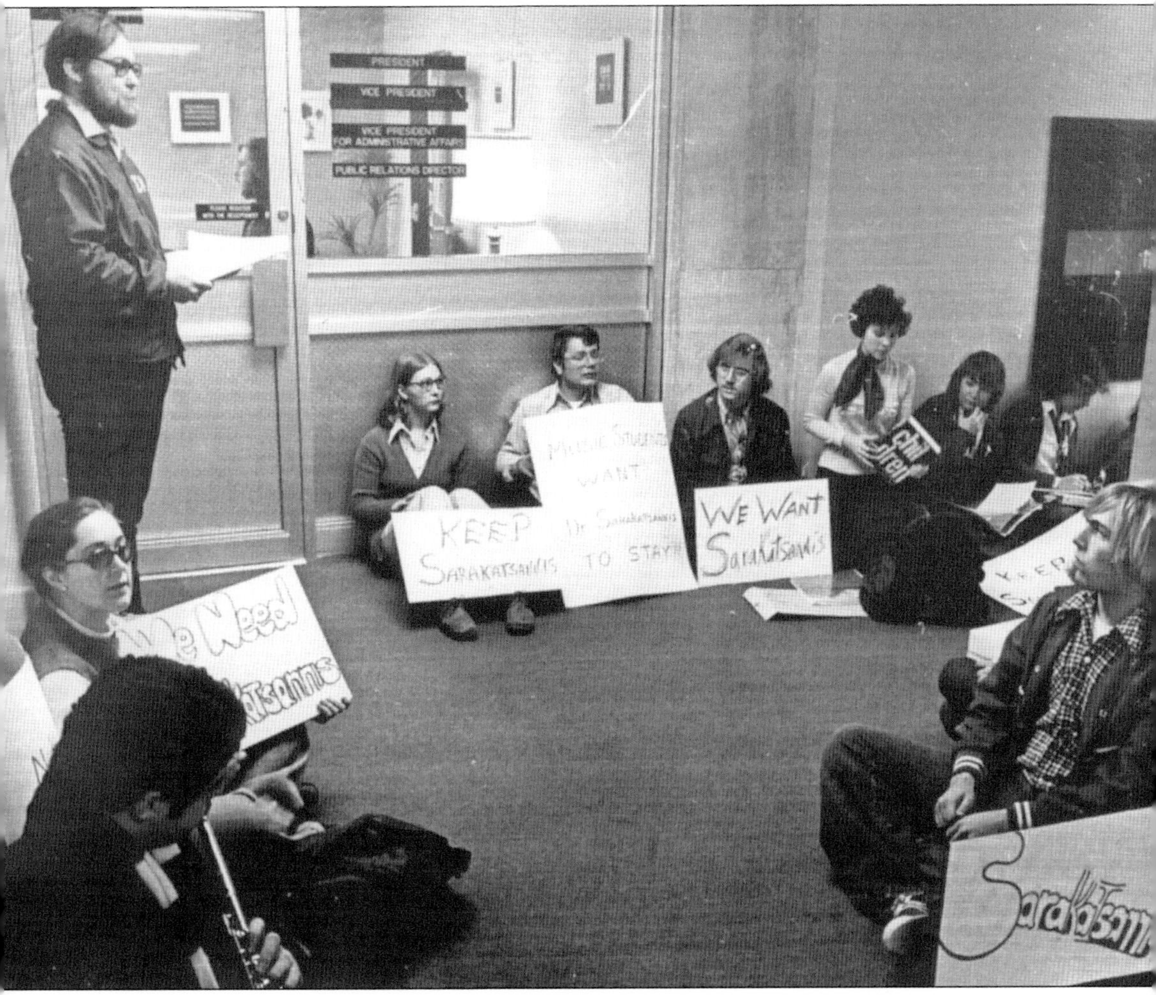

Despite the positive momentum, all was not smooth sailing on campus. Student protests and general unrest were fairly common on college campuses across the country in the early 1970s, and NKSC was no exception. This particular student protest was over the dismissal of Dr. Leonidas Sarakatsannis, a professor in the music department. The later dismissal of Dr. Leslie Tihany and the controversy it engendered would eventually lead to Steely's decision to resign as president of the university. He would accept a teaching position, joining the ranks of NKSC faculty.

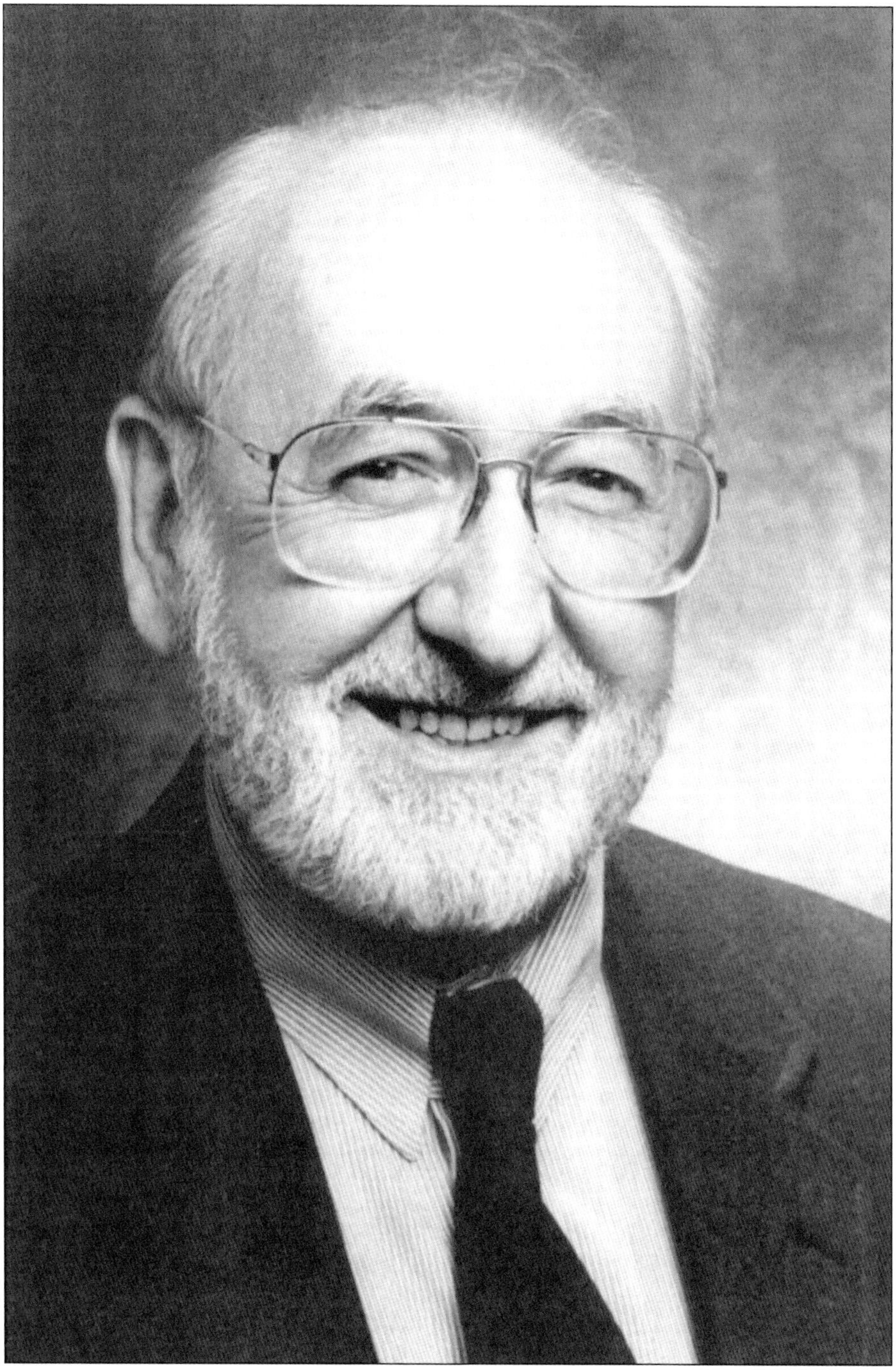

After many years teaching history at NKU, where he was well regarded by his students, Dr. Frank Steely retired. Though he was no longer teaching, he continued to write and research local history. His book *Northern: The Birth of a University*, recounting his view of the events of his presidency, was published in 1993 and dedicated to "all my relatives . . . who may never have a book dedicated to them." He is still seen on campus regularly, where he occupies an office on the top floor of Steely Library.

Three

UNIVERSITY STATUS
The Era of Tesseneer and Albright

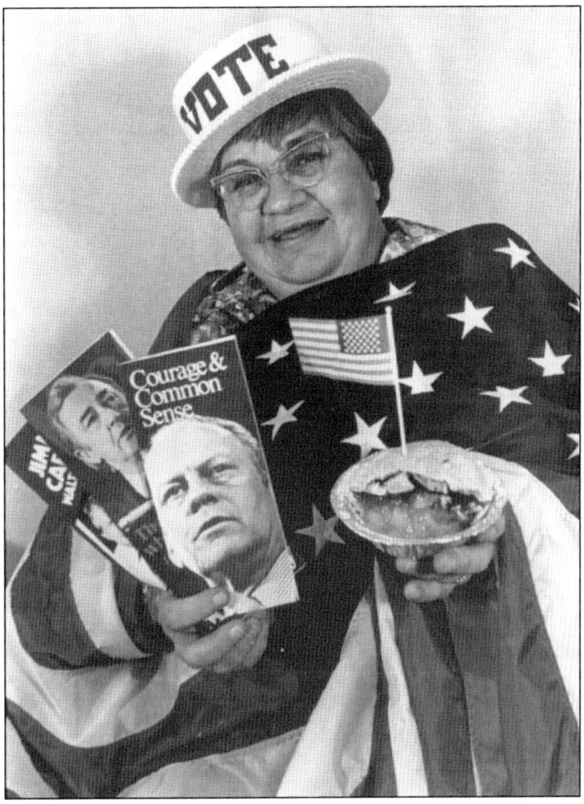

In a photograph titled "Mom, Flag, and Apple Pie," journalism professor Lois Sutherland shows off her patriotic spirit during the 1976 campaign season.

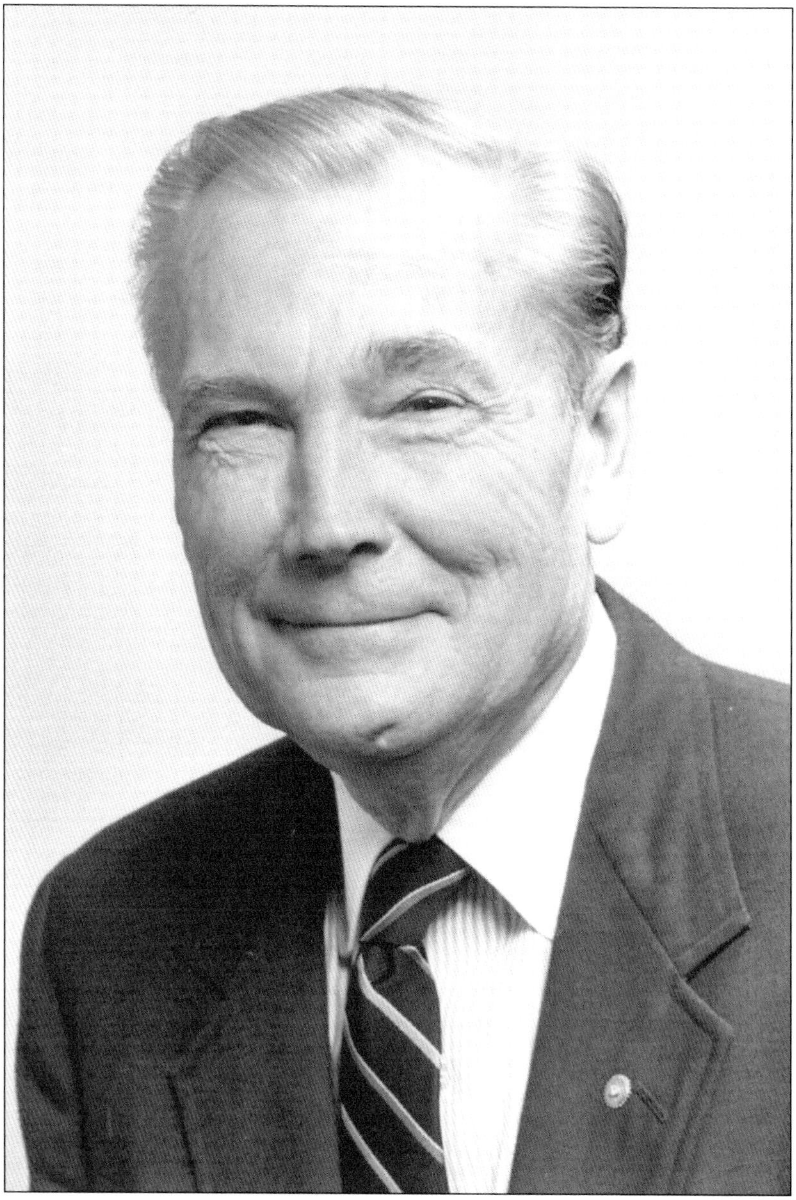

Dr. Ralph Tesseneer was vice president of academic affairs under the administration of the first president, Dr. W. Frank Steely. The two worked closely to build NKSC in its infancy. While Steely dealt with funding issues in Frankfort and other "big picture" items, Tesseneer hired the actual faculty. For this reason, Steely took over a former dance studio across the street from the Covington campus for his office, while Tesseneer was given the nicer administrative office in Hankins Hall. The faculty interviews were all conducted in Tesseneer's office, which gave a better impression to potential faculty than the pink-painted, mirrored room Steely was using. After Dr. Steely's resignation in 1975, Tesseneer was appointed interim president, a position he held for the next year. Though he applied for the position and was among the five candidates to be interviewed, Tesseneer was not favored by the faculty. The Board of Regents eventually chose Dr. A. D. Albright for the post. Tesseneer was elected as the first president of the NKU Foundation in 1977, a post he held until 1986.

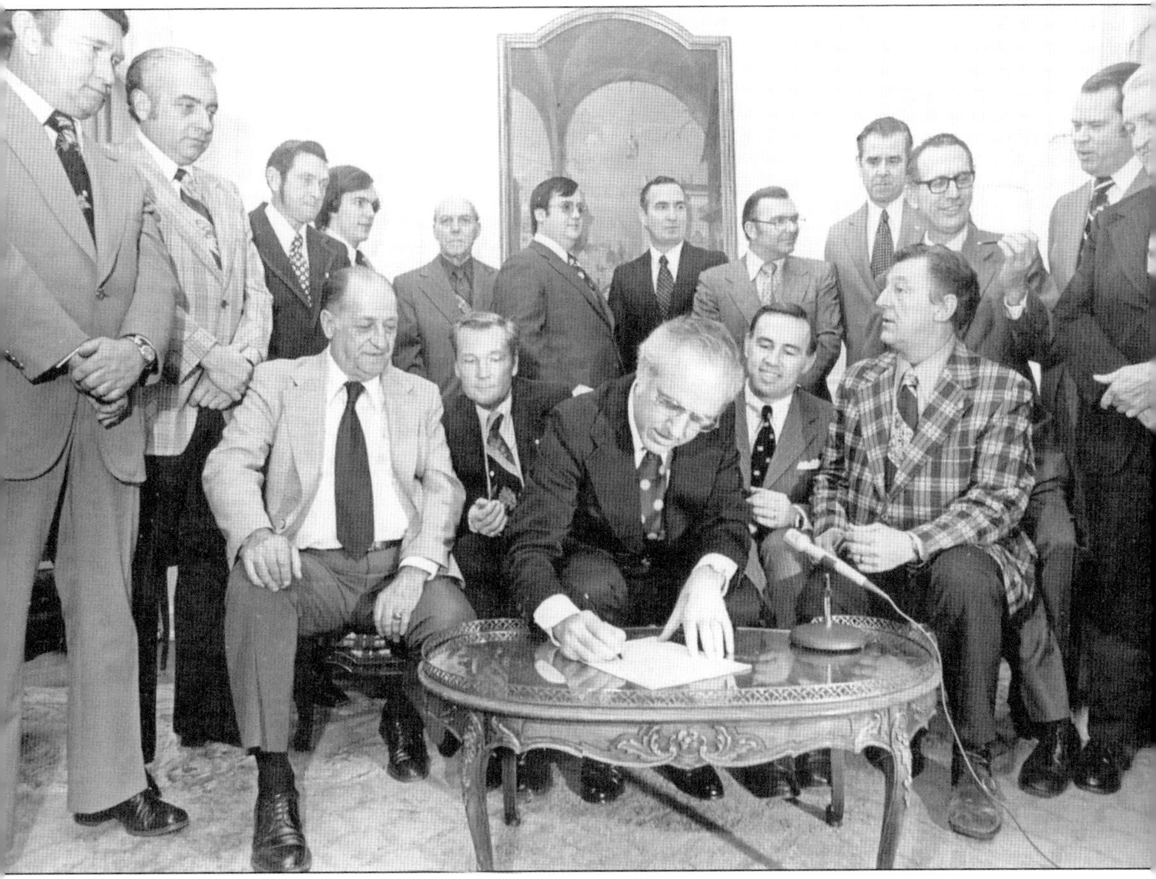

While the Northern Kentucky Caucus looks on, Gov. Julian Carroll signs the house bill granting NKSC full university status June 19, 1976. He signed a number of copies, all with different commemorative pens, which were distributed to each of the representatives present. One of these is available for viewing in the University Archives. With the Chase law school merger, NKSC had ceased to be a state college in truth and had begun the move to a full-fledged university. This was only reemphasized when the College of Education began a master's degree program. Signing the house bill shortly after the first master of arts in education degrees were awarded, Governor Carroll was acknowledging what had been a recognized fact among Northern Kentucky residents for several years: NKU wasn't just a state college anymore.

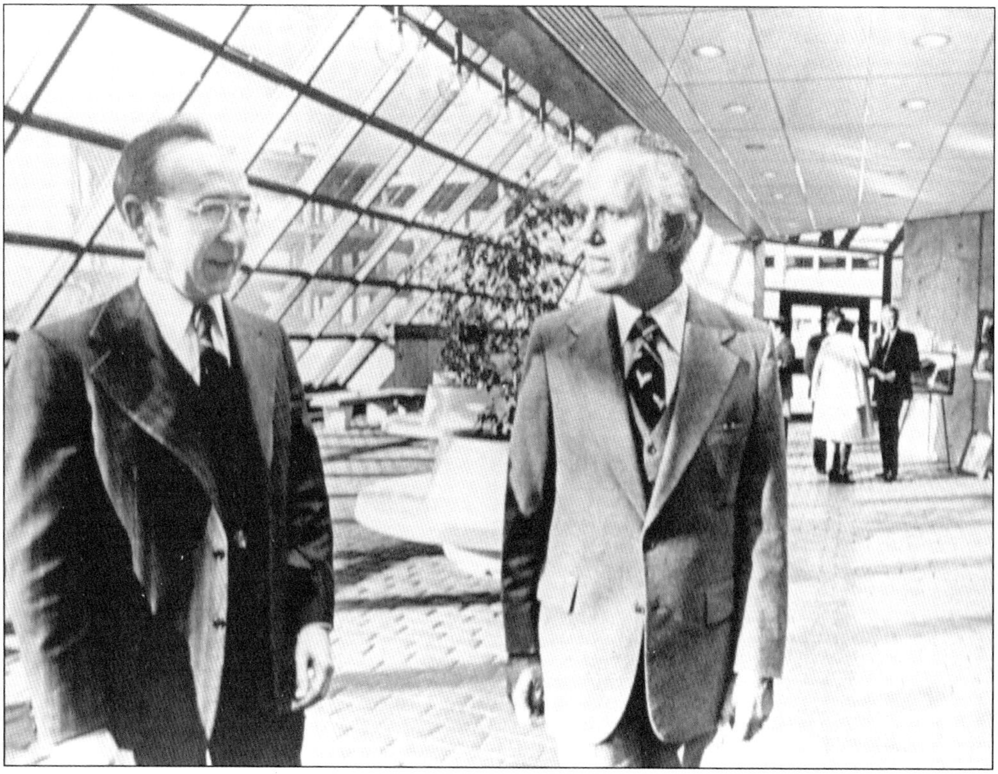

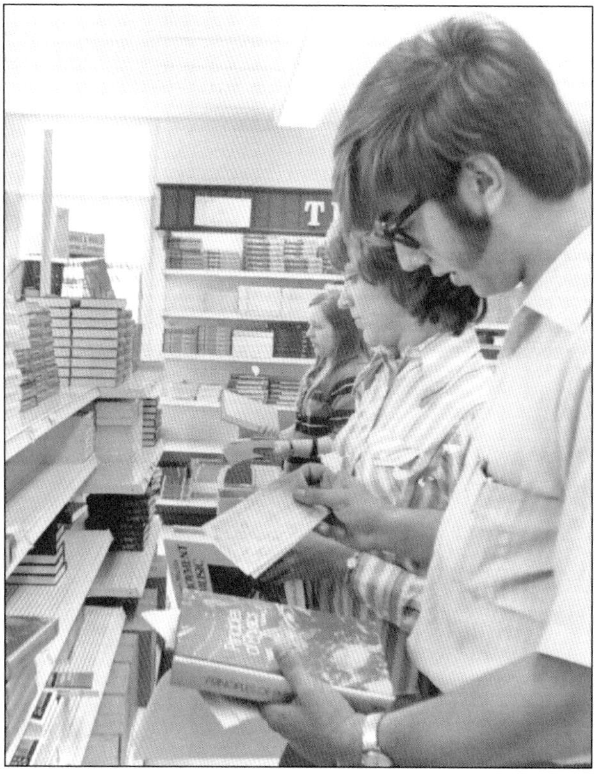

The W. Frank Steely Library was dedicated in November 1975. Steely, seen above, participated in the ceremony officially opening the new library that was named for him, the final building legacy of his presidency. Moving the library out of Nunn Hall gave much-needed space to the woefully overcrowded bookstore, seen at left. The space in Nunn that the two areas occupied had been specially built to accommodate the weight of stored books, an important factor several years later, when the time came to move the law school and its library to the main campus.

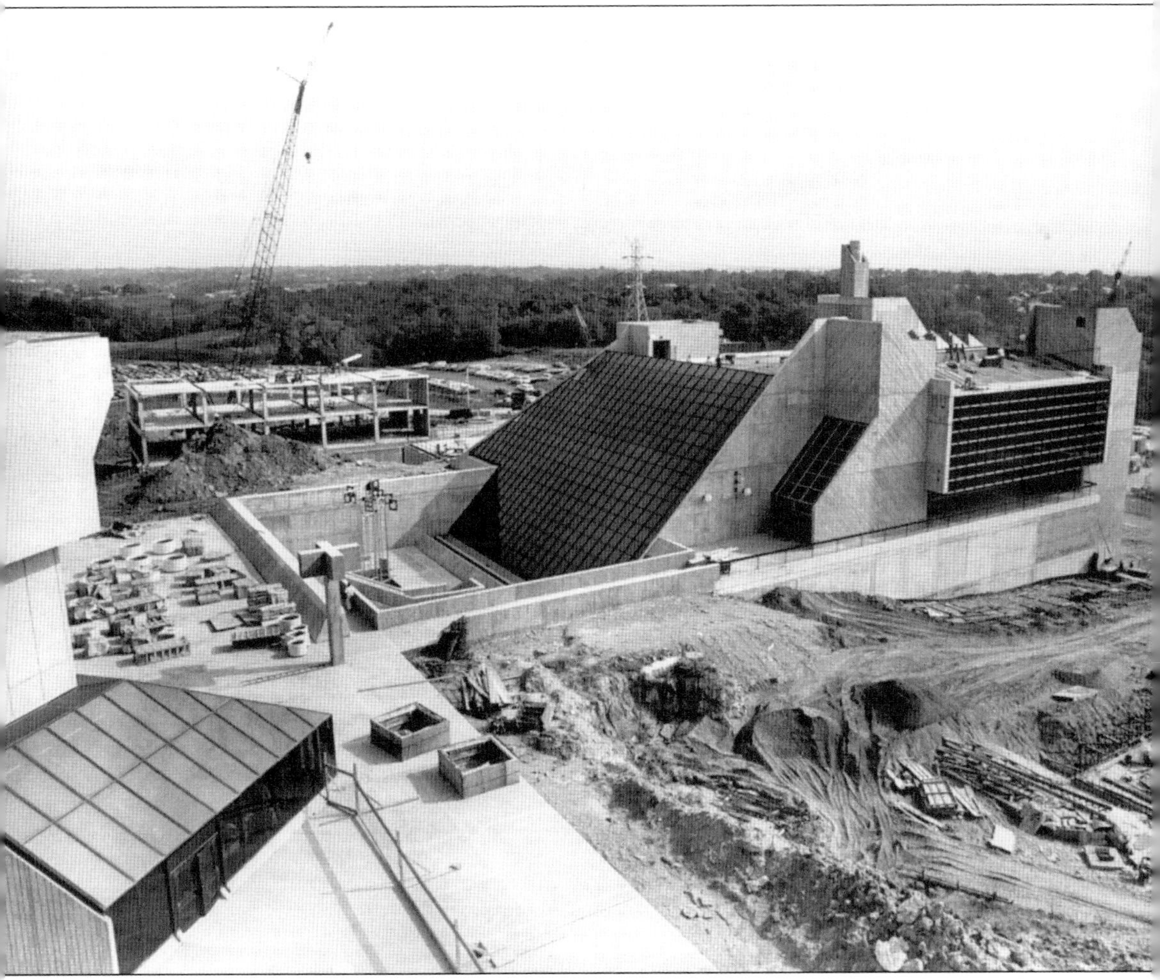

It has never been uncommon to see more than one building project on campus at any given moment. In this case, the W. Frank Steely Library is bracketed by the construction of the Landrum Academic Center and the Fine Arts Center. The two buildings were the first step in moving academic departments out of Nunn Hall. The long-range plan was to empty Nunn and to renovate it to house the Chase College of Law, at that time located at the original Covington campus. The large sunken plaza in front of the library was eliminated during a later library renovation. The area is now stack space in the building's lower levels.

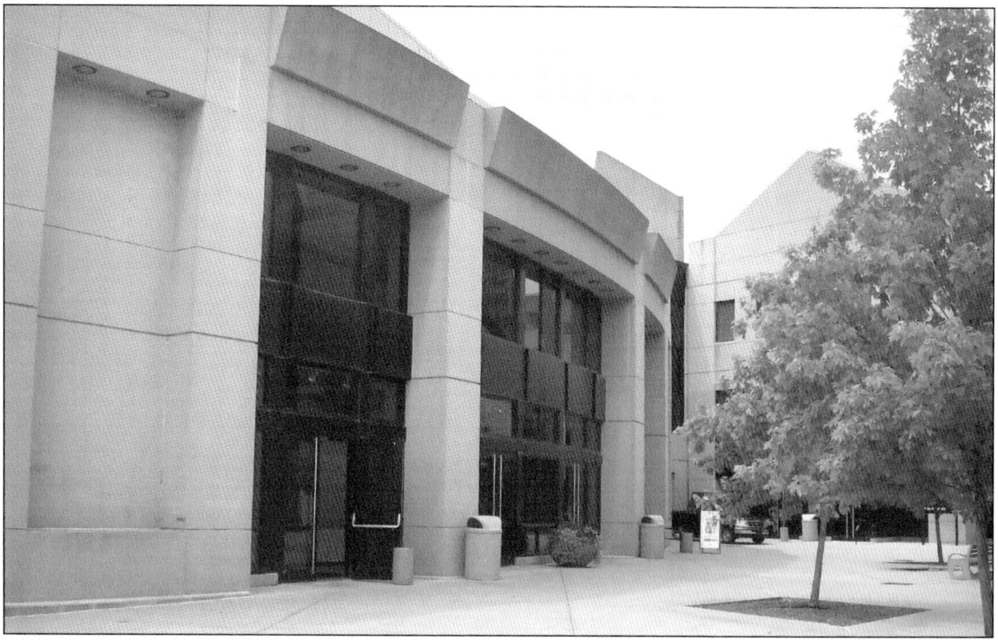

The Fine Arts Center finally opened in the spring of 1977, allowing the art, theater, and music departments to move out of the science building, where they had been temporarily housed during construction. It was hoped that they would be moving from their previous overcrowded quarters directly into the new building, but increasing enrollments prevented the departments from waiting any longer. Housing them in the science building was a stopgap measure until construction could be completed. The Fine Arts Center included a theater, music practice rooms, and several much-needed art galleries. The faculty and students of the various departments finally had the resources they needed. The later addition above included a new auditorium, Greaves Concert Hall. Below, art students and faculty prepare for a mixed-media exhibition in one of those galleries.

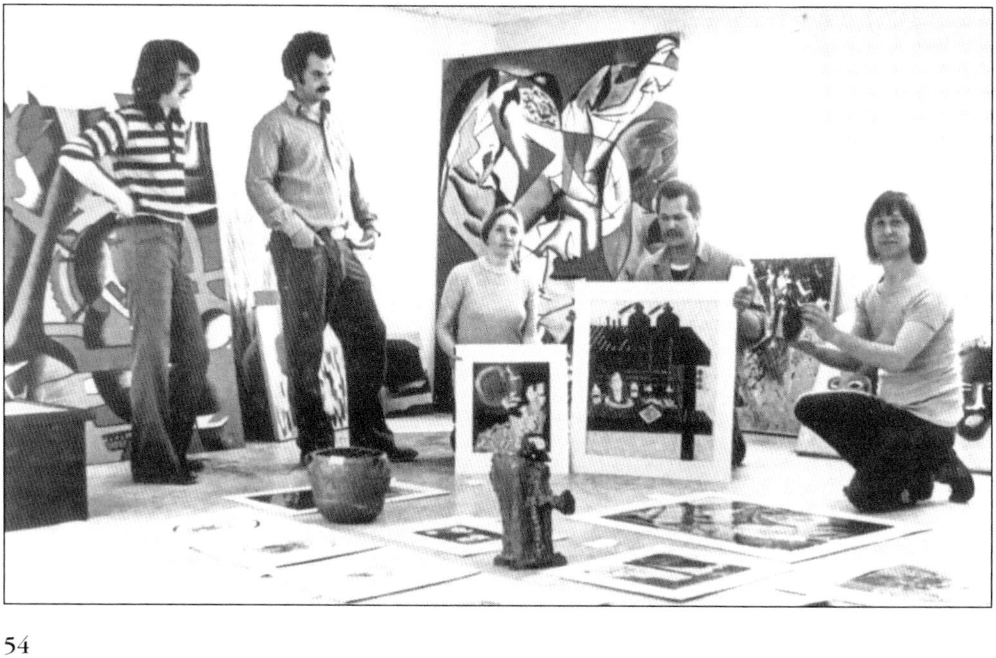

The Landrum Academic Center, opened for classes in the fall of 1976, became the home for a number of humanities and social sciences departments. Clearing those departments out of Nunn Hall was another step toward freeing up the space for the Chase College of Law to move to the main campus. Not long after the completion of Landrum, the building began to have problems. This was first noticed when doors refused to close and chalkboards fell off walls. An unusual layer of shale in the ground under the building, the first such layer ever found in Northern Kentucky, swelled, causing walls and floors to buckle in the building. A hole was excavated in room 107 as part of the investigative and repair work. The building didn't suffer any major structural damage, but the jokes it inspired continue to circulate on campus.

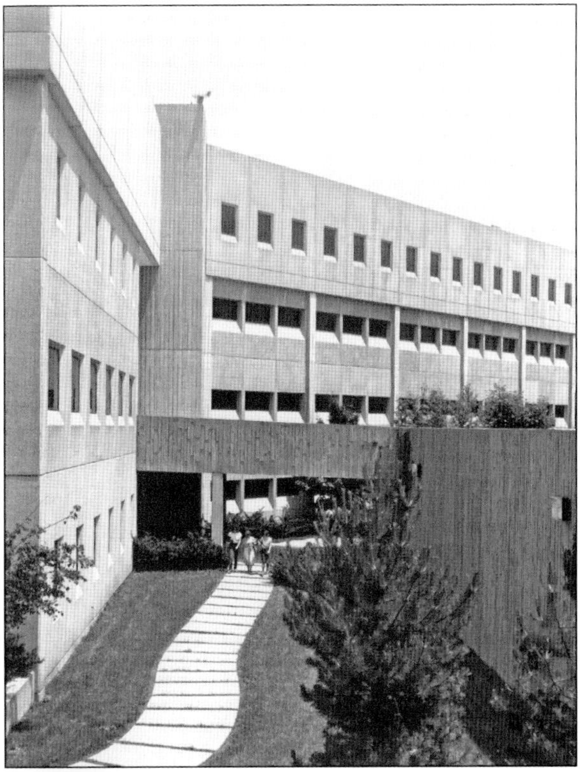

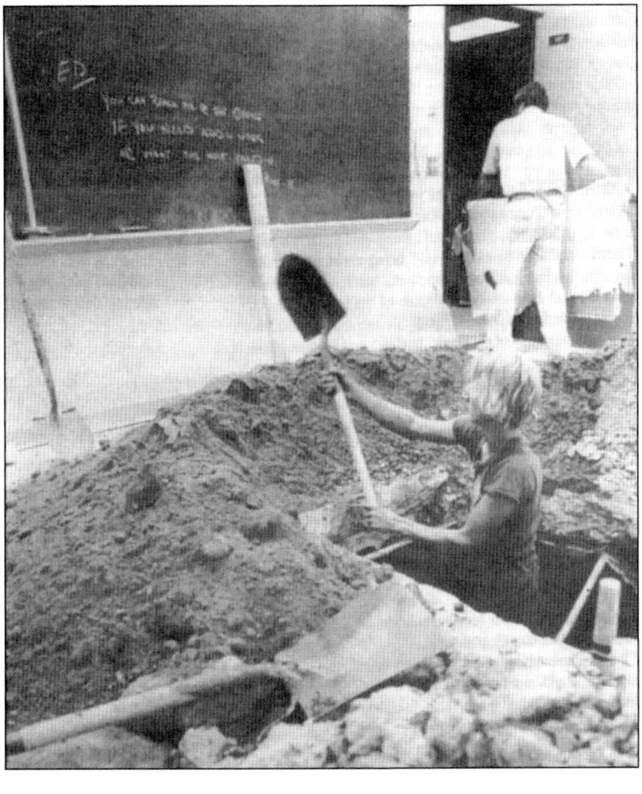

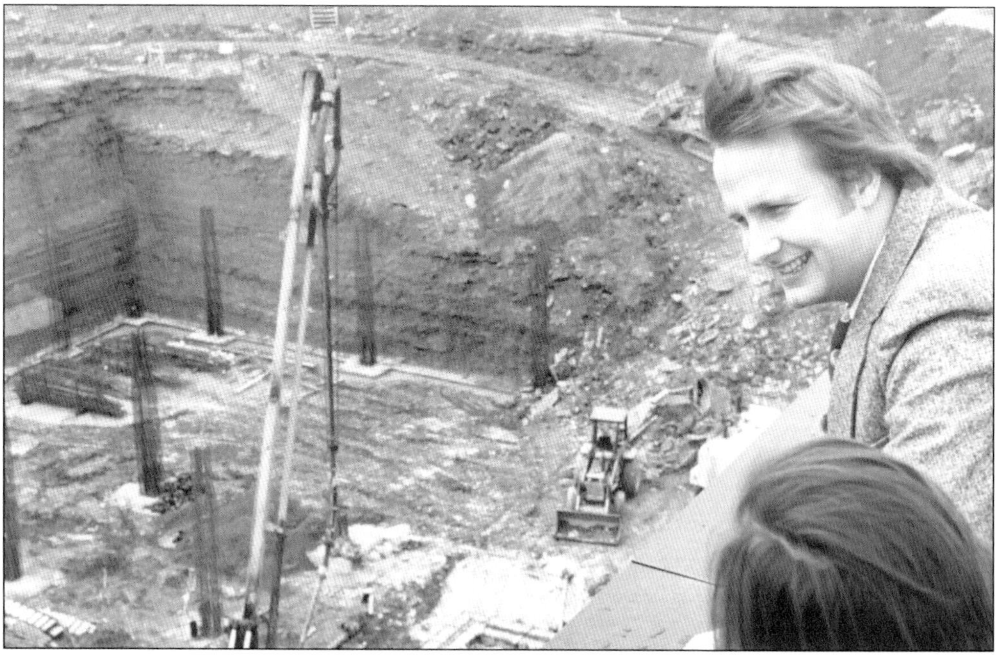

Above, administrator Gary Eith looks out over the construction site for the Lucas Administrative Center, begun in 1979. The first floor of the eight-story structure is below ground. It was hoped that the completion of this building, along with the Business, Education, and Psychology Center begun the previous year, would relieve the perennial overcrowding on campus. The space was also vital if Nunn Hall was to be emptied out for the Chase College of Law. Moving the administration into new quarters would clear the way for renovation work on Nunn, which would then become the permanent home of the law school. Below, the finished administrative building, named for congressional representative and former regent Ken Lucas, is the tallest building on campus.

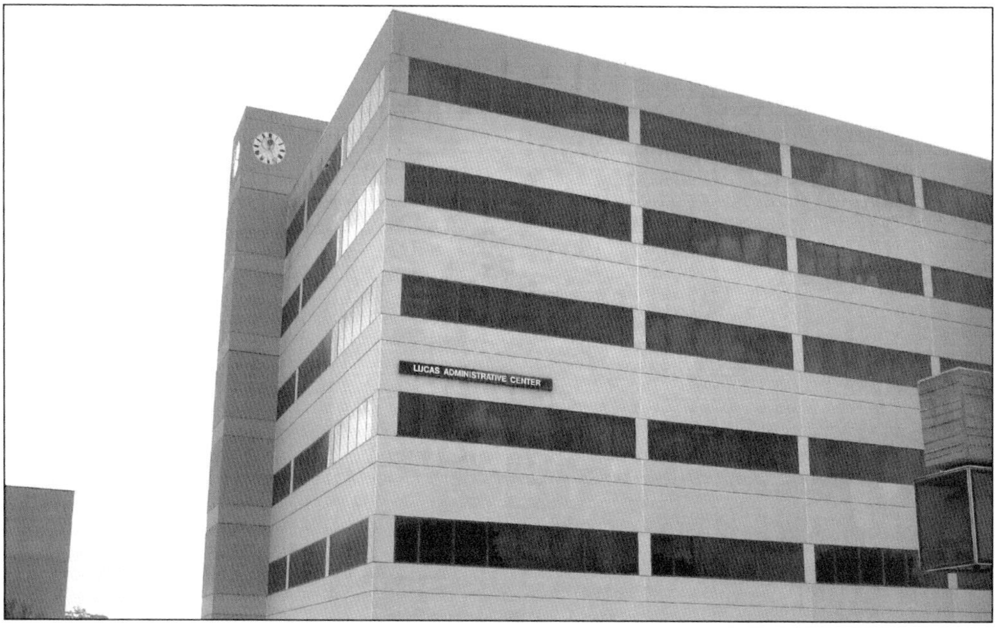

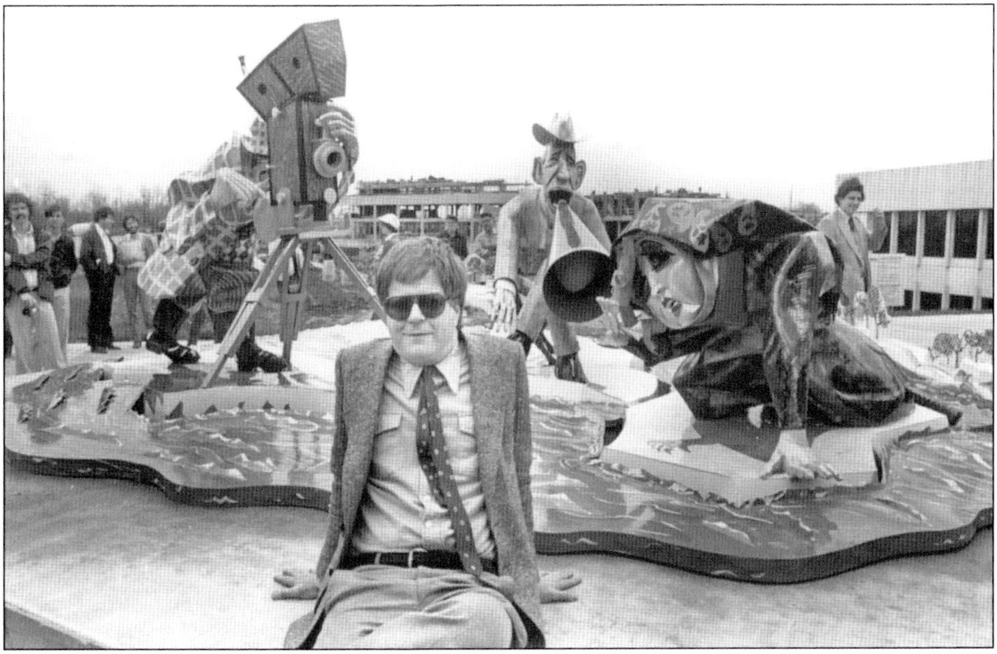

Above, artist Red Grooms is shown seated in front of the sculpture he created for the campus. *Way Down East* depicts the filming of the silent movie of the same name by controversial director D. W. Griffith. To the left is Prof. Howard Storm, who wrote the grant that funded the work. To the right is art professor Kevin Booher, who was also instrumental in bringing the sculpture to life. Originally installed on campus in April 1979, the piece was sent on loan to the Smithsonian Institution for its traveling exhibit "Hollywood: Legend and Reality." The sculpture opened the exhibit in 1985 with a two-month stint in front of the museum entrance in Washington, D.C., before touring the country for the next two years. Red Grooms answers questions at the sculpture's dedication below.

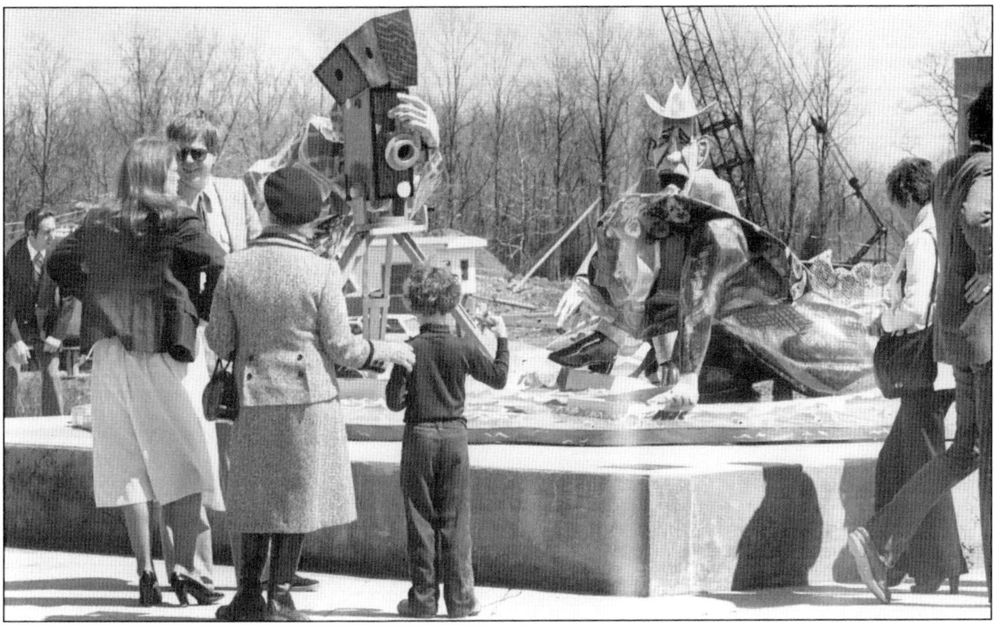

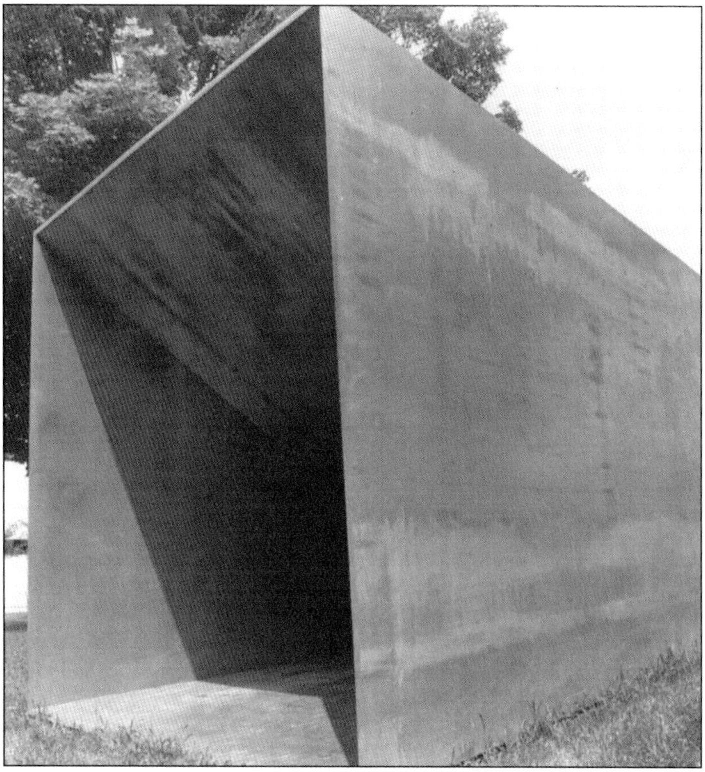

The National Endowment for the Arts grant that paid for Red Grooms's sculpture also paid for this minimalist work by artist Donald Judd. Now known by students simply as "The Box," the aluminum piece symbolizes and, some say, comments on the plain facades and sharp angles of NKU's concrete campus. Judd's sculpture resides on the main plaza in front of Nunn Hall.

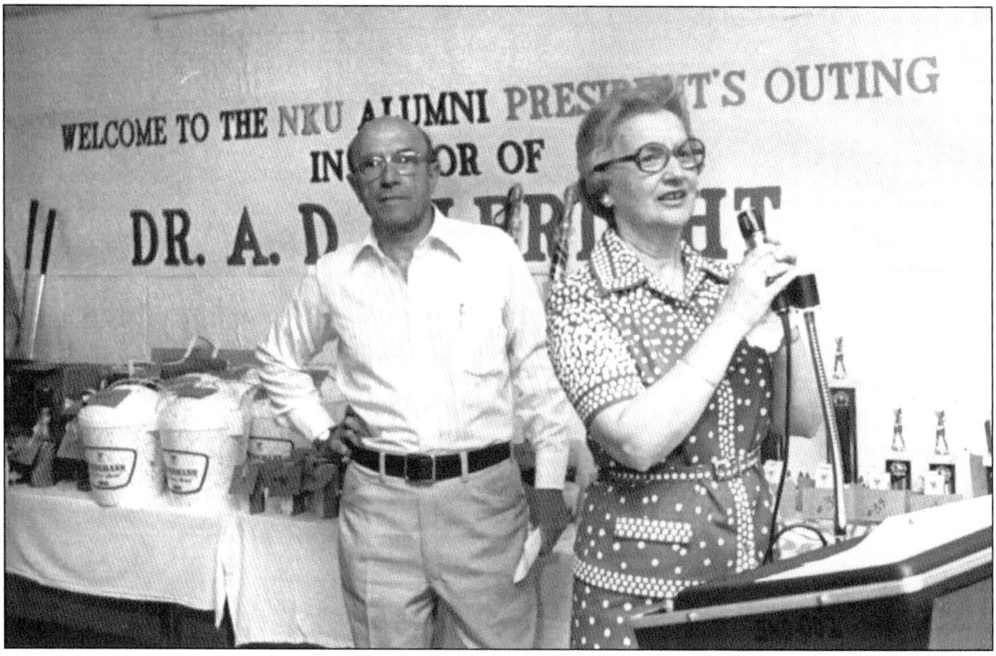

In the late 1970s, one of the older traditions of the campus began. The annual President's Golf Outing began as a way to get back in touch with alumni, bringing them together for a fun-filled day. It eventually became two events: the President's Invitational, sponsored by University Development, and the Young Alumni Society Golf Outing.

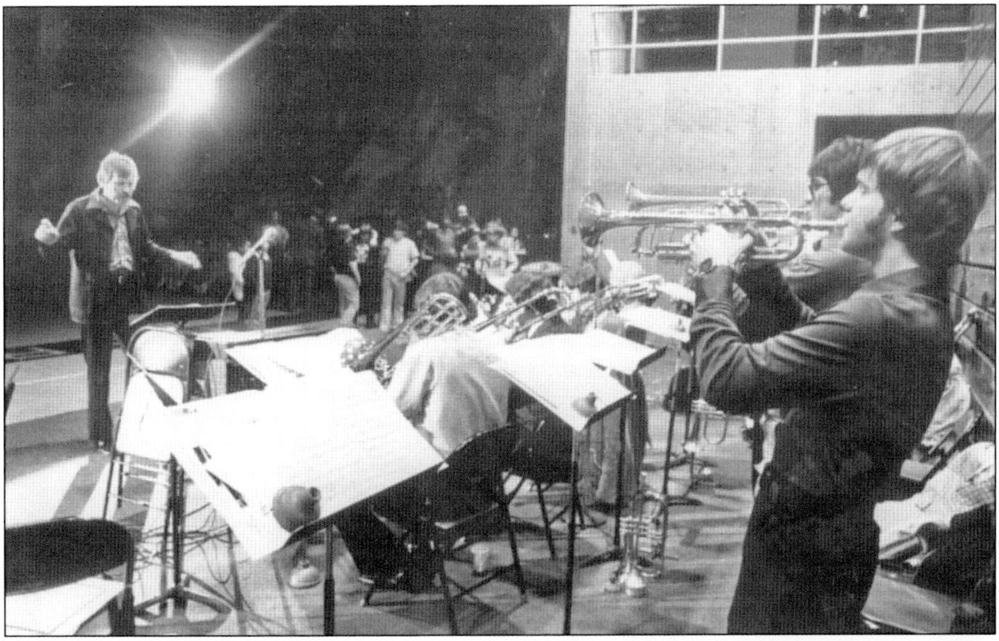

The NKU Jazz Ensemble, at that time under the direction of Prof. Gary Johnston, makes a halftime appearance at a 1978 basketball game in the photograph above. Dr. John Westlund, professor of music, conducted the group during this performance. In the photograph at right, Westlund directs the university choir at the Hanging of the Greens, which celebrates the holiday season. The choir is singing from the second-floor walkway overlooking the lobby of the University Center. The choir was later divided into two groups, the Northern Chorale and the Chamber Choir, both of which still perform.

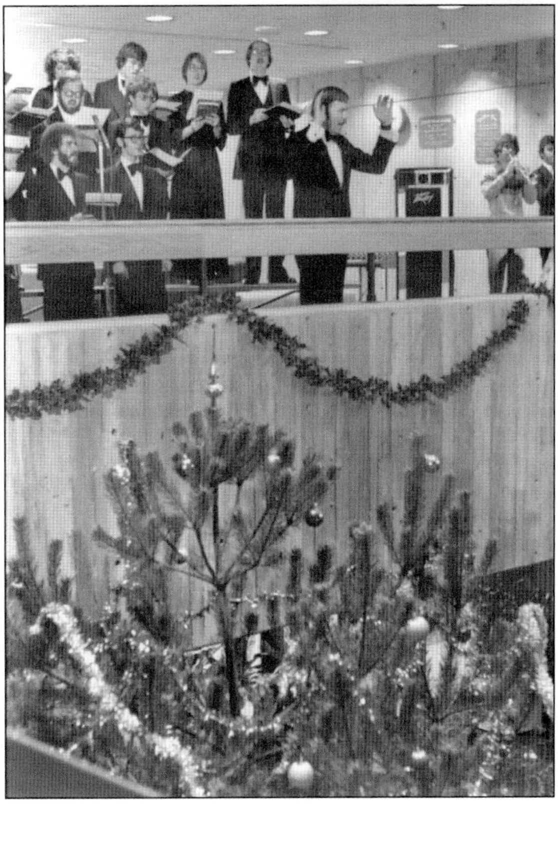

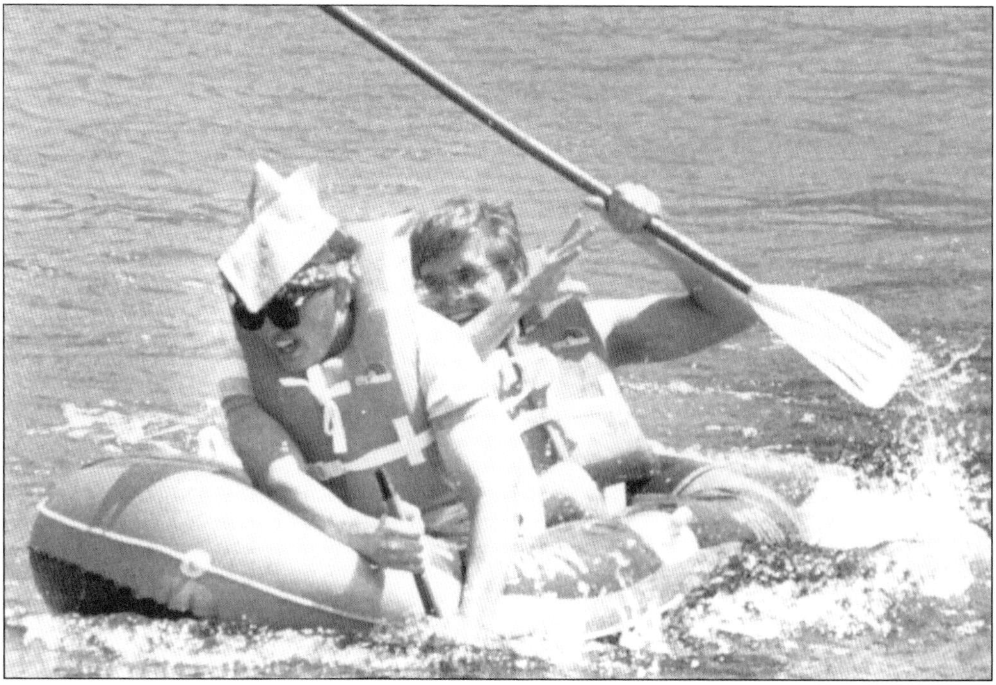

And they're off! The students above are paddling furiously in a bid to win the raft race across Lake Inferior at the annual Rites of Spring. As claw-footed bathtubs nearly disappeared from American homes, fewer and fewer were available for race day. Due to this overall decline in bathtub availability, the annual Bathtub Regatta was eventually replaced by racing rubber rafts. Of course, the lighter-weight rafts were not necessarily easier to handle, as demonstrated by the students below who are attempting to separate their rafts after a collision in mid race.

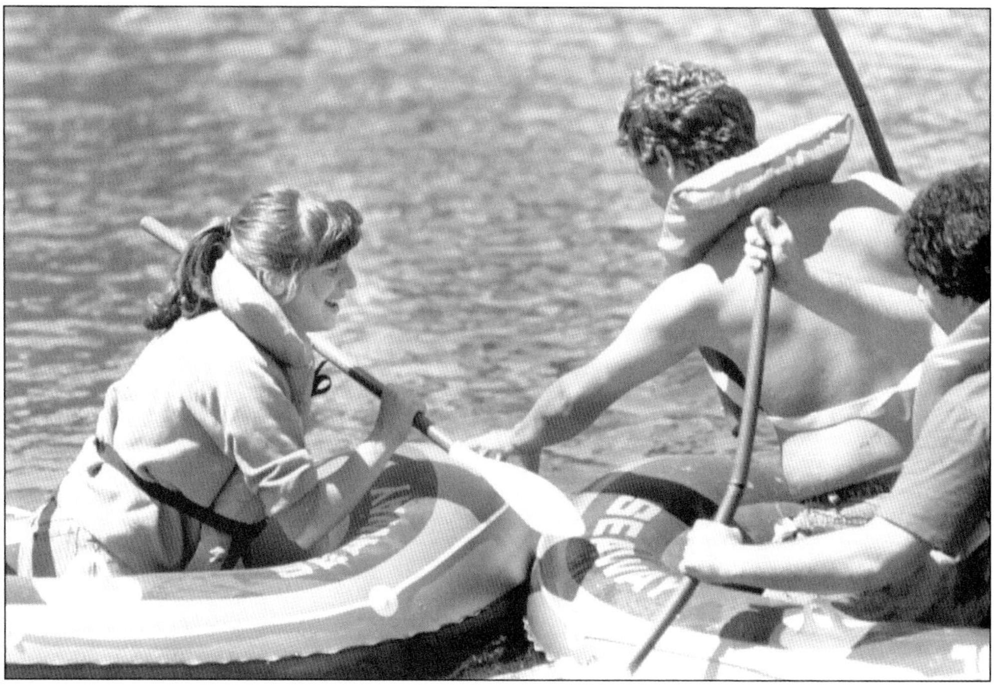

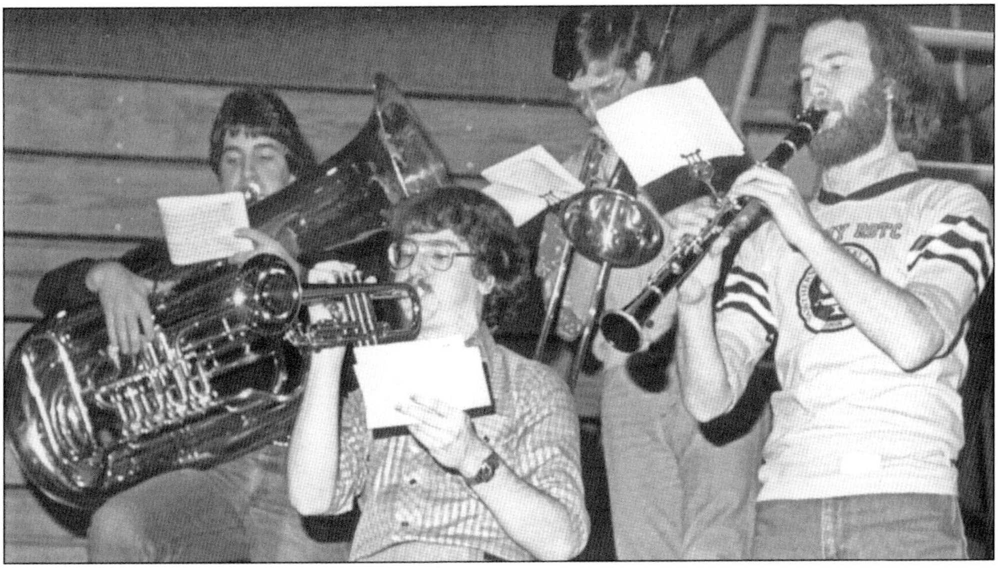

The NKU Pep Band is a common sight at university basketball games. The *c.* 1980 incarnation shown here featured Ralph Schroer on the tuba, Dan Bramwell on trumpet, Mark Schnitzleron on trombone, and Marty Poshkar on clarinet. A more recent version of the band shows the members' school spirit, complete with funny hats, in the photograph below. Though still officially known as the Pep Band, they did wear "Basketball Band" shirts for a time. They are now under the direction of William Brian Hogg, lecturer of saxophone and jazz studies in the Department of Music.

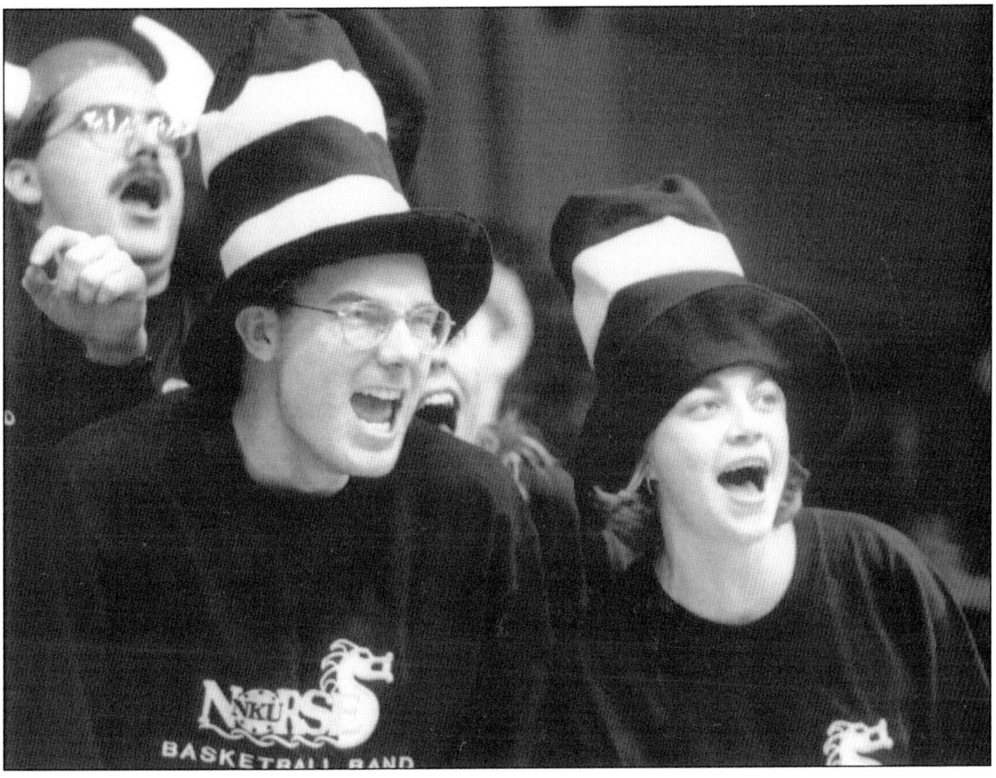

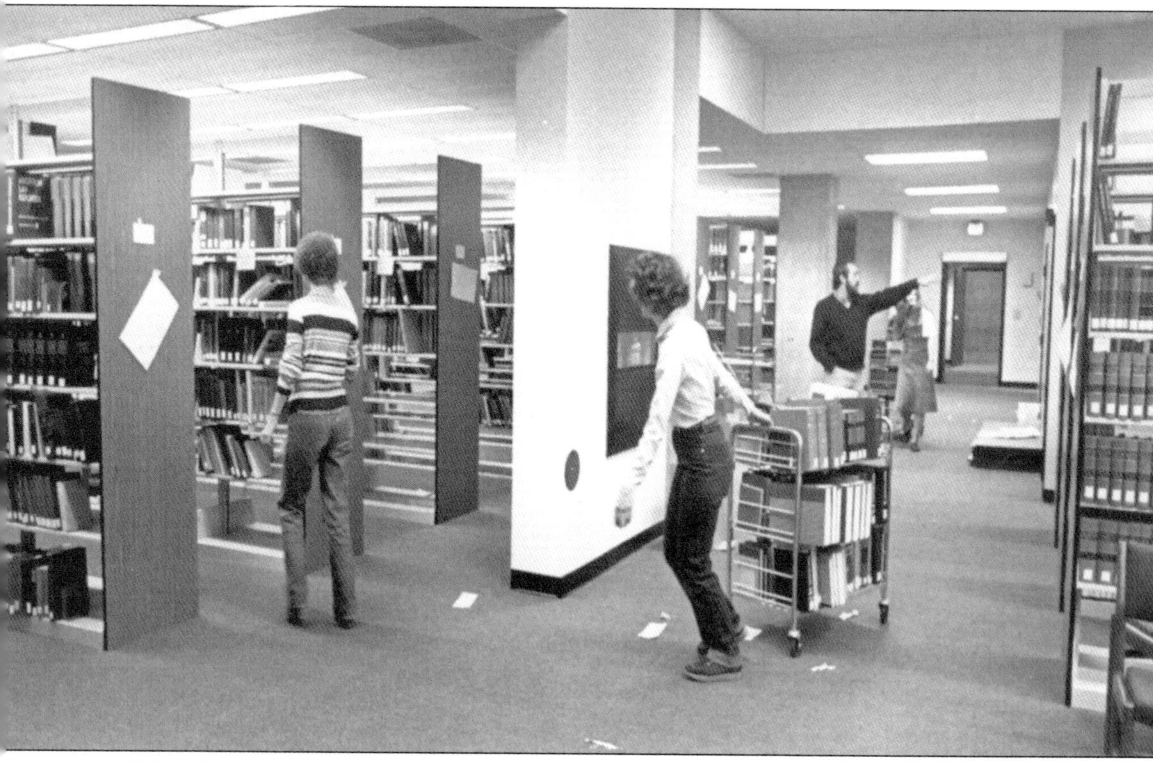

In 1982, the renovations to Nunn Hall were complete, and it was time for Chase College of Law to finally move onto the main campus in Highland Heights. The move didn't come a moment too soon, as the American Bar Association had been pressuring Chase for some time to move out of its exceedingly cramped quarters in Hankins Hall on the original Covington campus. In the spring of that year, Chase began the laborious process of moving across two counties. The law library was moved into space on the bottom two floors, which had originally housed the main campus library and the bookstore when the building was first built. Moving the incredible collection of thick, heavy, legal tomes was regarded as the worst part of the entire move. Here Tom Heard, associate professor of law library services, orchestrates the carts of books moving into the library. The law faculty members were so impressed by the hard work and leadership of the law librarians and staff that they awarded them a special commendation in appreciation of their untiring efforts.

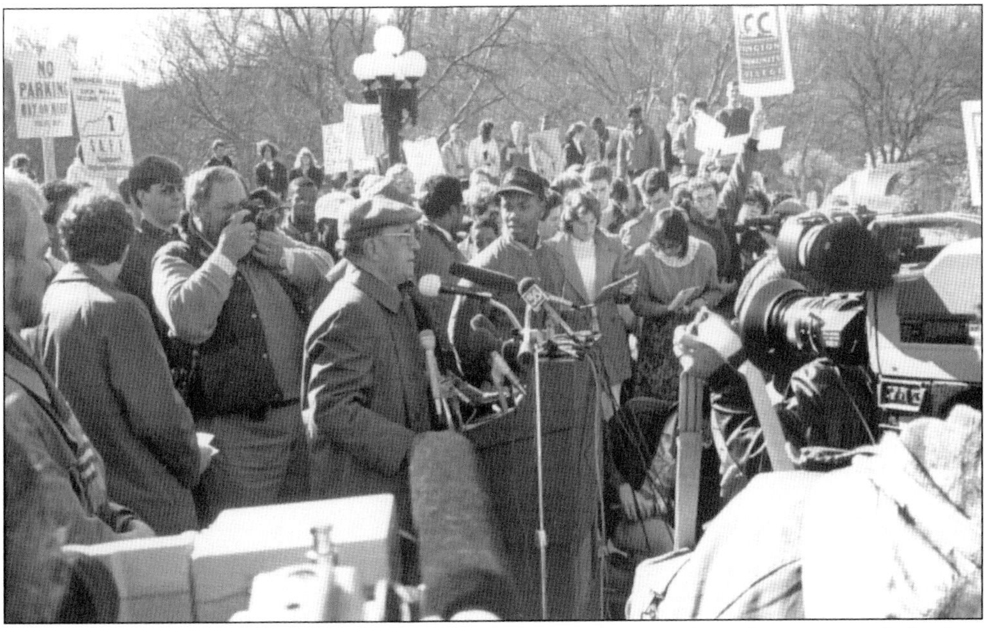

Budget cuts are an oft-heard cry in Kentucky state government. When those statewide budget cuts begin to have a heavy impact on public colleges, the higher education community responds with rallies, protests, and demonstrations in the state capital. This time it was Albright's turn to lobby for higher education funding. Here he speaks at a rally in Frankfort, Kentucky, attended by representatives from all of Kentucky's public colleges and universities.

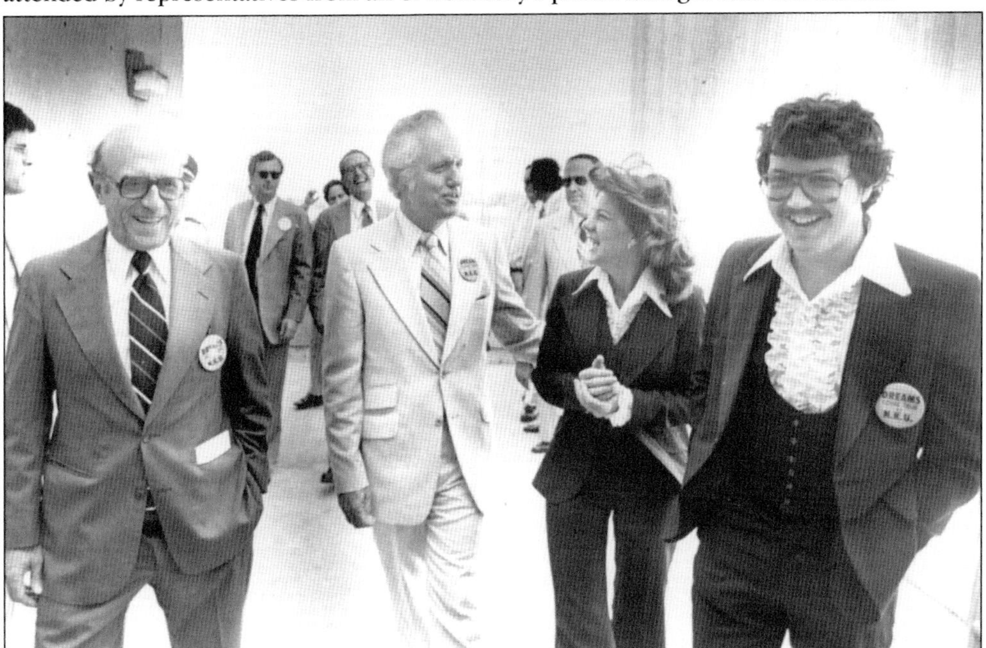

A great deal of excitement surrounded Kentucky governor Julian Carroll (far left) during his 1979 visit to campus. He was given a button that read "Dreams come true at N.K.U." In the photograph, he is accompanied to the site of his speech by the university president, Dr. A. D. Albright (second from left), and other university officials.

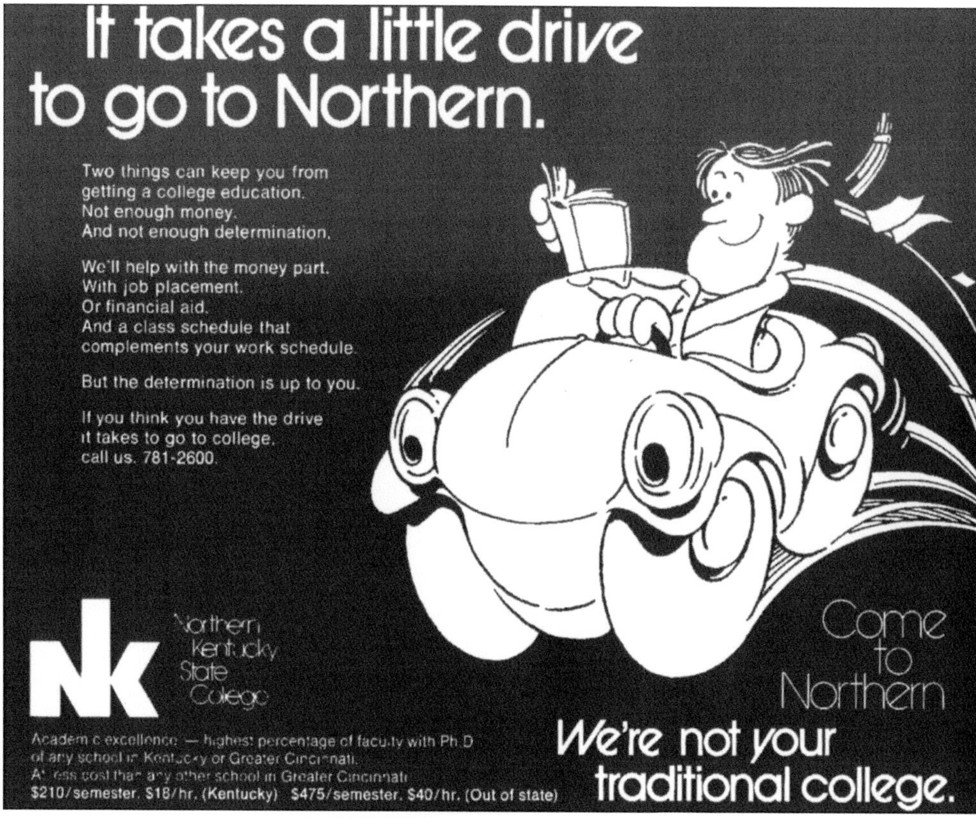

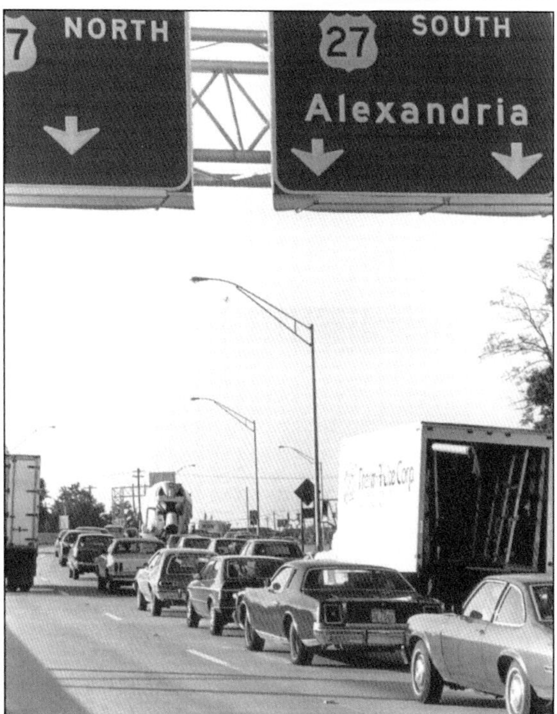

The newspaper ad above was meant to refer to the commuter nature of the campus. In fact, it did take quite a drive to get to NKU in the earlier years of the college. The campus site had originally been chosen because it was at the crossroads of the planned I-275 and I-471 highways. I-275 would become the outer belt for the greater Cincinnati region, while I-471 would directly connect Highland Heights with I-71 in downtown Cincinnati. Both together would make NKU one of the most accessible campuses in the state. Unfortunately the highways weren't completed until 1978 and 1980 respectively. Until then, all the traffic was confined to the old, two-lane highway, U.S. Highway 27.

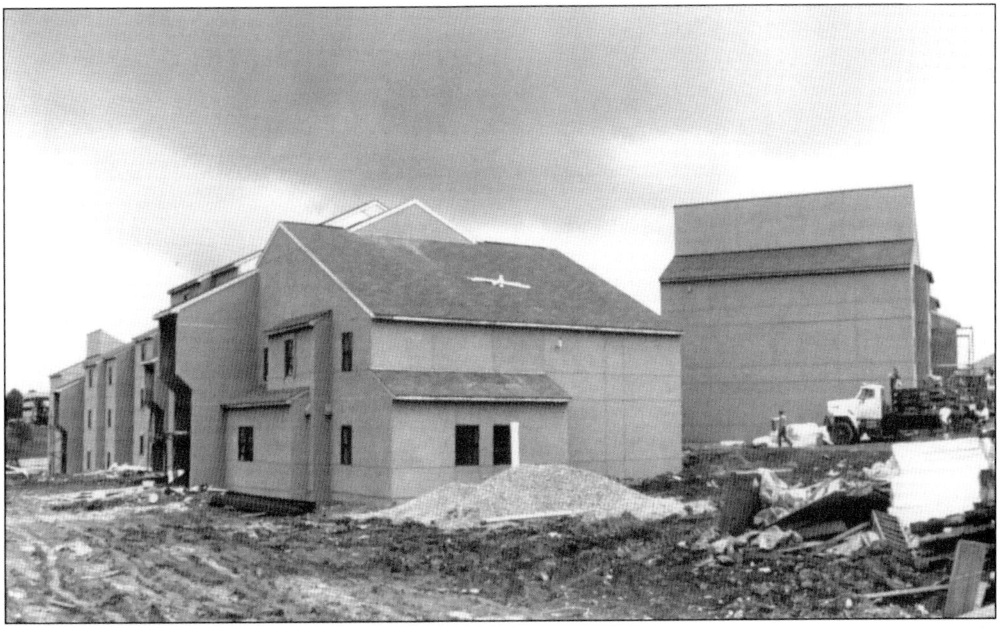

In the spring semester of 1982, NKU at last began to move away from its commuter-only status with the opening of its first residence halls. With this change, NKU finally began to bring in students from outside the immediate area. In addition to bringing in students from Kentucky and other states who lived too far to commute, on-campus housing also made it a viable campus for international students. Residential space has continued to be added over the years, most recently with the addition of suites. Initially holding only about 400 beds, the university now has enough space for approximately 1,500 students to live on campus.

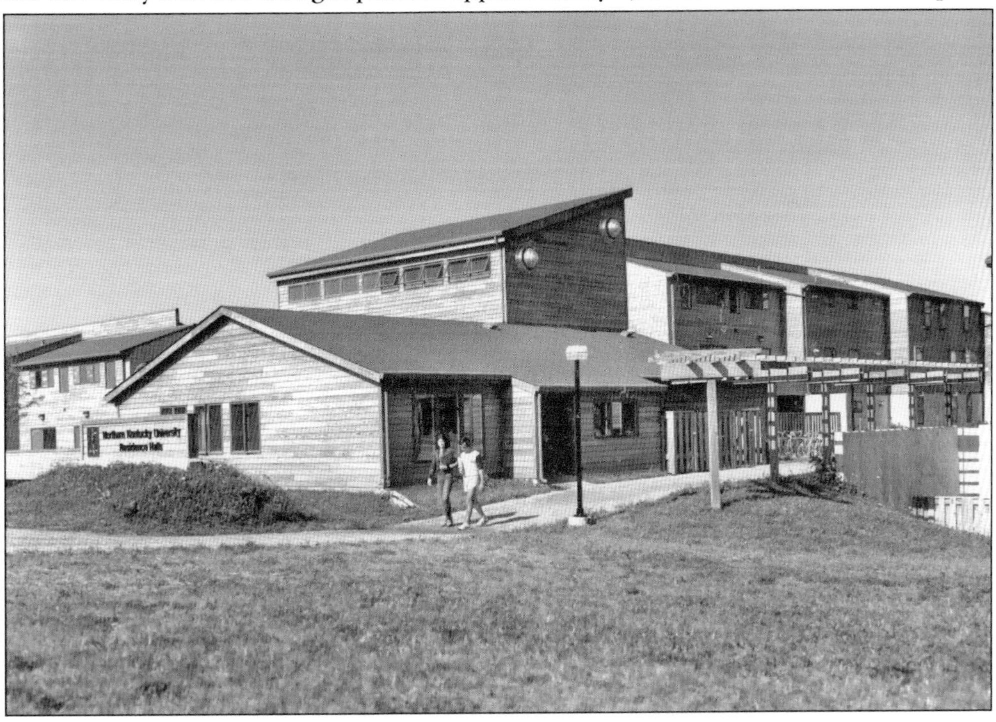

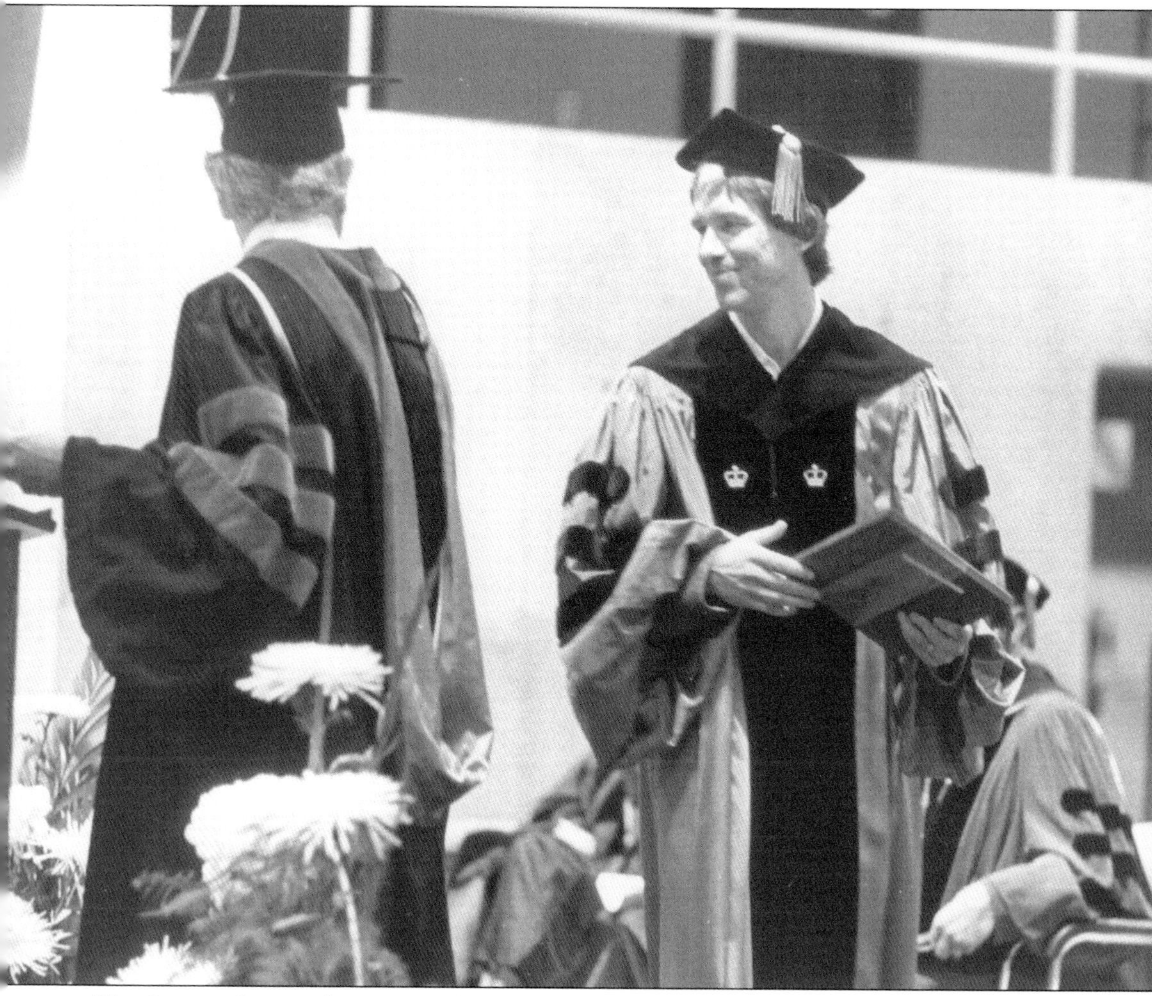

The Outstanding Professor Award began as an annual faculty award in 1970 and was first granted to Dr. William Byron, a professor in the Department of Literature and Language. After 1973, the award was suspended. It was restarted in 1981 with the naming of Dr. Robert K. Wallace above, another literature and language professor. In 1996, the award was endowed by Dr. Carol Milburn in memory of her husband. At that time, it was renamed the Frank Sinton Milburn Outstanding Professor Award. The award is considered a great honor for the faculty member on whom it is bestowed. As only tenured and tenure-track faculty are eligible for the Milburn Award, two other awards were started to cover the rest of the teaching faculty. These are the Michael C. C. Adams and Susan S. Adams Outstanding Non-Tenure Track Faculty Award and the Part-Time Faculty Excellence in Instruction Award.

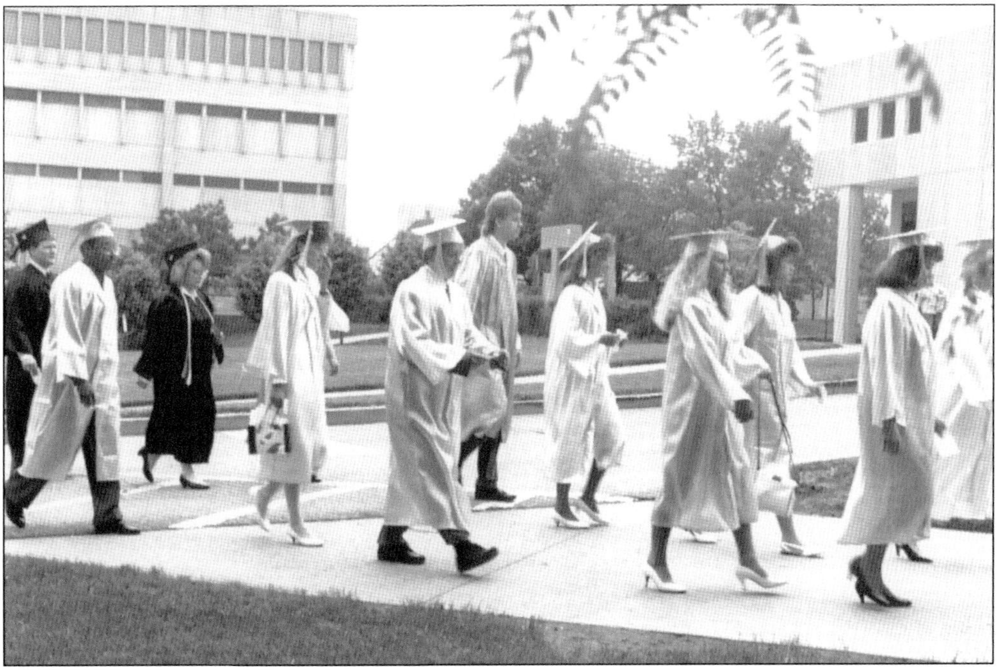

Early graduations at NKU included a march of the graduates across campus to Regents Hall, where their proud families awaited the commencement ceremony. This procession was a last tour of the campus, giving the more sentimental a chance to say goodbye. Sometimes the procession was a sedate walk through the sunshine, as it was in the picture above from the 1980s. Sometimes this was a harried hike through uncertain weather as seen below, when the 1979 graduates had to hang on to their caps in the high winds roaring across the central plaza.

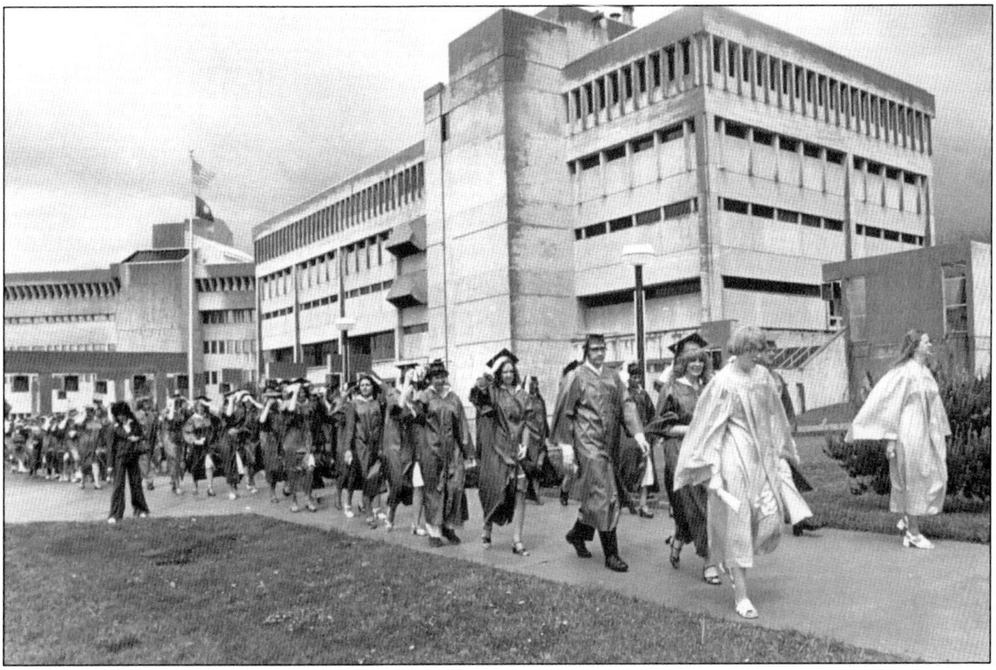

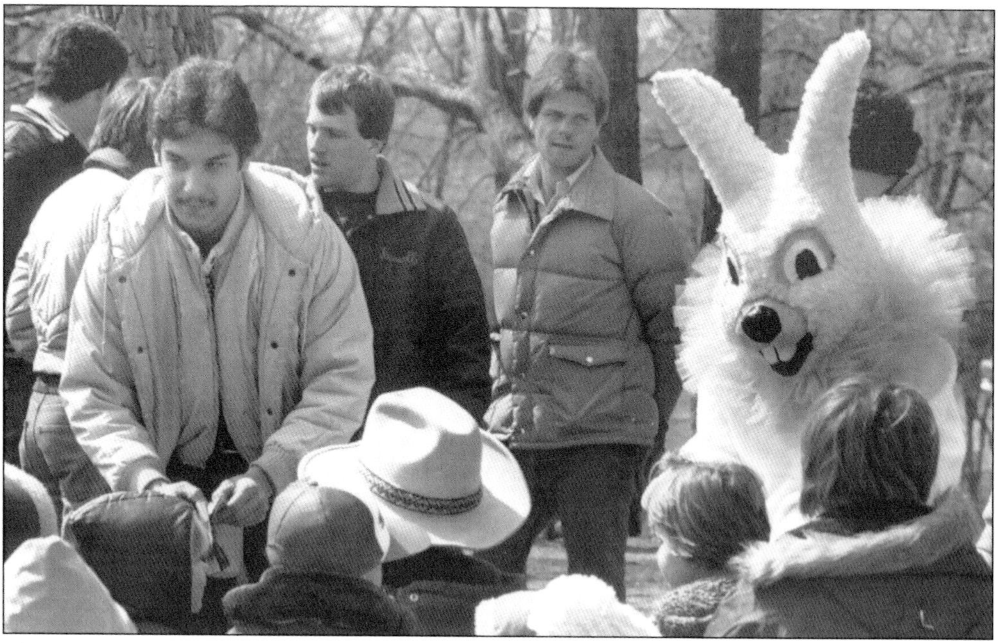

The Greek fraternity and sorority system has been with NKU from its earliest days. Community service is a major element in Greek life at the university. This photograph was taken at a 1982 Easter egg hunt sponsored by the members of Pi Kappa Alpha fraternity for the children of the Brighton Street Center, a local charity organization founded to create opportunities for individuals and families to reach self-sufficiency. Pictured from left to right are member Ted Pappas, fraternity president Russell Alexander, and associate member Darren Dawson. The Easter Bunny is portrayed by sister sorority member Becky Riffe.

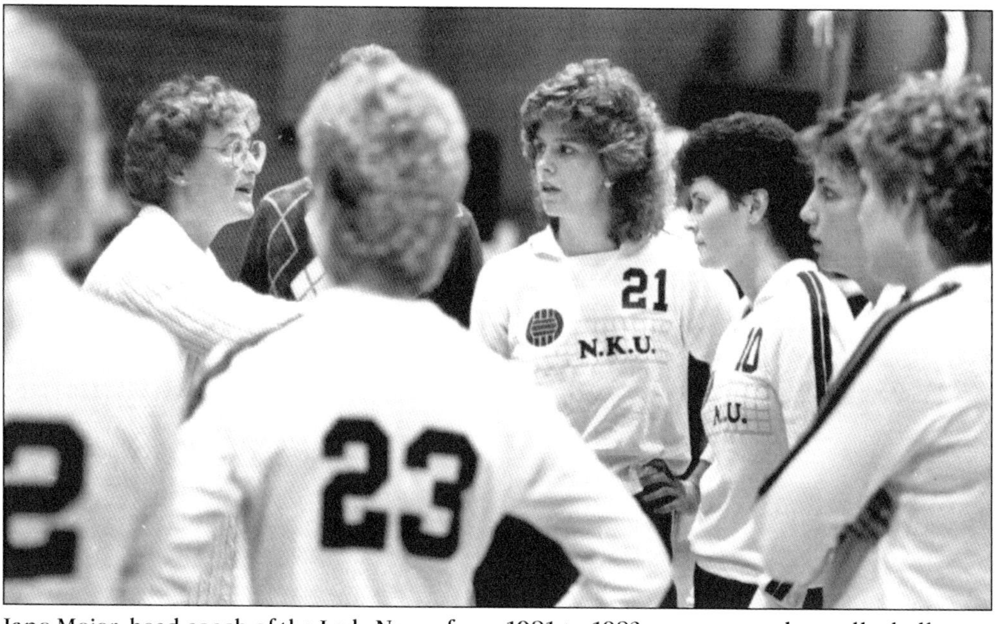

Jane Meier, head coach of the Lady Norse from 1981 to 1983, encourages her volleyball team players during a break in the game. The volleyball team had been one of the few survivors of the statewide budget cuts at the beginning of the 1980s.

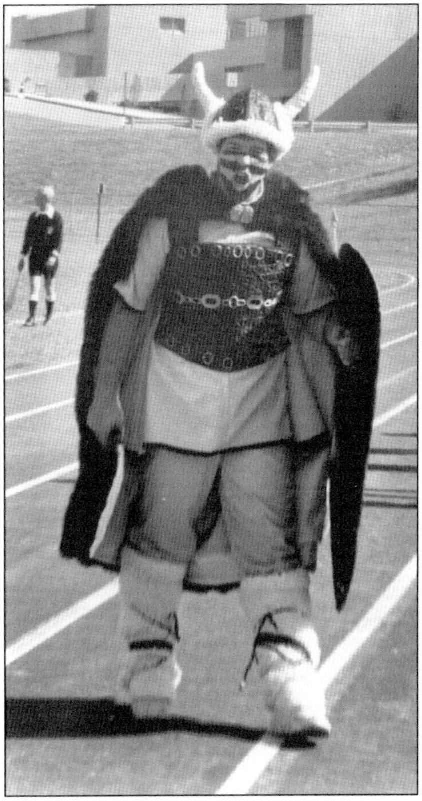

The original mascot for the university was a Norseman, portrayed by Mark Buerger in the photograph at right. Used to more-modern-looking college and professional mascots, this fantastical version of a Viking warrior appears hopelessly outdated. The Norseman was later replaced by the Norse dragon seen below. A group of student athletes who were also graphic arts majors developed and designed the dragon. A professional costume company created the costume, and the athletics department held a contest to name it. Despite some resistance from administrators, students preferred the name "Hey U!" It won the student vote. The new mascot was officially unveiled in a dramatic ceremony where the dragon was anointed as the new representative for NKU athletics.

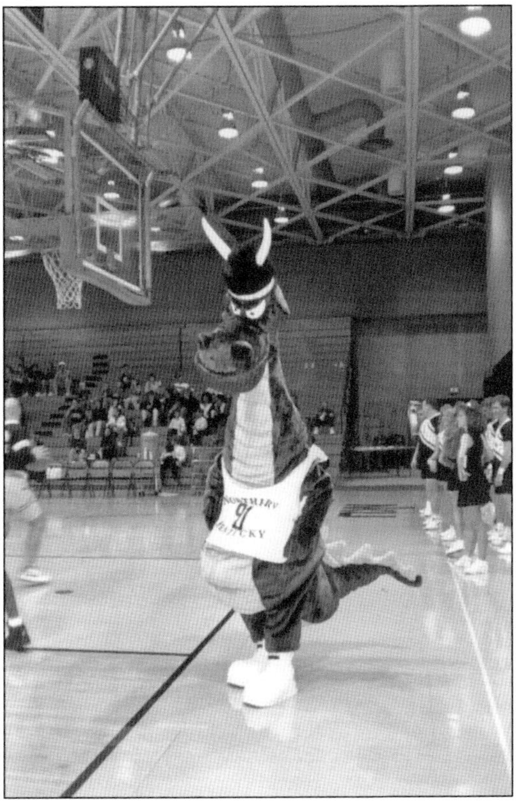

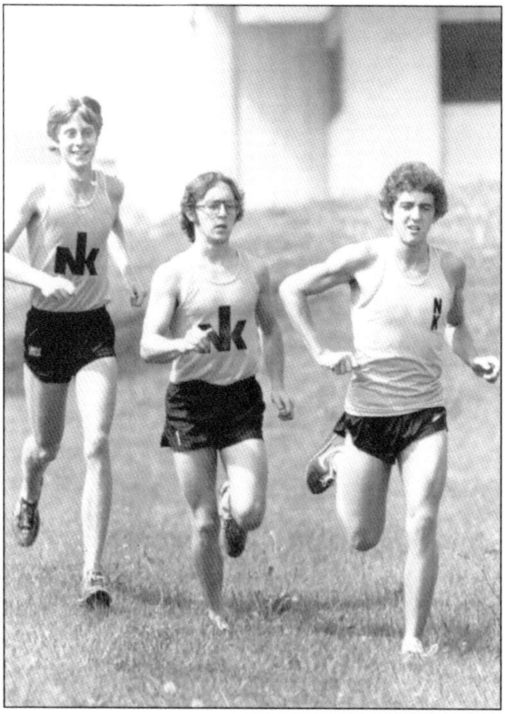

Cross-country is another of the sports that has been offered at NKU almost since the beginning. The students pictured here, Tom Ashe (left), Joe Lunn (center), and John Lott (right), were expected to be the cornerstone of NKU's cross-country team in 1979. This photograph is from a workout before a meet the previous season.

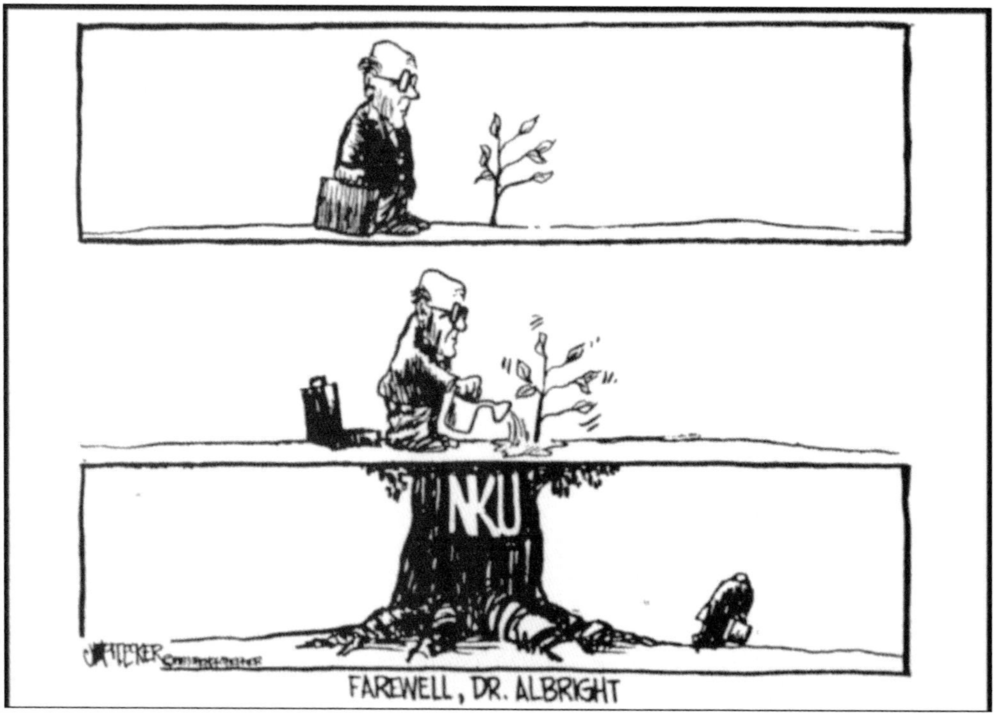

Having previously joked that he was soon to reach the mandatory retirement age in Kentucky, Dr. A. D. Albright announced his retirement at the October 1982 meeting of the university's Board of Regents. At the age of 70, Albright left NKU. The student newspaper, *The Northerner*, ran this cartoon in tribute to his presidency.

Four

THE BOOTHE ERA
Changes for Northern Kentucky University

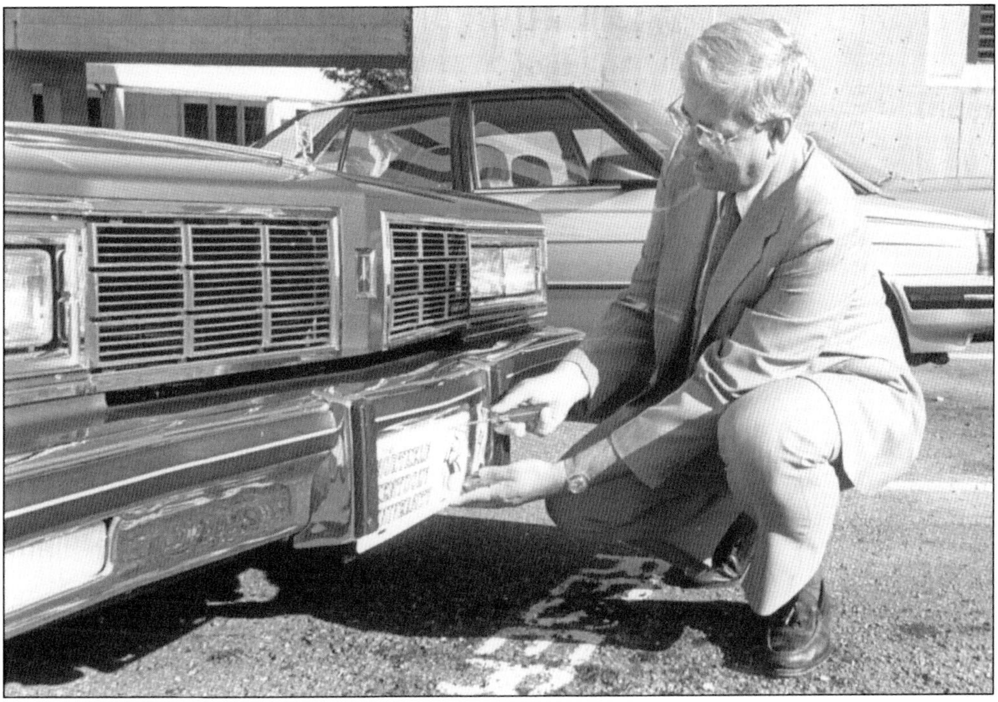

Newly appointed president Leon Boothe shows his Norse pride by attaching a Northern Kentucky University license plate to the front of his car.

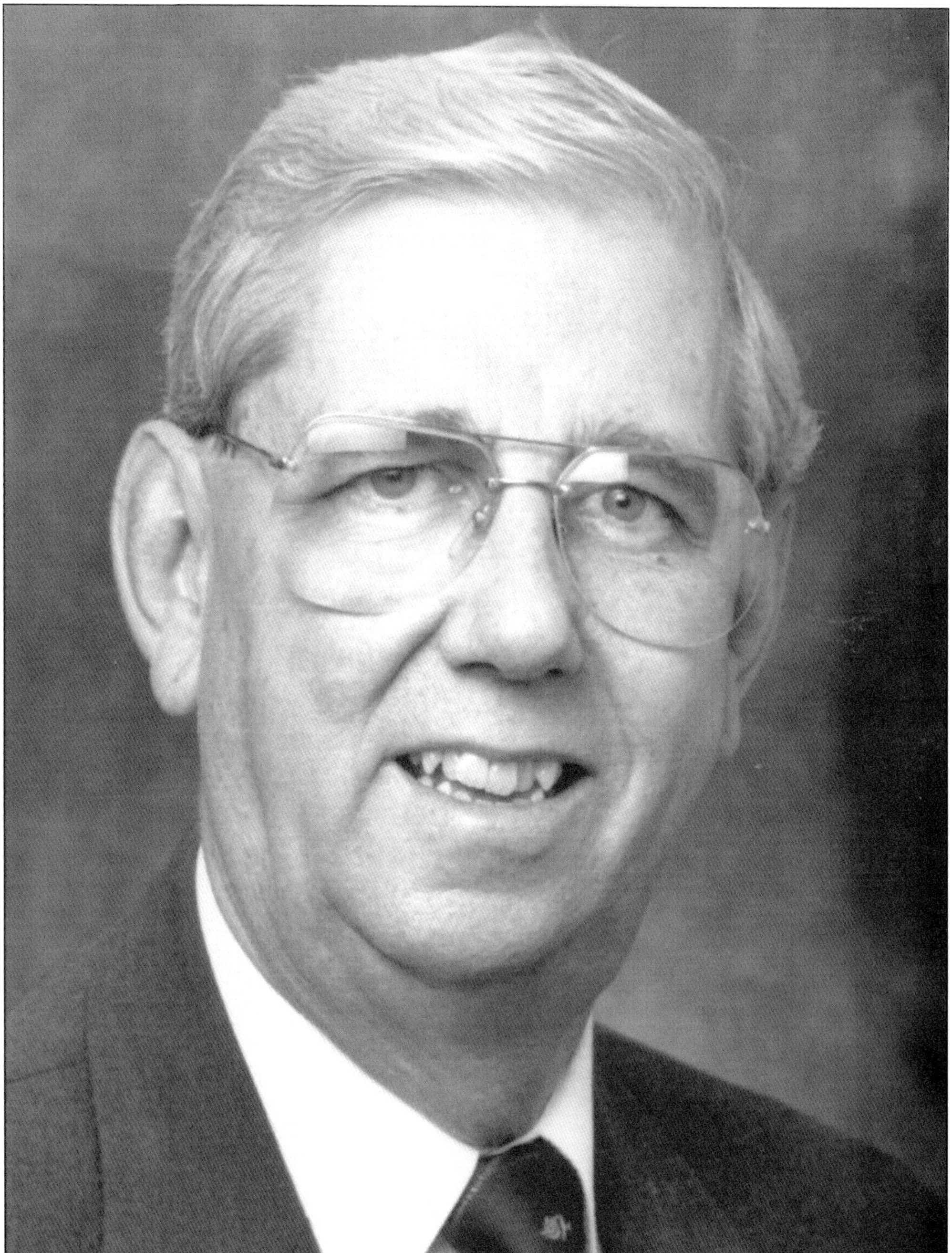

Following the retirement of Dr. A. D. Albright, Dr. Leon Boothe became NKU's third president in 1983. Boothe had been a contender for the position of provost under Dr. A. D. Albright in 1976. At that time, he commented on the tremendous potential he saw in the growing campus. As the new university president, he finally had his chance to shape the potential he had seen years before. Boothe served the campus for 13 years before his wife's increasingly ill health caused him to resign the post. He later returned to campus to spend another six years as a professor of history, retiring in 2006.

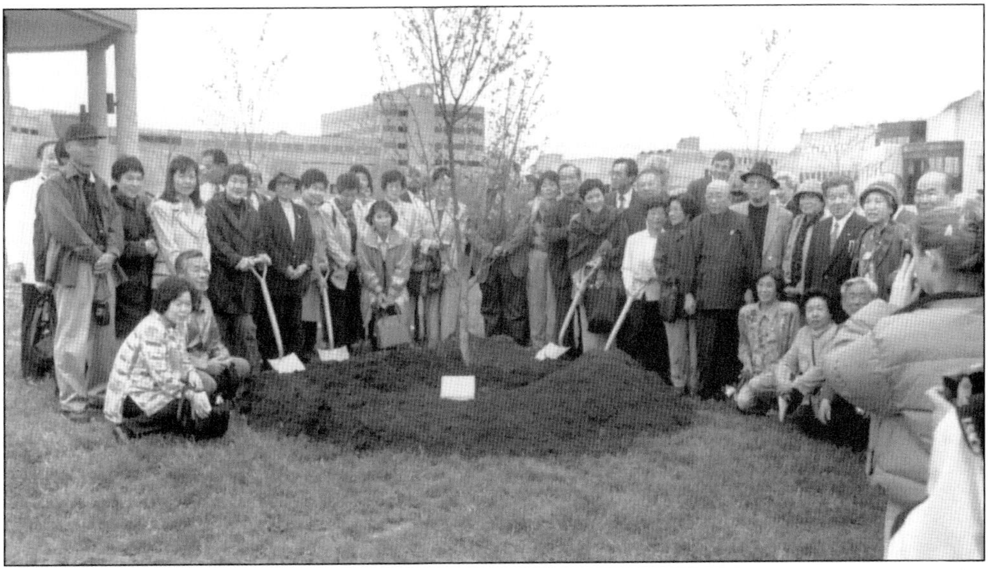

Among Boothe's many interests was the culture of the Orient. He introduced NKU to the East when he signed the document that made NKU a sister to a Japanese university. He also paved the way for a Japanese studies program and classes in the Japanese language. The Japanese cherry trees above were planted on campus as a symbol of the ties between NKU and Japanese cultural groups. In the photograph below, Boothe poses between NKU history professors Dr. Michael Washington and Dr. Yasue Kuwahara. The two professors collaborated to research the influence of American values on Japanese society.

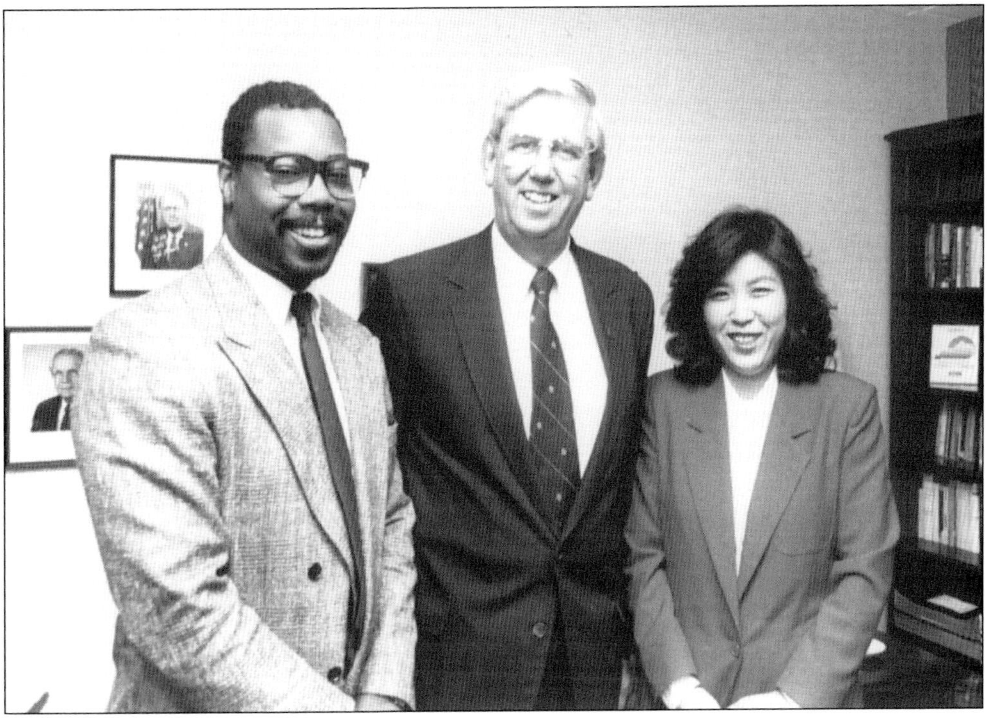

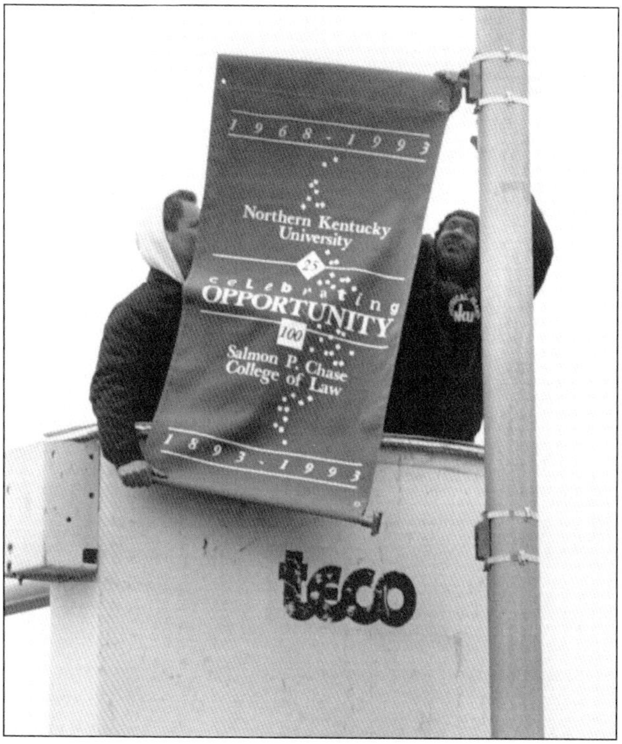

The year 1993 was a banner anniversary year for NKU. The university celebrated its 25th year, while the Chase College of Law celebrated its 100-year mark. A number of festivities surrounded the anniversaries. The university even commissioned emeritus English professor Frank Stallings to write a book for the occasion. His 74-page *Groundbreakings* told the complete story of the university's first 25 years, marking the time with the numerous groundbreakings on the rapidly expanding campus.

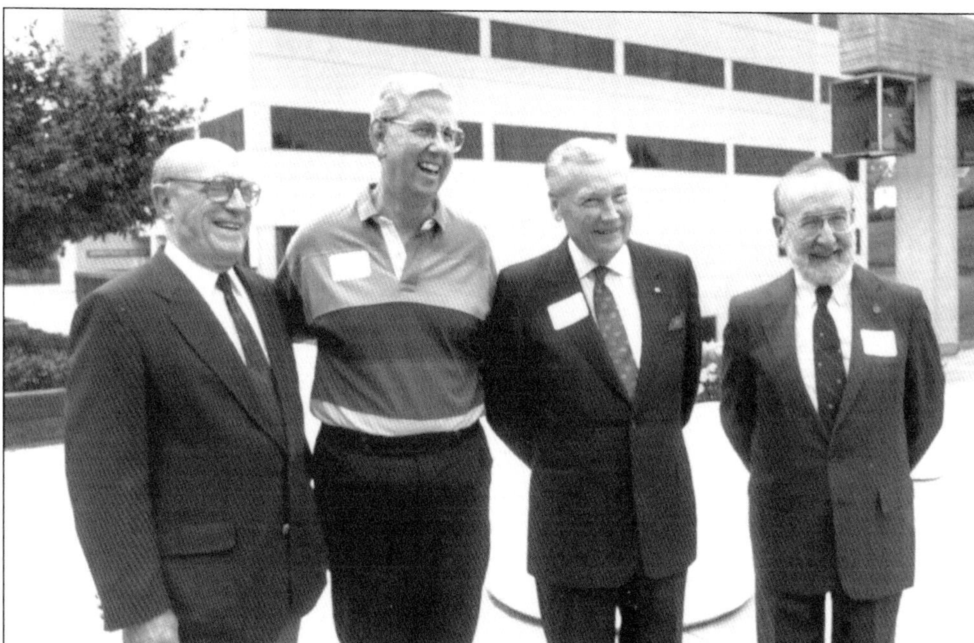

University presidents never wander far from their NKU home. Many take up teaching positions on campus, while none of them are strangers at university special events. They are often brought together on these occasions for a group photograph. Here we see every president through Boothe. They are, from left to right, Drs. A. D. Albright, Leon Boothe, Ralph Tesseneer, and W. Frank Steely.

Originally licensed in 1982, WNKU, the National Public Radio–affiliated station on campus, went on the air in 1985. For 20 years, the voice of WNKU was News and Public Affairs Director Maryanne Zeleznik. She left NKU in 2005 to join the news team at WVXU, the NPR-affiliated station at Xavier University in nearby Cincinnati.

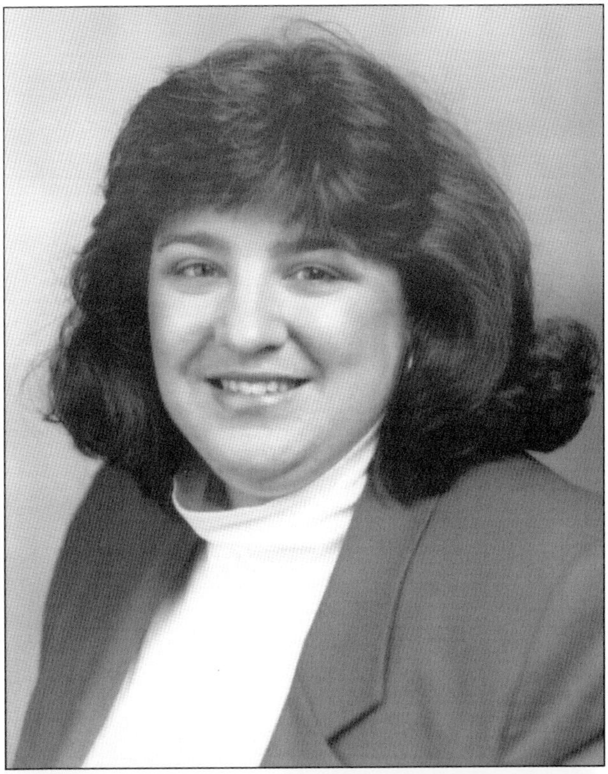

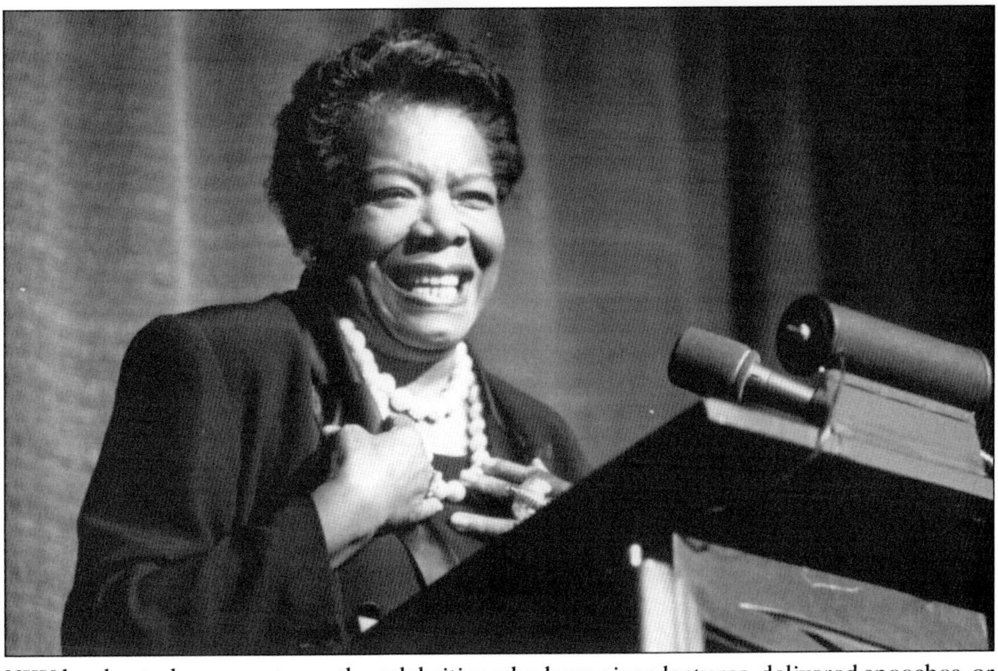

NKU has hosted many noteworthy celebrities who have given lectures, delivered speeches, or performed on campus. These include musicians such as David Crosby and opera star Eileen Farrell, international scholars such as Jacques Barzun, artists such NKU alumnus David Mack, and writers such as Neil Gaiman and Pulitzer Prize–nominated poet Maya Angelou.

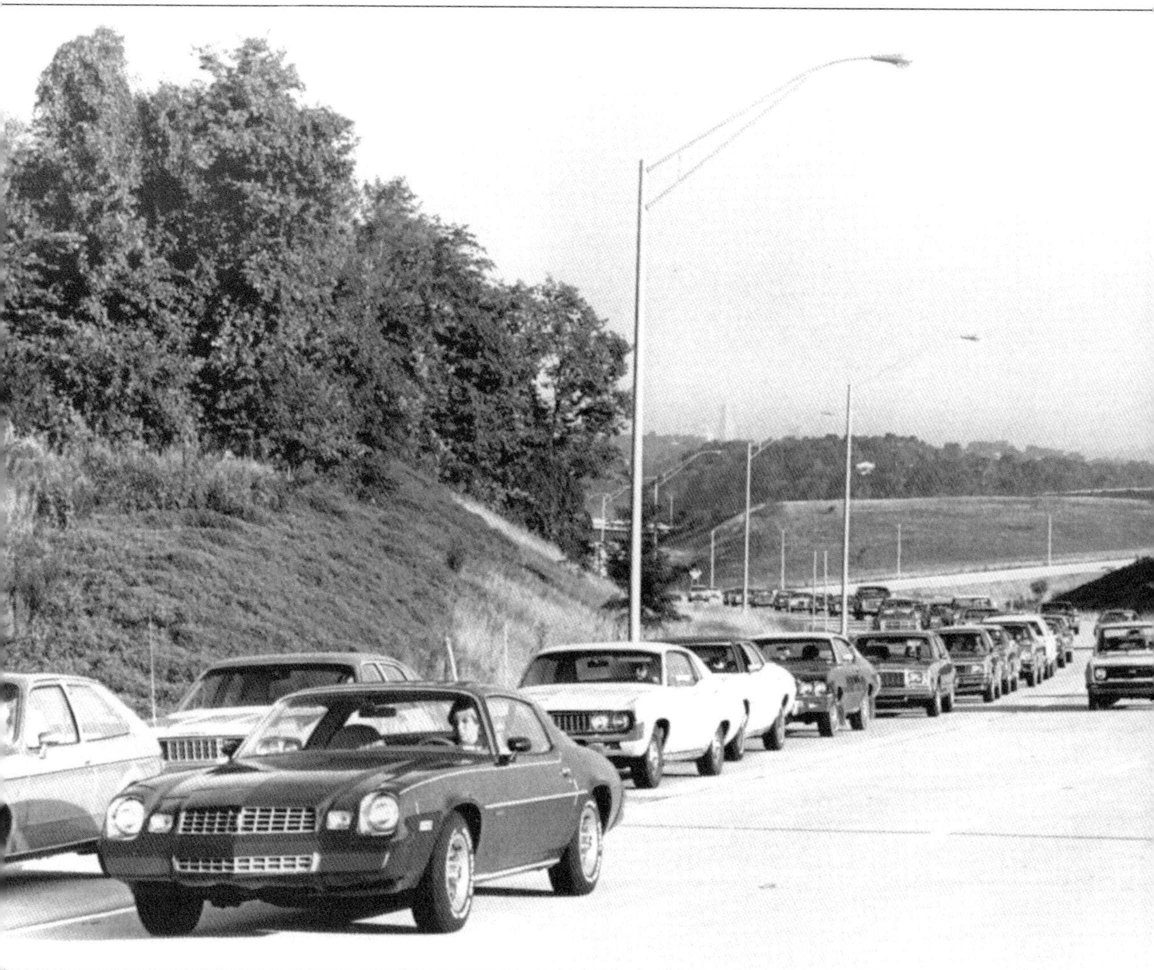

Even after the I-275 and I-471 highways were completed, traffic continued to be a problem trying to get to a campus that had grown faster than anyone's wildest dreams. This photograph is a sample of what it was like trying to get to class in the 1970s. The solution was an additional eastbound exit off I-275, an exit that brings traffic directly onto campus from the highway. That exit was finally completed in 1987. As the campus continues to grow, traffic grows with it. Congress has now approved the building of a federally funded connector road from the nearby AA Highway to ease the problem.

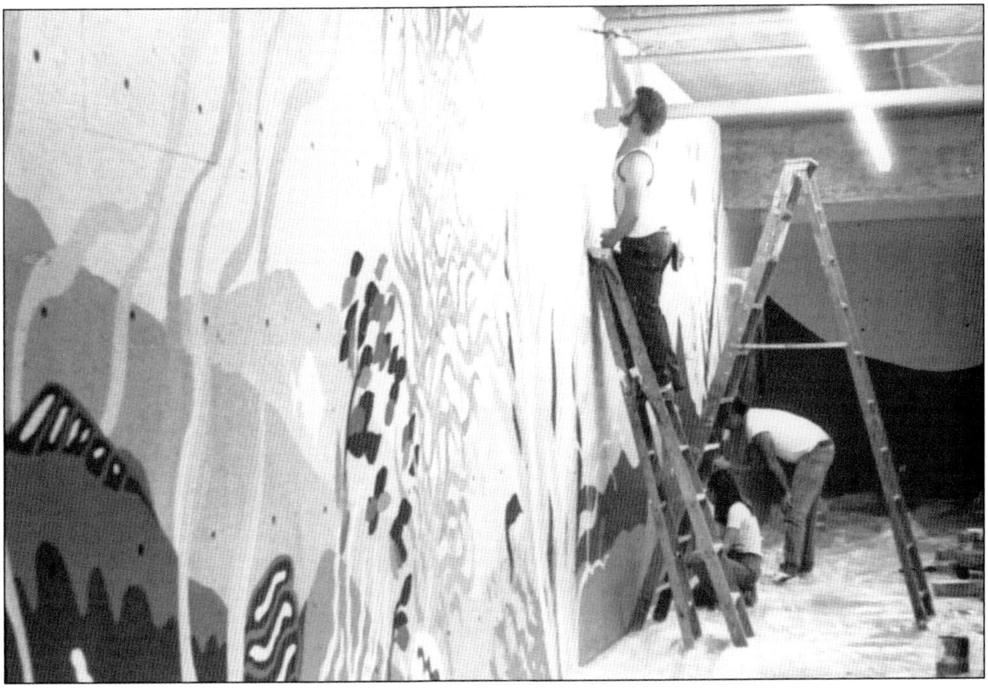

A partially underground tunnel connects the ground floor of the University Center to the second floor of the Lucas Administrative Center. Above, art students Dennis Beckner (left) and Teresa Padgett (center) work under the direction of Prof. Howard Storm (right), painting the undersea mural that adorns the walls of the tunnel. The mural features the mythological sea god Neptune, some very large fish, and a sunken Viking longship, another reference to the Norse mascot. The longship is given a prominent place at the bend in the tunnel. The mural was completed in 1982 by Professor Storm's students Dennis Beckner, Robert Moore, Craig Davis, and Teresa Padgett.

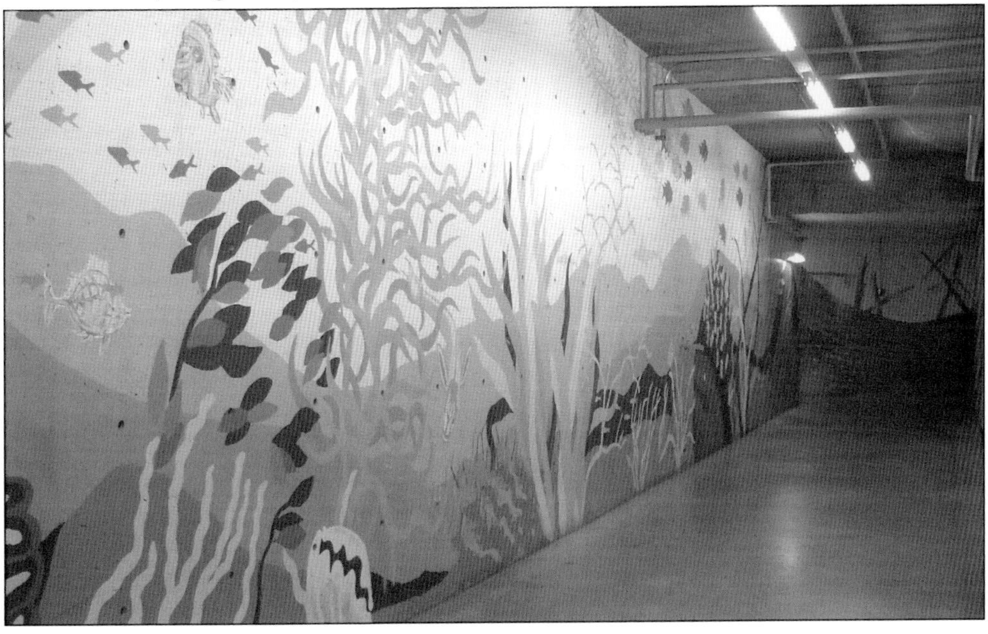

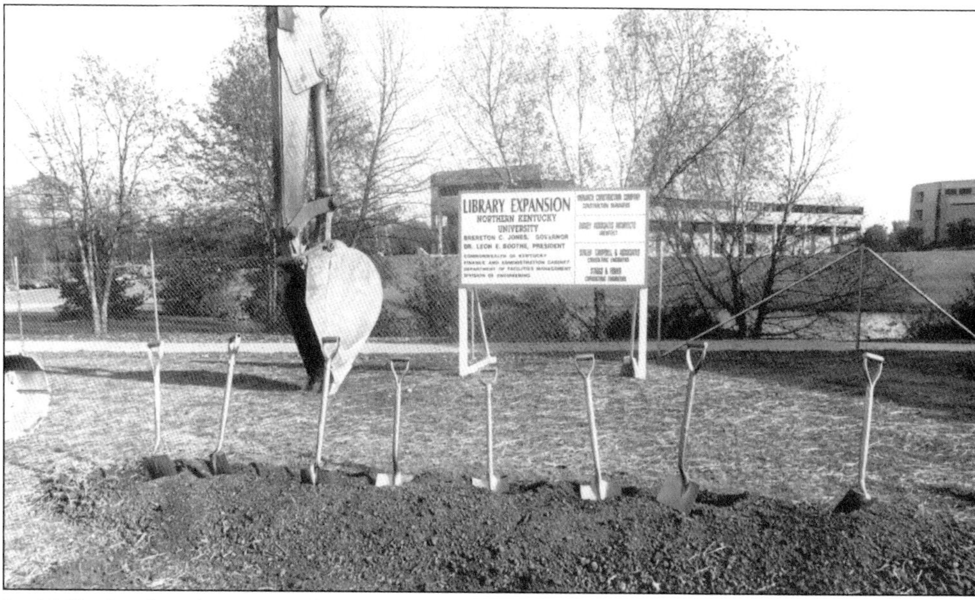

In 1993, Steely Library needed more space to continue to build collections and services to support an ever-growing campus community. Ground was broken for an expansion that would take the library in two directions. The front library plaza, or "the Pit" as it was sometimes known, was filled in. That area became additional book stack space for the first and second floors of the library. An entirely new section was added on the backside of the library as well. This section now houses special collections and archives, technical services, and government documents, among other areas. Entrance to the library was through a narrow corridor of plywood and plastic sheeting. The construction side of this corridor can be seen in the photograph below. Library faculty and staff were commended by the teaching faculty for their patience while working in the incredibly noisy and dusty conditions.

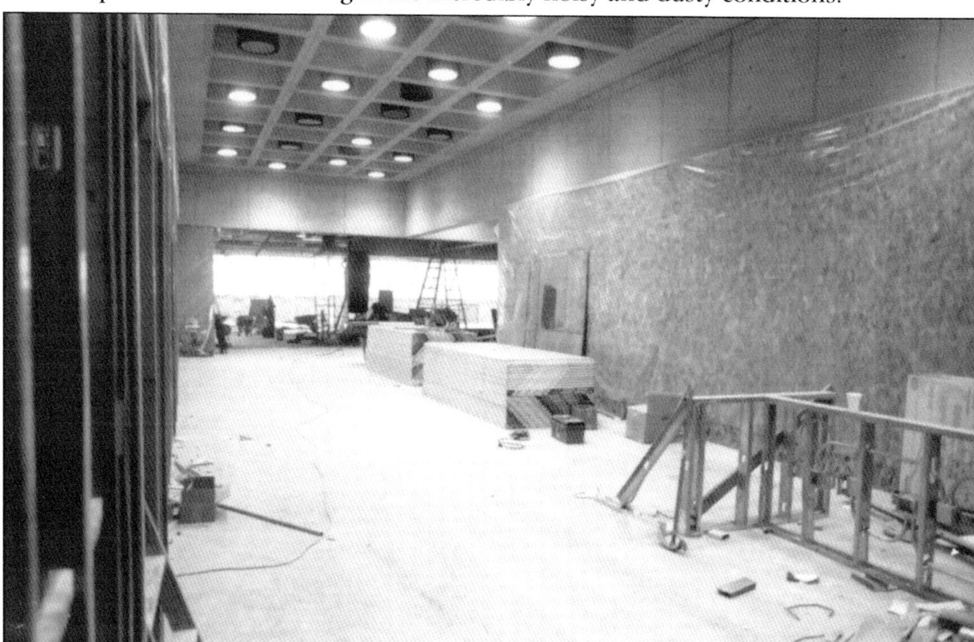

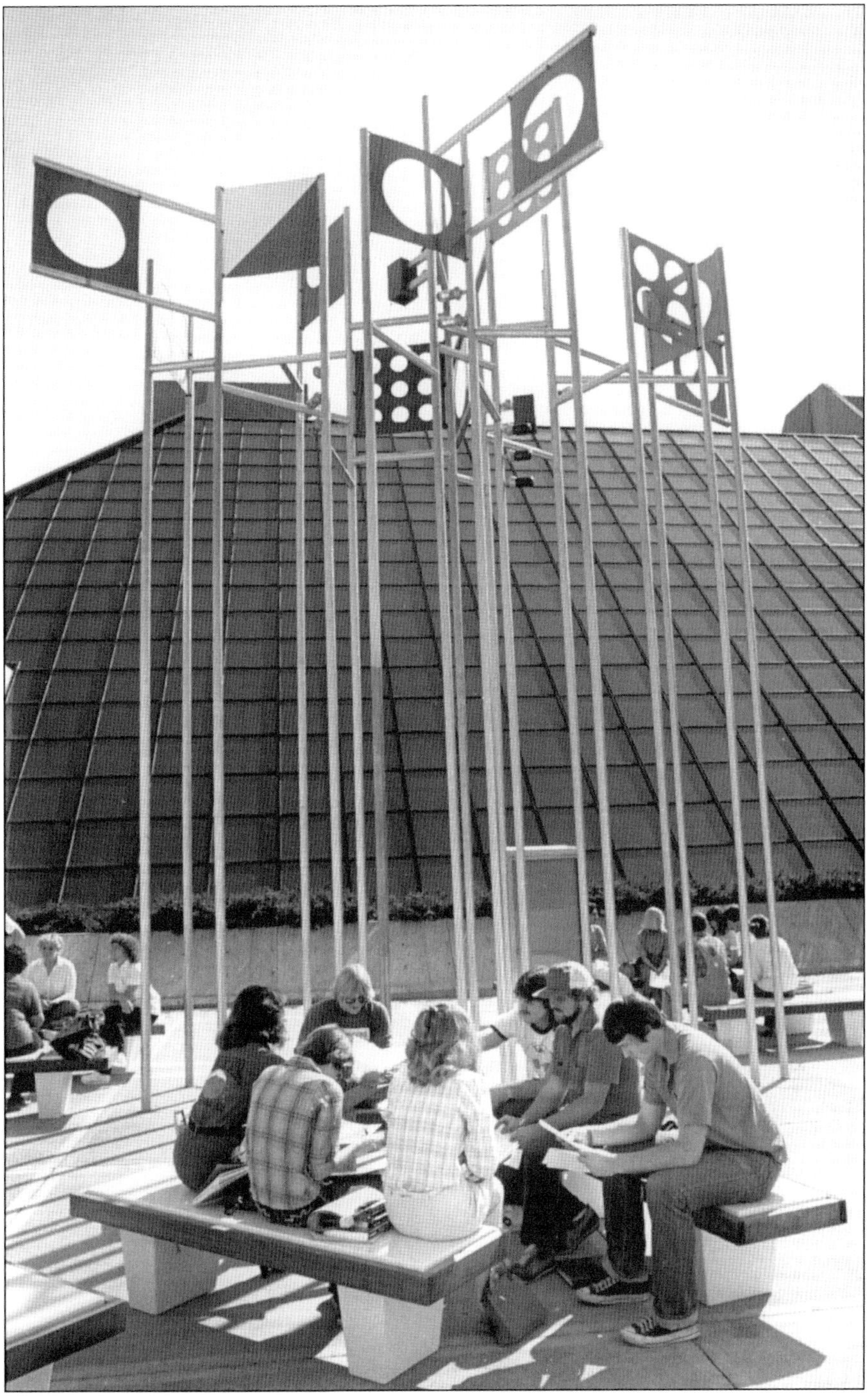

Dr. Joseph Patrick's philosophy class takes advantage of a warm, sunny autumn day to take small-group work out to the library plaza. The plaza, or the Pit as it was sometimes known, was filled in during the 1993 library renovation. The space is now taken up by book stacks and the faculty development center. The sculpture in the background, the flag-like *Superstructure*, was moved to a new location outside the residence halls.

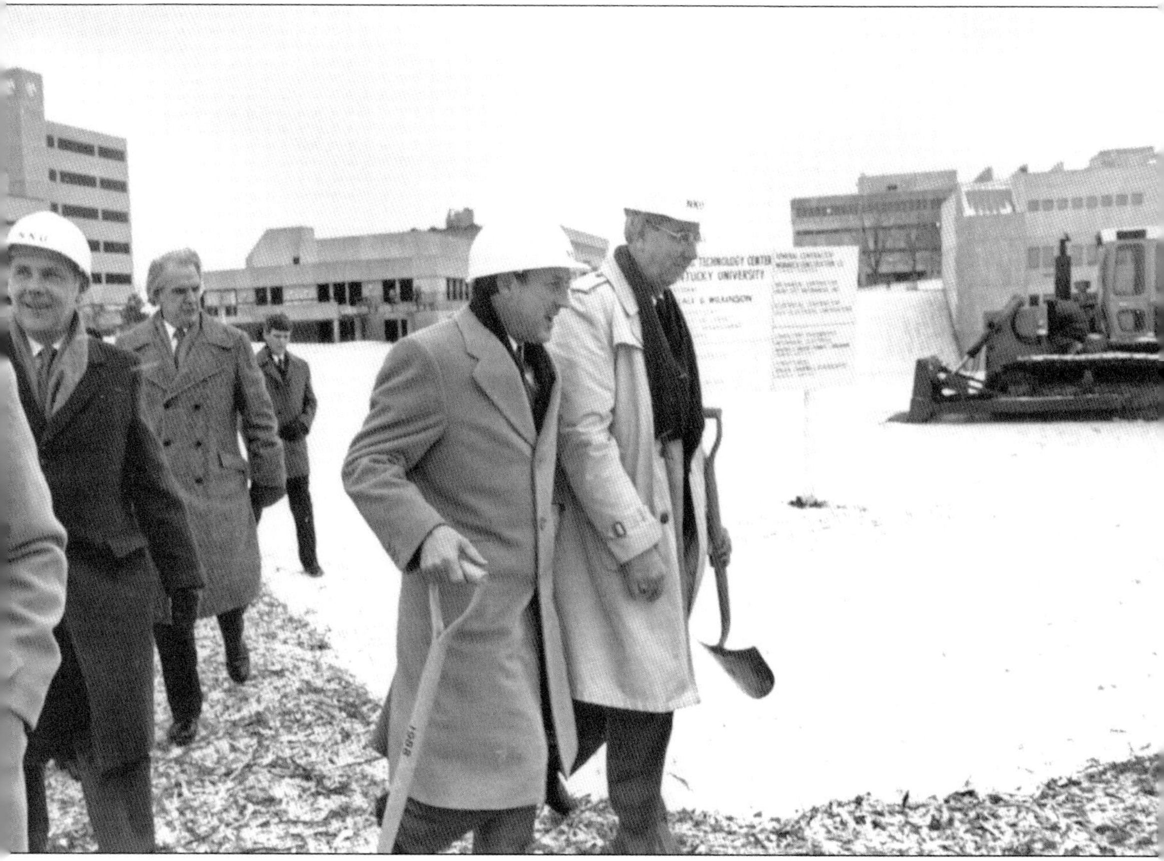

On a cold day in January 1988, Gov. Wallace Wilkinson and NKU president Leon Boothe carry their shovels to another groundbreaking ceremony, this time for the Applied Science and Technology Center. Completed in 1990, the building became the home for all the technology programs on campus, eventually including computer science.

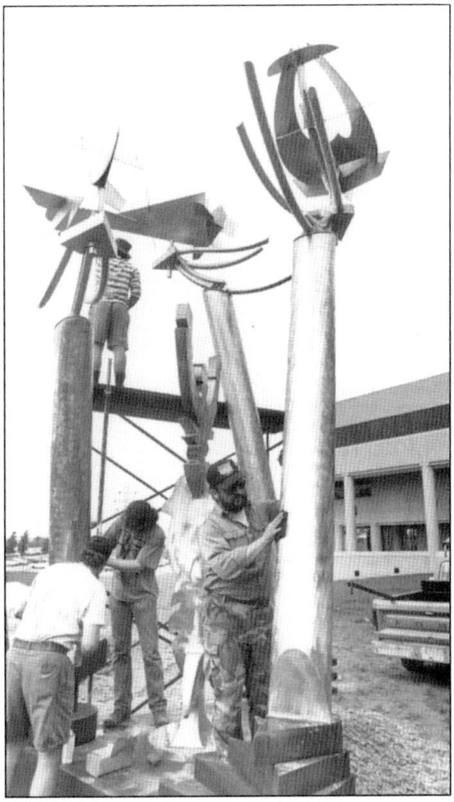

This piece created by sculptor Jack Gron was installed in front of the Applied Science and Technology Center in 1990. The formalist sculpture is intended to represent humanity's use of technology in the eternal quest for knowledge. This is symbolized by a figure and winged forms that move in the wind. Gron used a number of different metals to achieve this effect, including the bronze used for the figure representing humanity. In the photograph at right, Gron oversees the installation of the piece on campus. Quite a crowd turned out for the sculpture's dedication, as seen below.

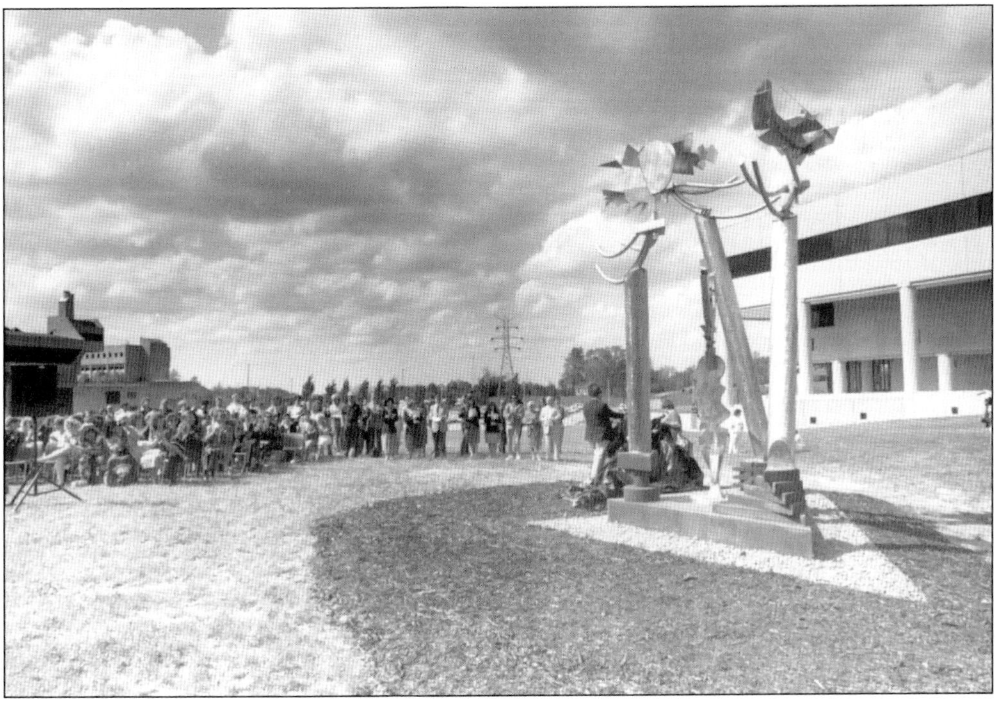

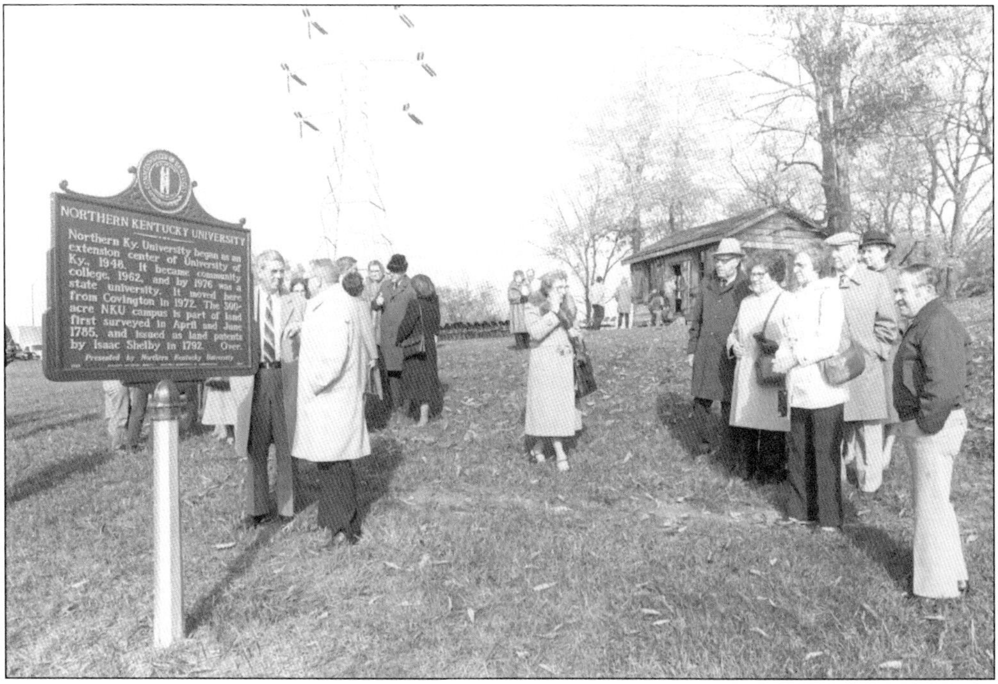

The log cabin in these photographs began life as a pioneer home out near Grant's Lick, Kentucky. To save it from demolition, the cabin was first moved to Alexandria, Kentucky, then later to Campbell County's A. J. Jolly Park. It was eventually moved to NKU's campus as a reminder of the region's history. Local legend says that when the schoolhouse in Grant's Lick burned down, the cabin was used as a school for several years until a new one could be built. The dedication for the cabin took place in May 1984. It now resides on a grassy hillock along the main campus drive.

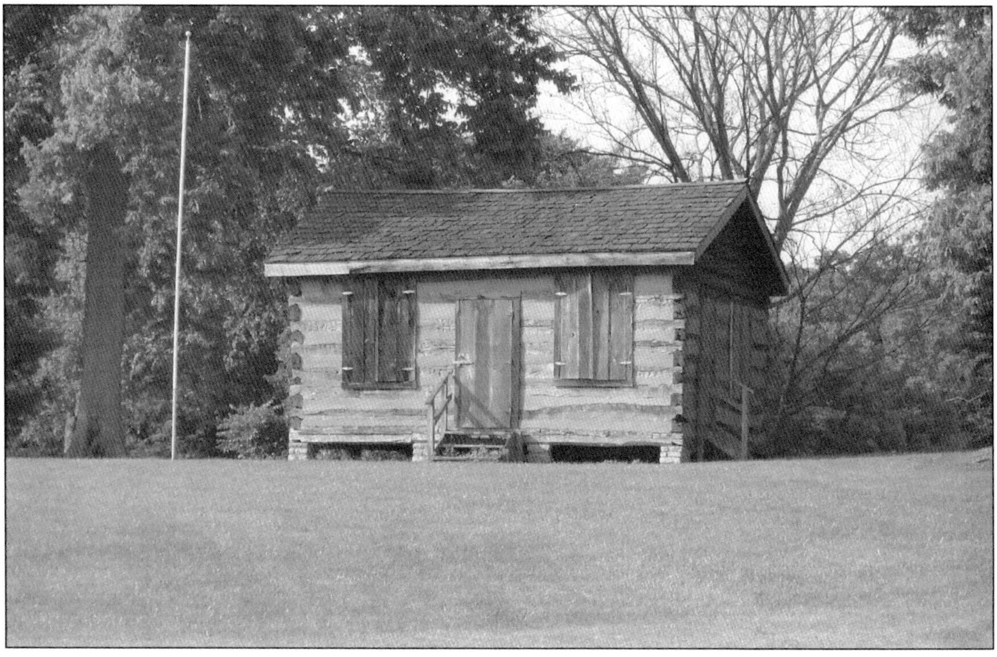

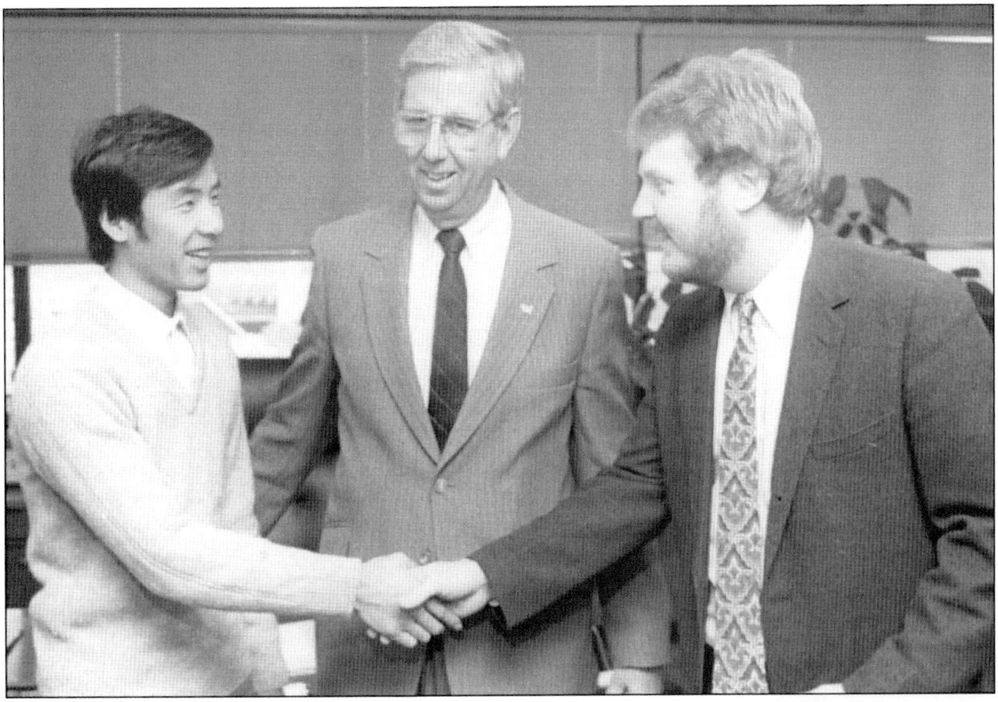

Boothe was known for encouraging a more global view at NKU. He pushed the growth of international student enrollments, study-abroad programs, and the study of foreign languages. These two photographs are excellent examples of his influence in internationalizing the campus. Above, Jianhua Liang was welcomed to NKU by Boothe and Duane Froelicher, student government president. Liang was the first student from mainland China ever to attend NKU. He came to Kentucky to pursue a master of business administration degree. At right, two undergraduate students from Zimbabwe, Paula Nyika-Makore and Honest Mamutse, compare their class schedules.

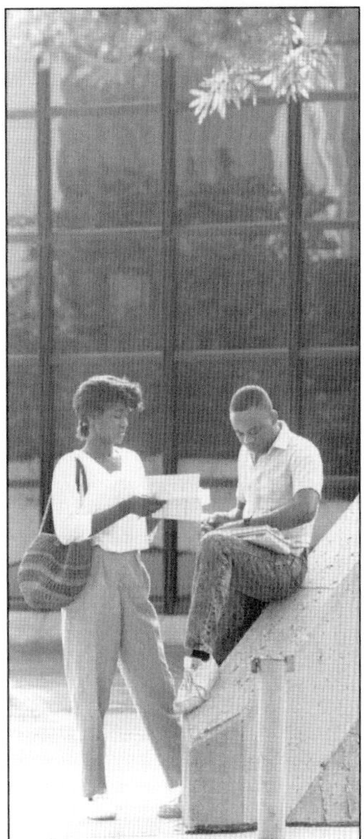

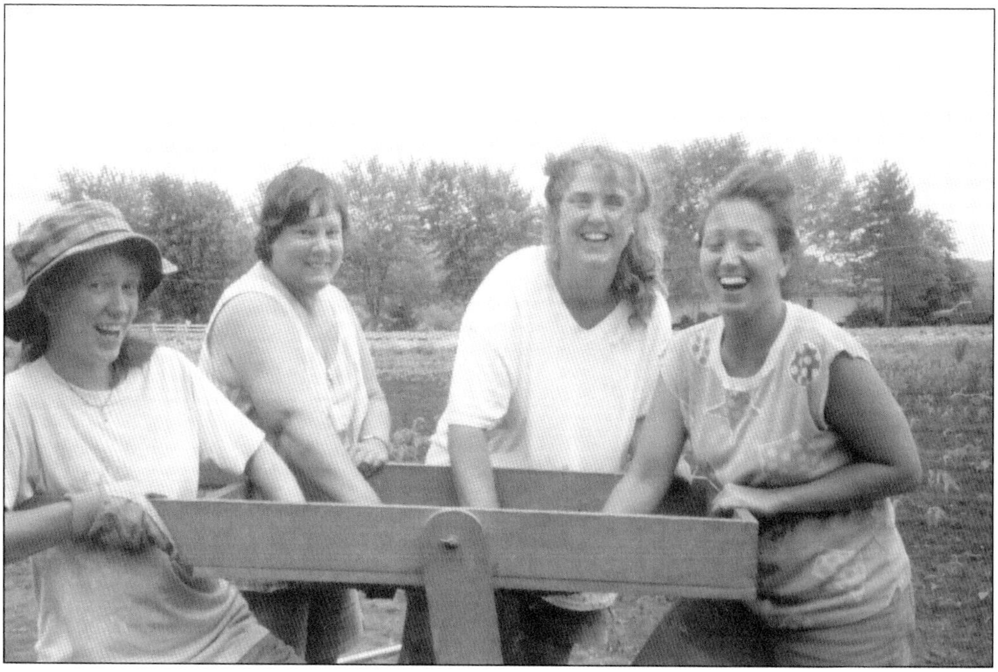

Students in anthropology conduct digs throughout Kentucky under the supervision of NKU faculty. They may be sent in search of Native American artifacts, proof for a suspected Underground Railroad station on a Kentucky farm, or the remains of people buried in a previously unknown African American cemetery in Kentucky's capital. In the photograph above, students on a 1999 summer anthropology dig carefully sift through dirt at a site near Mentor, Kentucky, under the watchful eye of Dr. Barbara J. Thiel (second from the left). The students below are hard at work in a cornfield during an August 1991 dig.

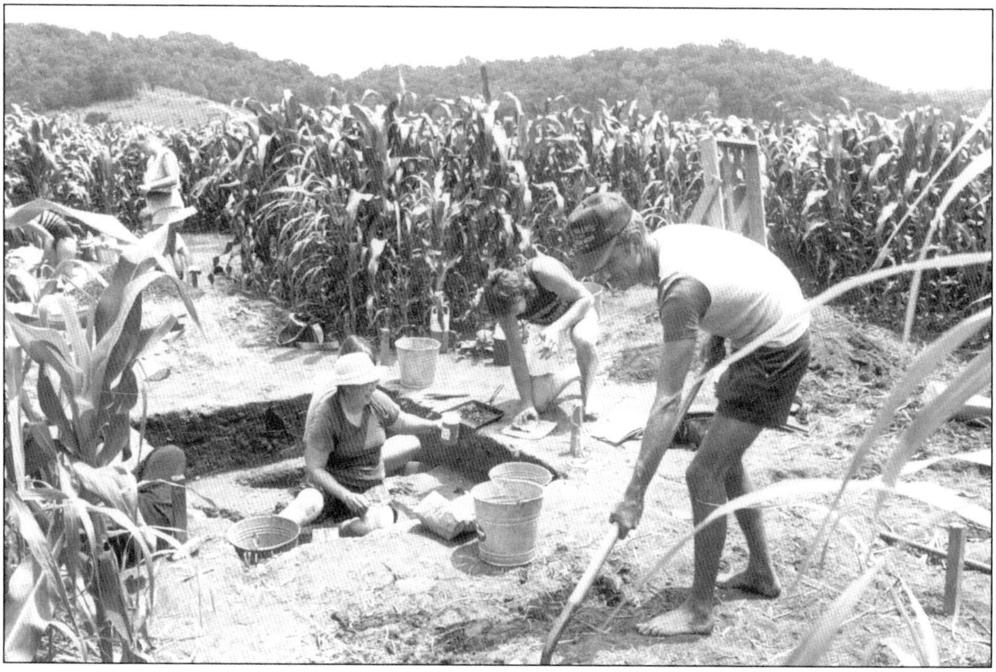

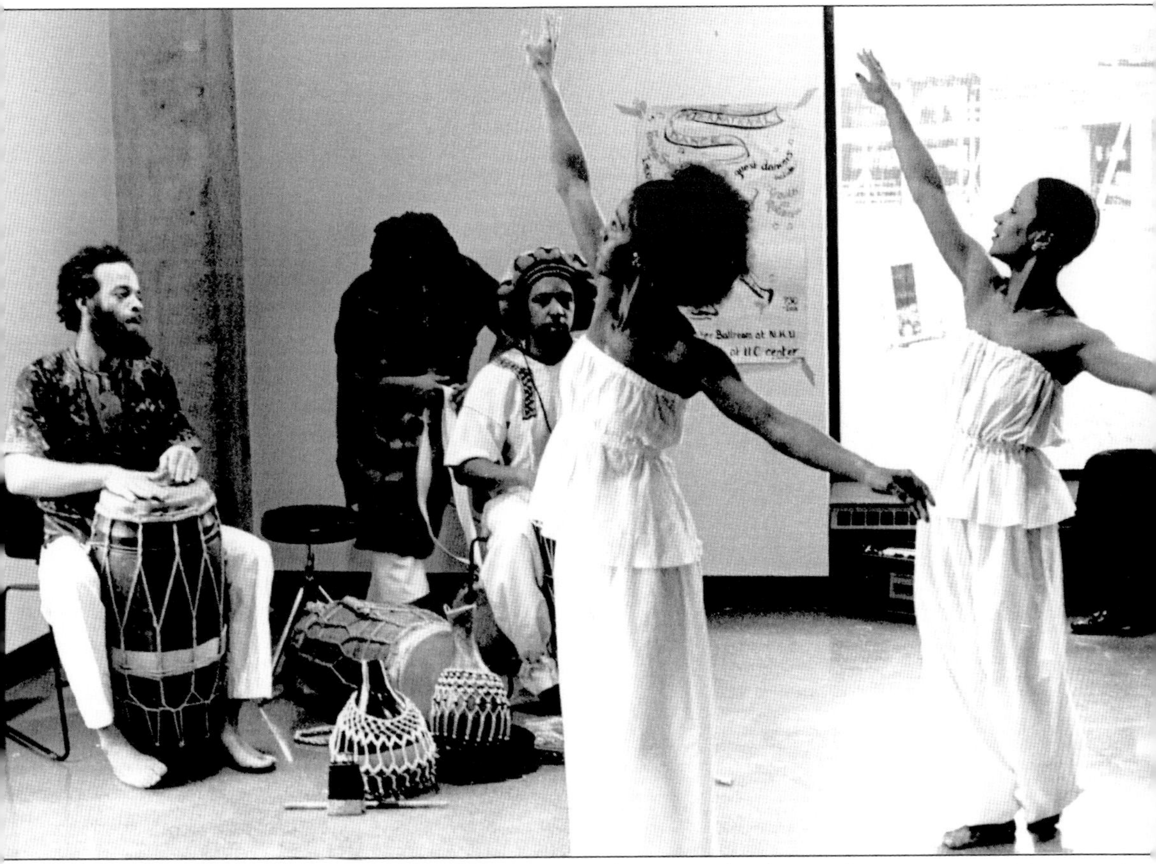

International students have been a vibrant part of the NKU landscape for many years. Here a group of international students perform a traditional dance to a drum accompaniment. Through the window is a typical view of the seemingly unending campus construction.

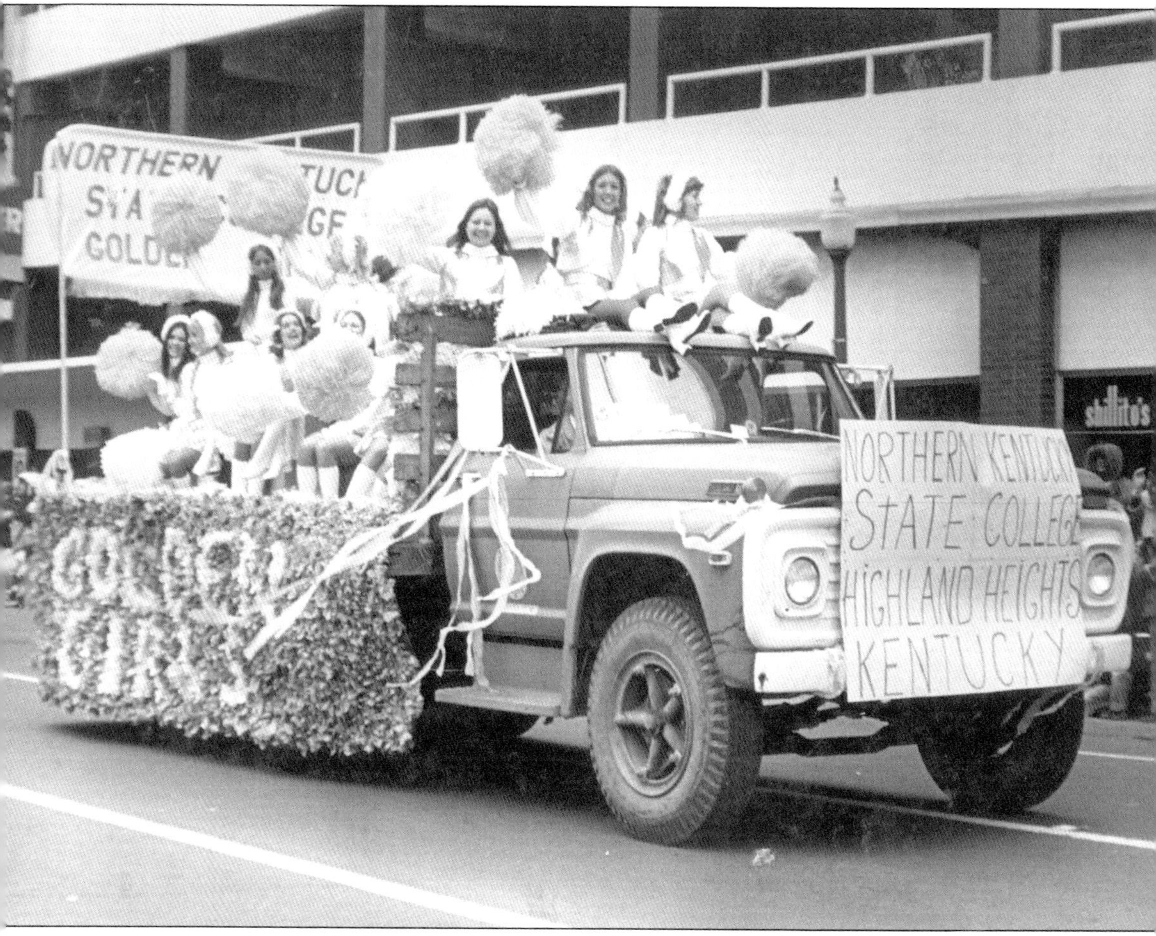

A float in the annual homecoming parade features the Golden Girls drill team. The team was founded in 1971 under the direction of Irene Brownfield, the secretary of academic vice president Dr. Ralph Tesseneer. The team performed in the halftime shows at NKSC basketball games, marched in parades such as the annual homecoming parade, and turned out for many campus events. The team continued representing NKU until 1989.

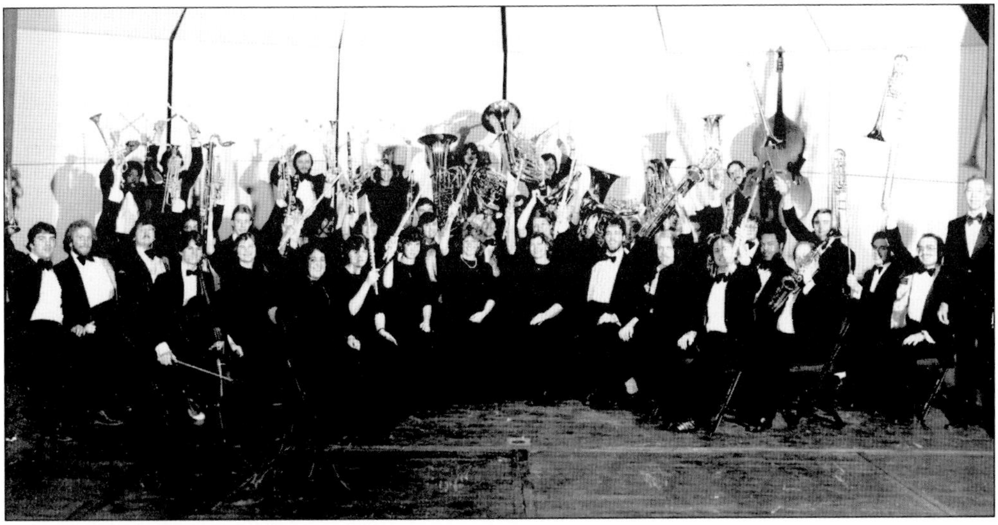

NKU didn't have a symphony orchestra until very recently, but the campus did have a symphonic band. The band members salute the camera for a newspaper photograph. The university also has many choral groups and small ensembles, several of which date back to the earliest days of the campus.

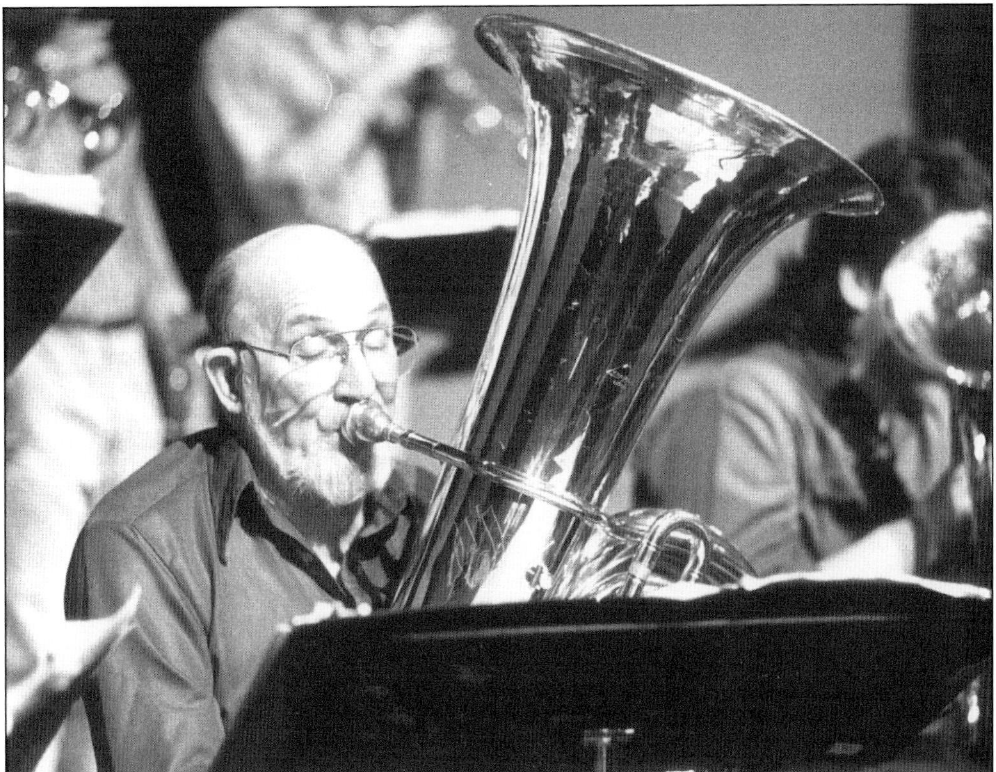

NKU has always had a large population of non-traditional students. With the current provisions for Kentucky senior citizens to take classes for free, the university's popularity with an older generation is unlikely to wane. Many of these students take part in campus activities, such as Raymond Neufarth, who at the age of 60 was playing the tuba in the symphonic band.

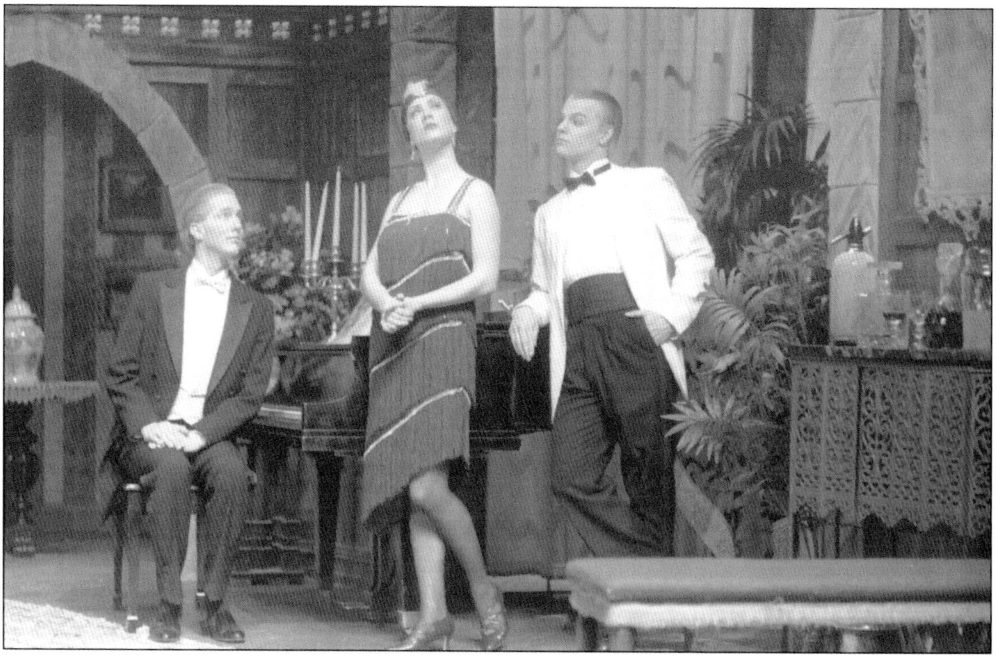

Theater has always been an important part of the campus community. The first production was launched while the new college was in its original location at the Covington campus. The tradition of summer dinner theater was also launched in the early days, after the move to Highland Heights. Here theater students perform a scene from *The Royal Family*, starring Kevin Sketch and Heather Burns in the main roles. The production ran from April 20 to April 30, 2000.

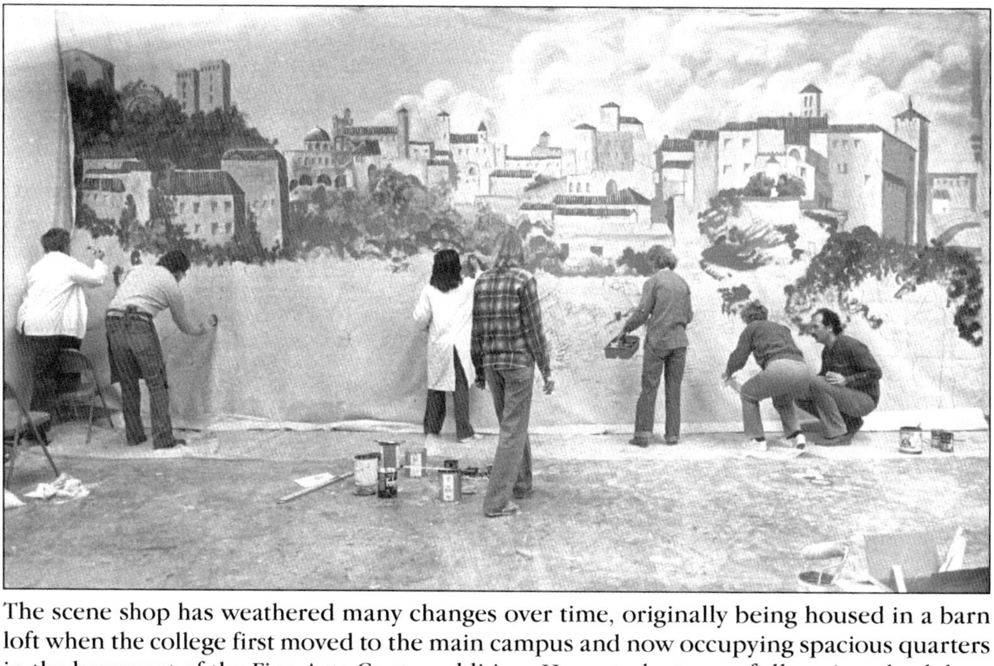

The scene shop has weathered many changes over time, originally being housed in a barn loft when the college first moved to the main campus and now occupying spacious quarters in the basement of the Fine Arts Center addition. Here students carefully paint a backdrop for another theater production.

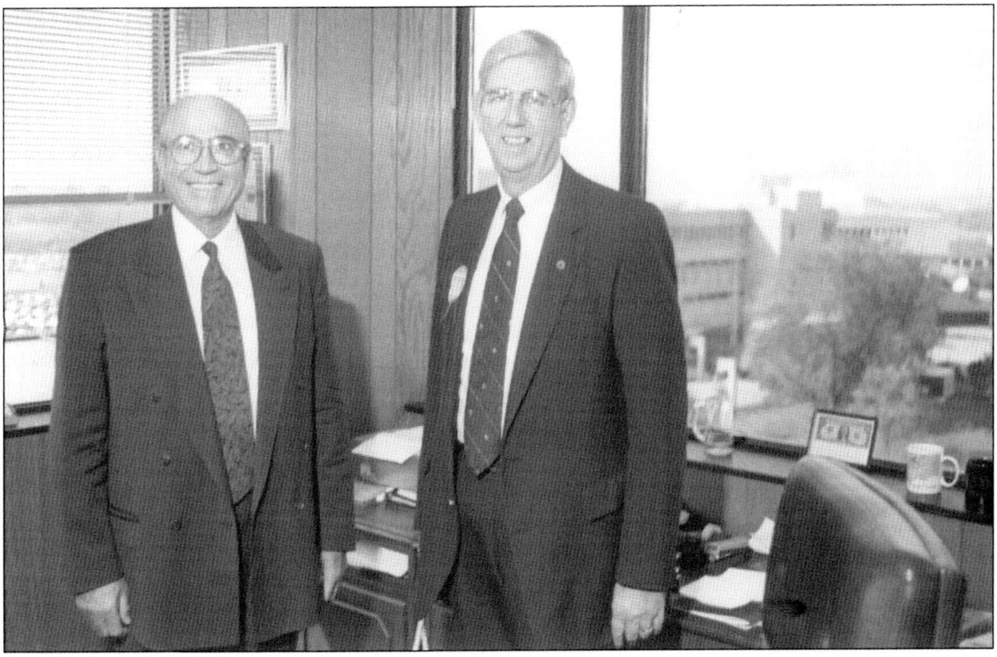

NKU's excellence was recognized when the campus was honored by a visit from the minister of education for the island of Cyprus. Sponsored by the U.S. State Department, Minister Christophoros Christophides visited a number of American colleges to help him develop a plan for expansion and innovation in the schools and universities of Cyprus. Here the minister is greeted by university president Dr. Leon Boothe.

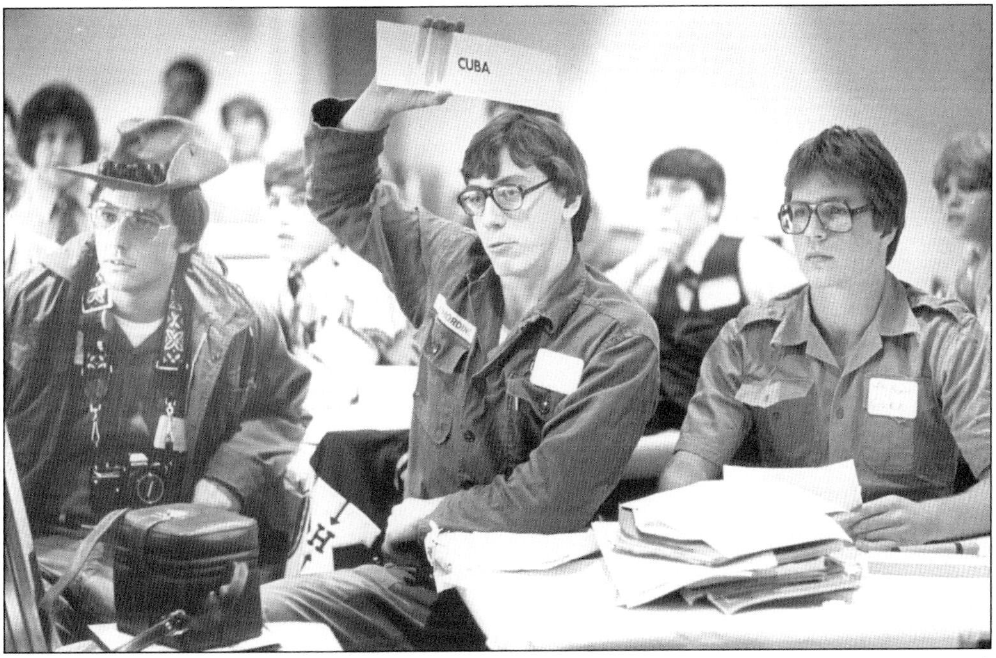

Unusual academic events are a highlight on any campus. A number of students at NKU took part in a university-hosted mock United Nations. In this photograph, the "representative from Cuba" wishes to be recognized by the secretary general.

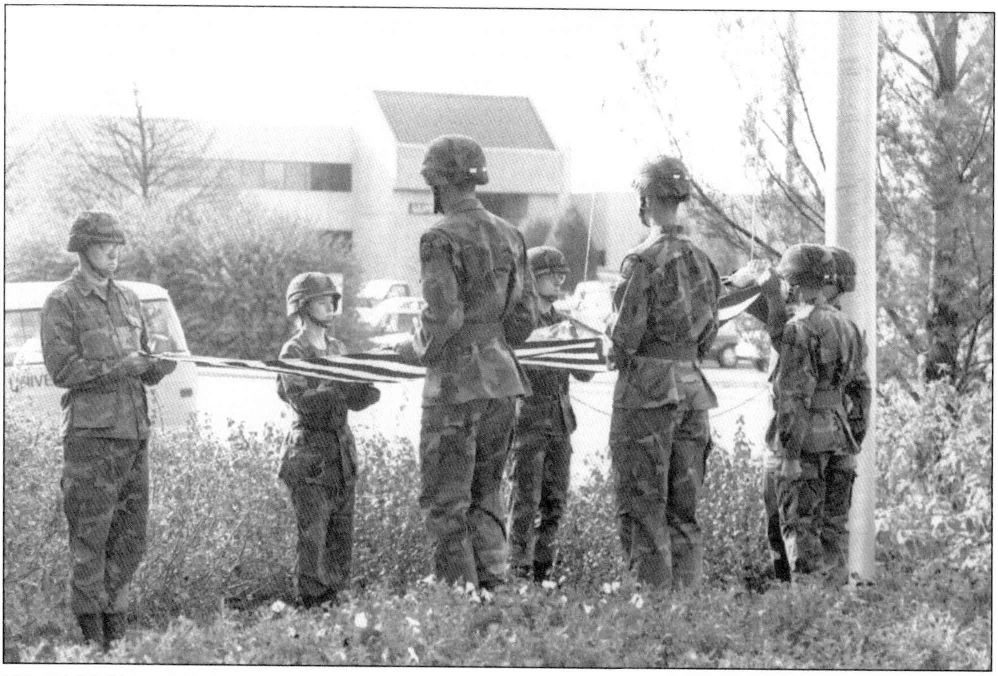

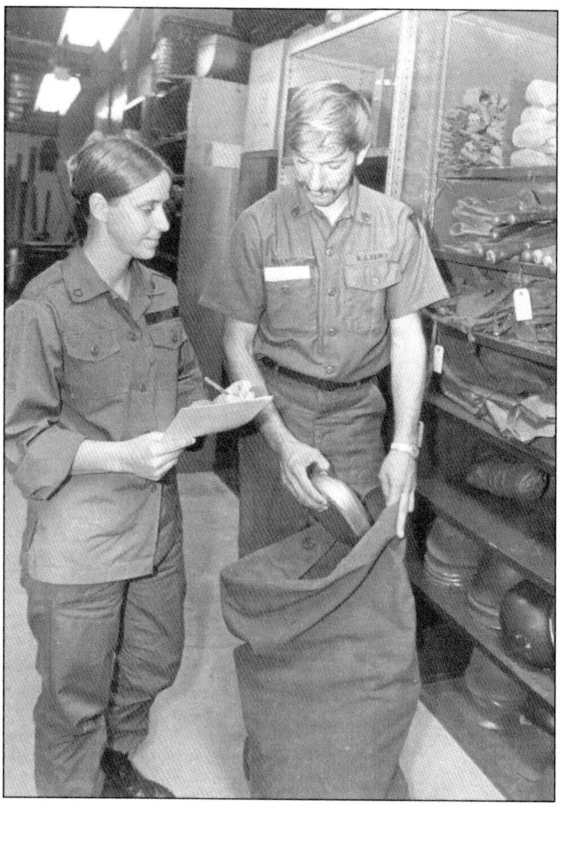

NKU had an Army ROTC post for many decades. They raised and lowered the American flag near Nunn Hall each day, hosted an annual Veterans Day event, and fired a 21-gun salute for campus memorial services. Due to military budget cuts in the Clinton administration, many campuses lost the funding for their ROTC programs. NKU was one of the campuses hit with this cut, and the ROTC program was discontinued. The students enrolled in the now-discontinued program became affiliated with the ROTC program at Xavier University, a private college in nearby Cincinnati. The photograph at left shows S.Sgt. Susan Sensel and Supply Sgt. Douglas B. Hillman packing a duffel.

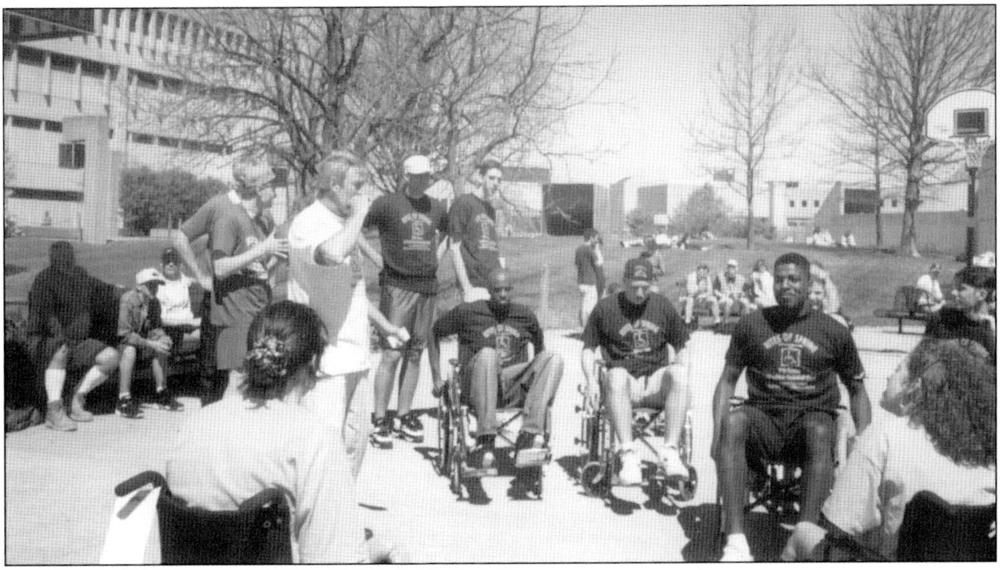

Dale Adams, director of disability services, is shown here with the teams at a wheelchair basketball game, part of the annual Rites of Spring festivities in 1995. This was the fourth annual game for disability awareness, organized to demonstrate to students the challenges faced daily by their disabled colleagues. Adams is blowing his whistle to signal the players who are divided into teams according to their shirt colors, NKU gold and black. In the scene at right, a player on the black team tries to shoot a basket without lifting himself out of the wheelchair.

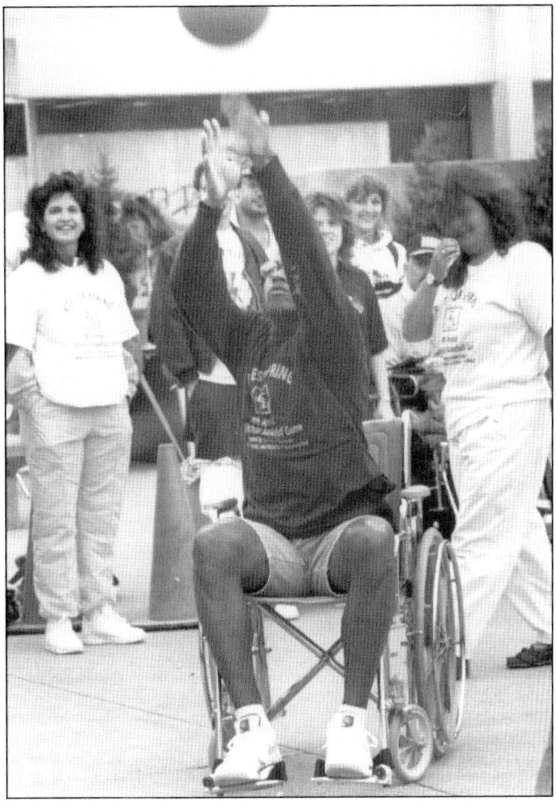

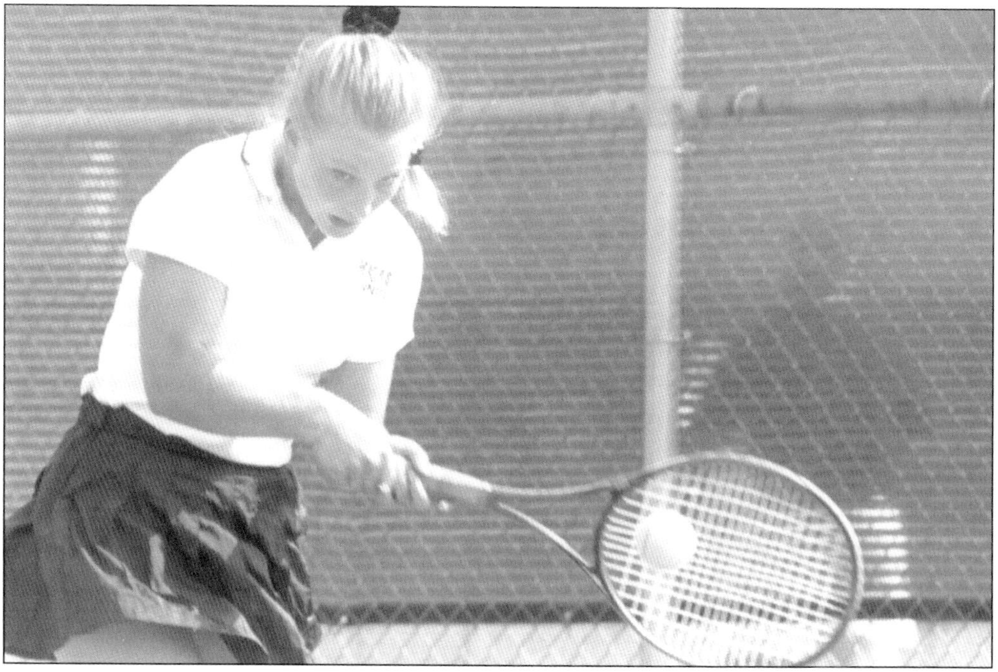

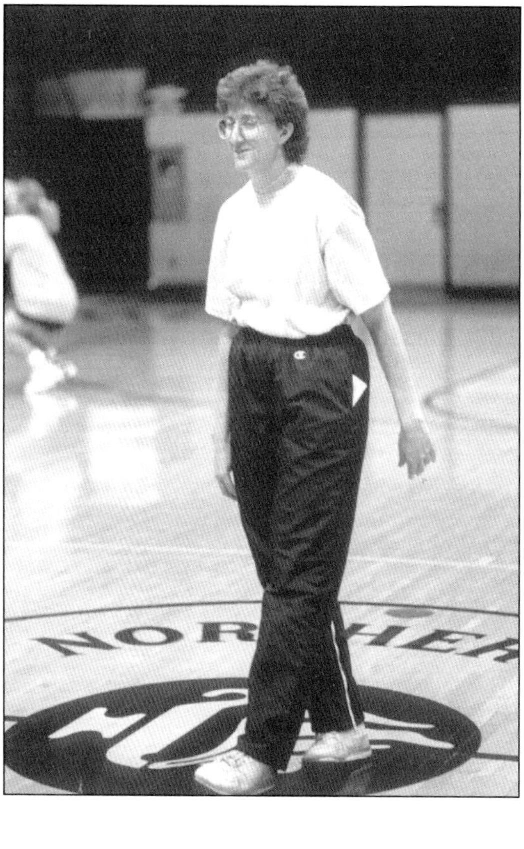

In the early 1980s, when Gov. John Y. Brown ordered a large budget cut, NKU athletics were hit hard. The university was forced to drop tennis, golf, and cross-country, and with them membership in the NCAA, which requires universities to participate in at least six men's and six women's sports. The athletics program came roaring back in the late 1980s after increased funding allowed these teams to be reinstated. In 1987, the Lady Norse secured a spot in the NCAA Division II Final Four. The men's basketball team was runner-up in the national tournament in both 1996 and 1997. However, athletics at NKU reached their current high point in 2003 when the Lady Norse, under coach Nancy Winstel (left), won the NCAA Division II national championship.

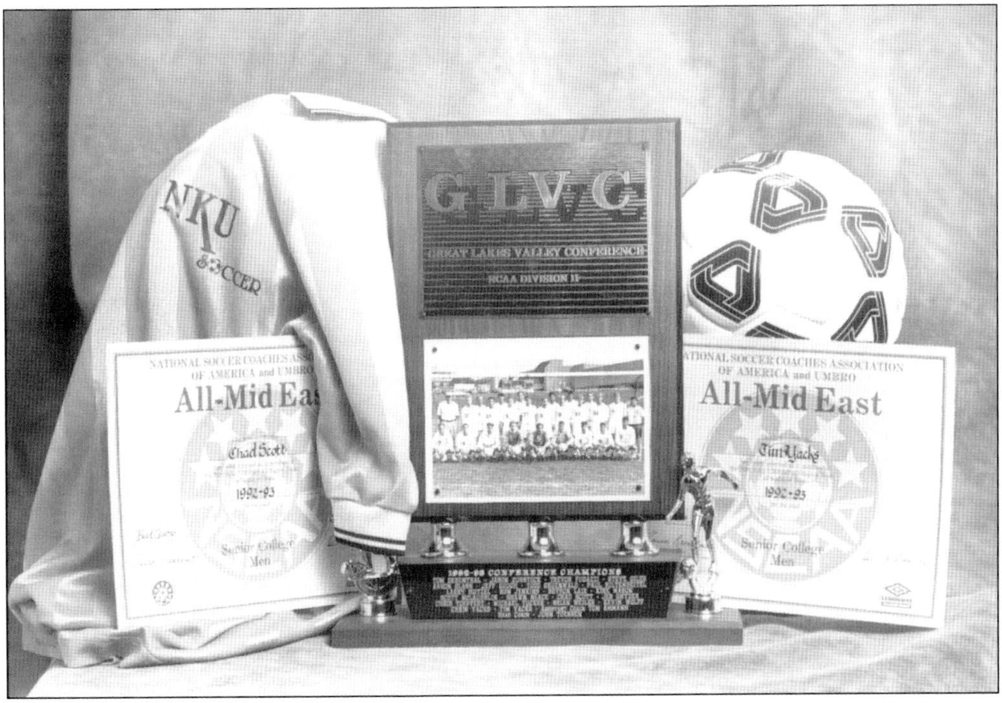

Soccer managed to survive the budget cuts of the early 1980s and has also done well in recent years, with the 1993 men's soccer team winning the Great Lakes Valley Conference championship. Two of that year's players, Chad Scott and Tim Yacks, were named to the All Mid-East regional team. Todd Gruenwald (in action in the photograph at right) was named the university's all-time scorer during the early 1990s. He was one of 22 players on the 1993 championship team under Head Coach John Toebben and Assistant Coach Tom Ammann.

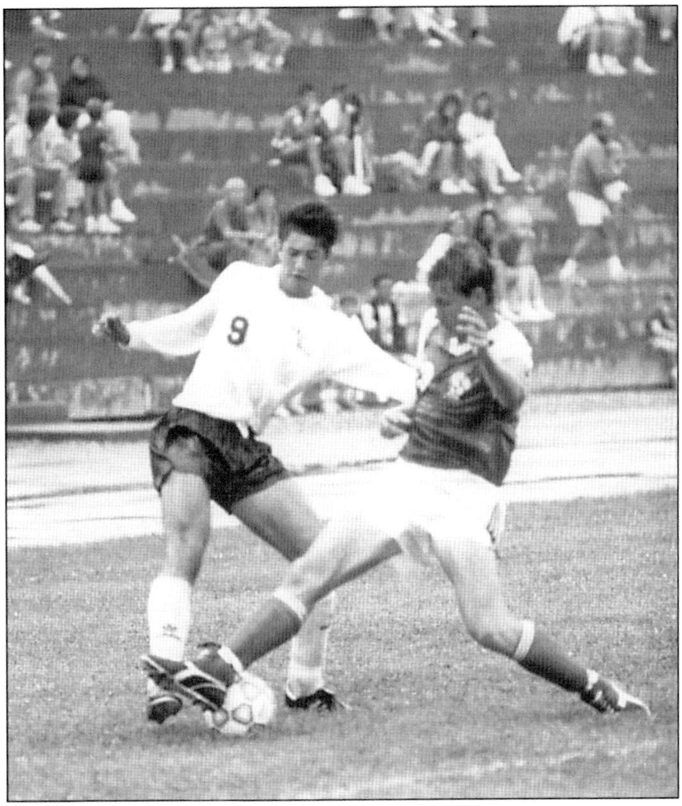

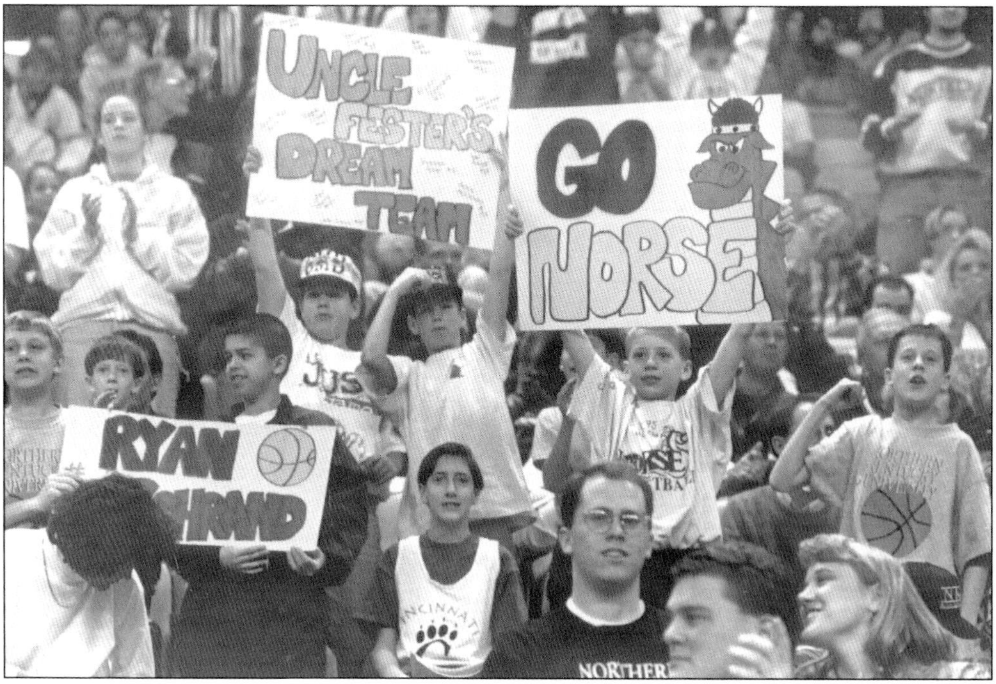

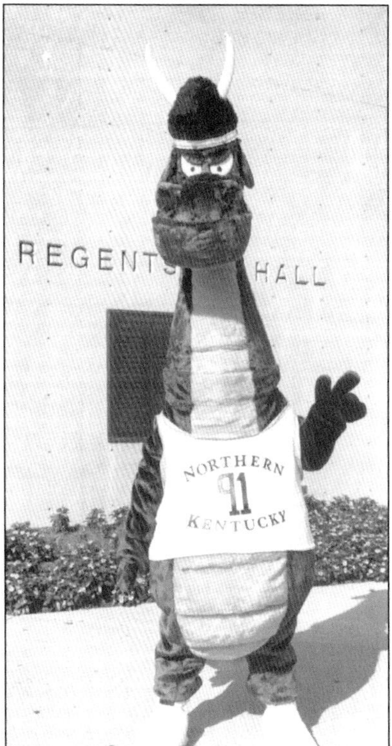

And the fans go wild! Nothing beats the excitement at NKU over basketball, especially with both the men's and women's teams playing so well over the last few years. Student support of the basketball teams is evident in the signs the crowd holds during the early-1990s game above. Students flock to the games, filling Regents Hall to overflowing. As can be seen in the photograph above, Regents Hall is too small to hold the crowds who wish to attend the games. The new arena under construction, the Bank of Kentucky Center, is being built to accommodate the largest NKU crowds. For now, fans will continue to be welcomed to Regents Hall by the NKU mascot, as in this photograph featuring Hey U! In 2005, the dragon mascot was succeeded by a return to the Norseman.

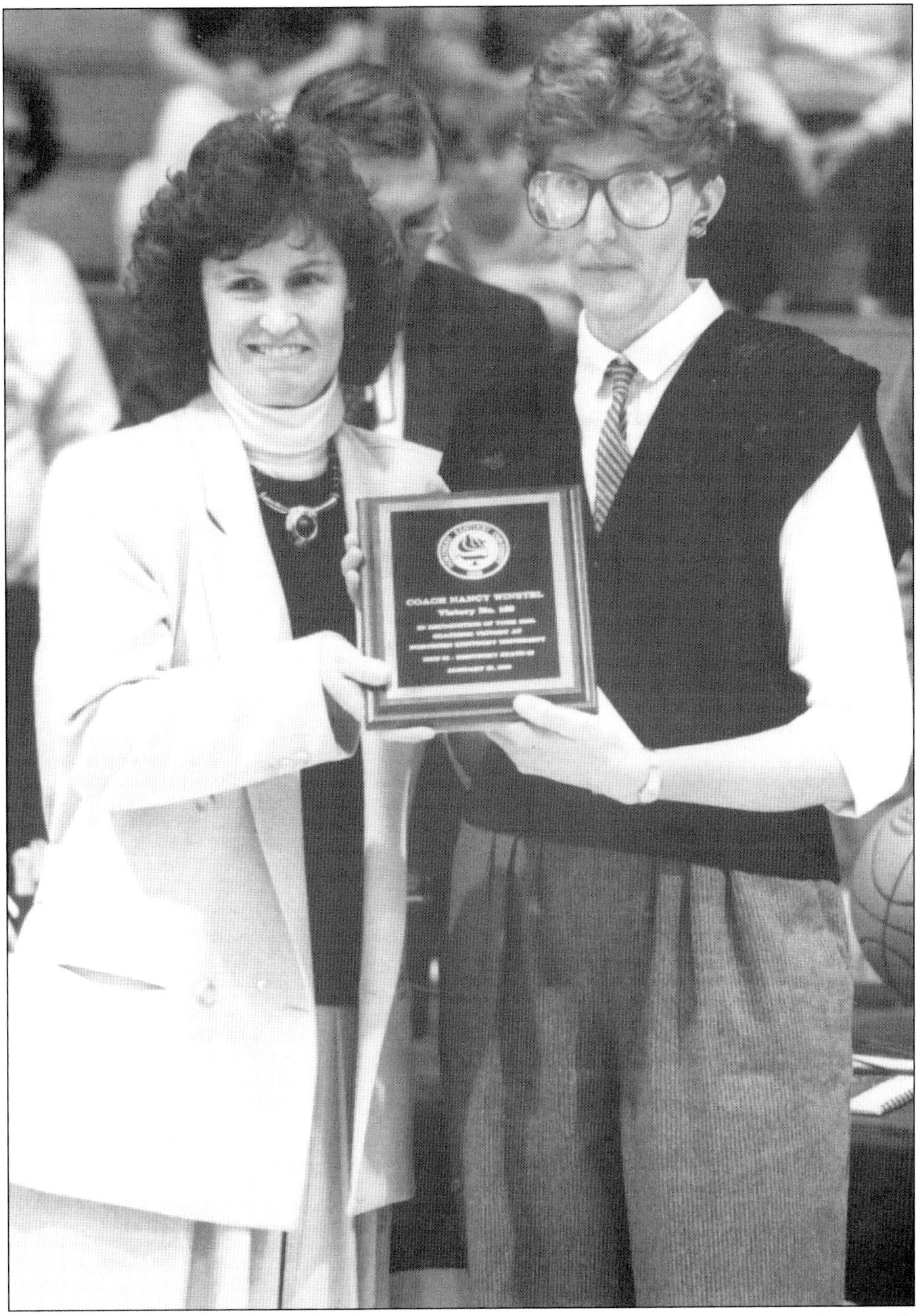

Lady Norse basketball coach Nancy Winstel receives a plaque from NKU vice president Cindy Dickens celebrating her 100th victory as head coach in the late 1980s. Winstel had played for NKU as a student before beginning her coaching career. She returned to NKU in 1983, taking over for Jane Meier.

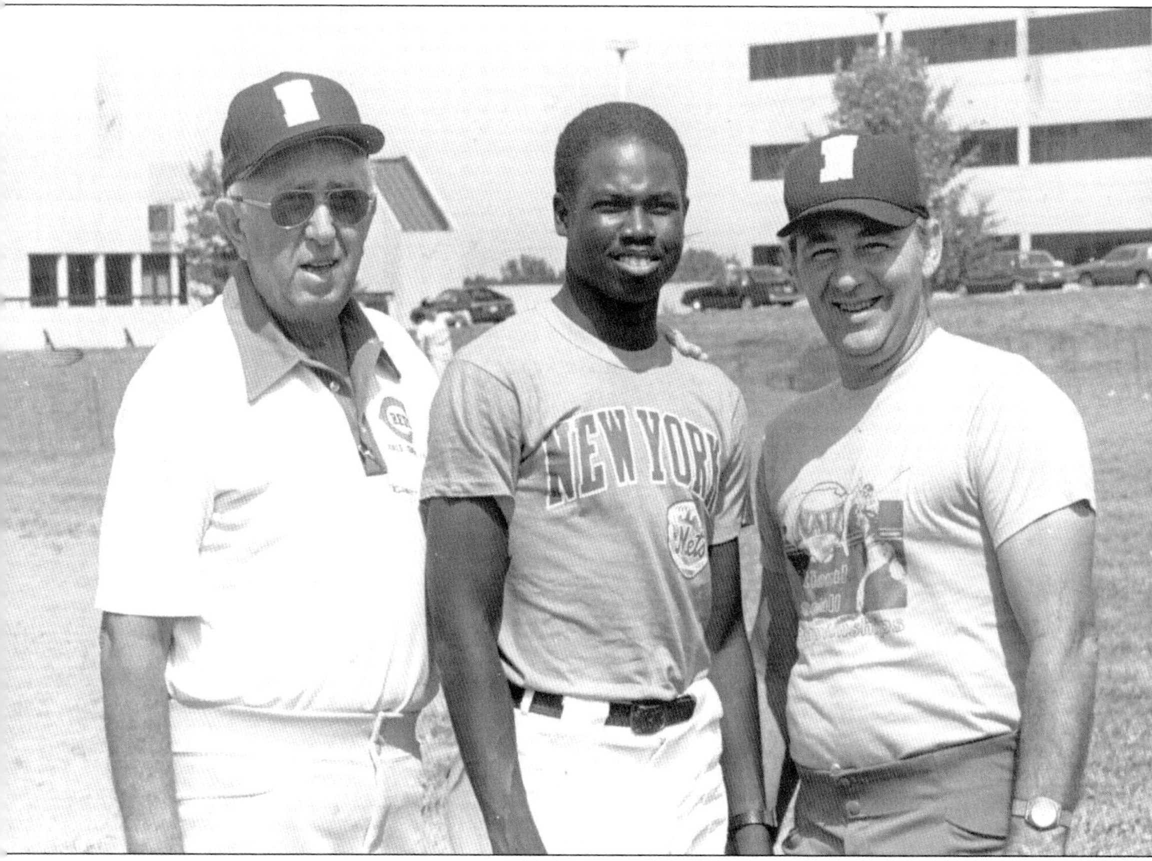

Though basketball often takes center stage in NKU athletics, the baseball program was actually formed a few months earlier in 1971. Though the first season was not one for the history books, the baseball team has been consistently successful through the years. Some former players have gone on to professional sports, such as Alan Hayden, who is shown here with assistant coach Charlie Leftin (left) and head coach Bill Aker (right). Hayden was drafted by the New York Mets in 1985 and played for their Kingsport, Tennessee, farm team.

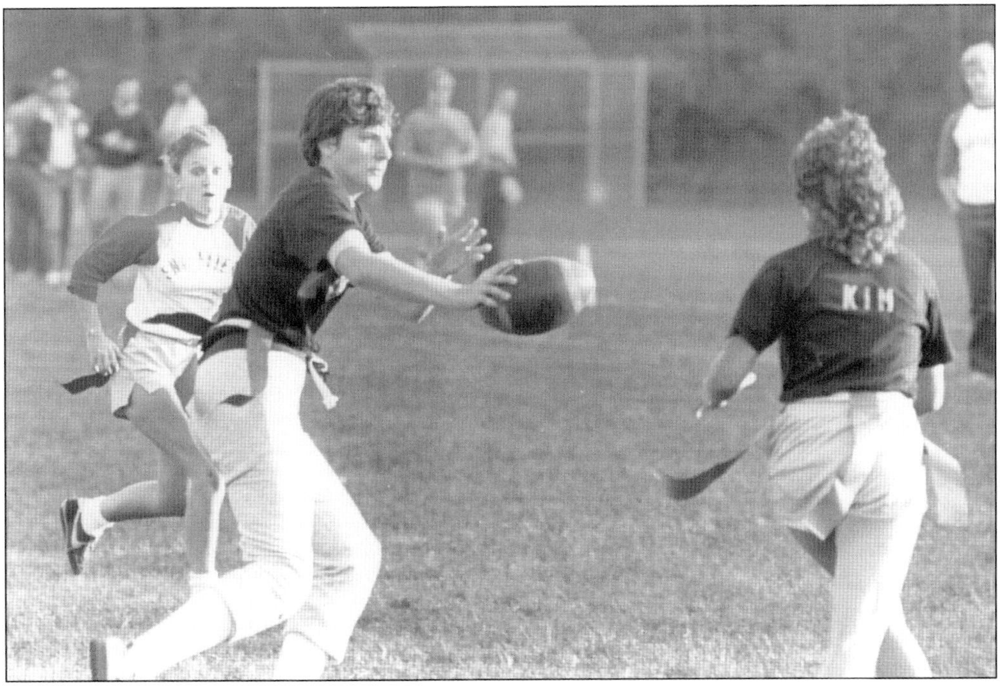

Though intramural coed flag football is a common enough sport on campus, full-contact football has never taken off. Every so often it is suggested, but basketball fanatics at NKU simply don't seem terribly interested. They would rather cheer on their favorite team in the arena.

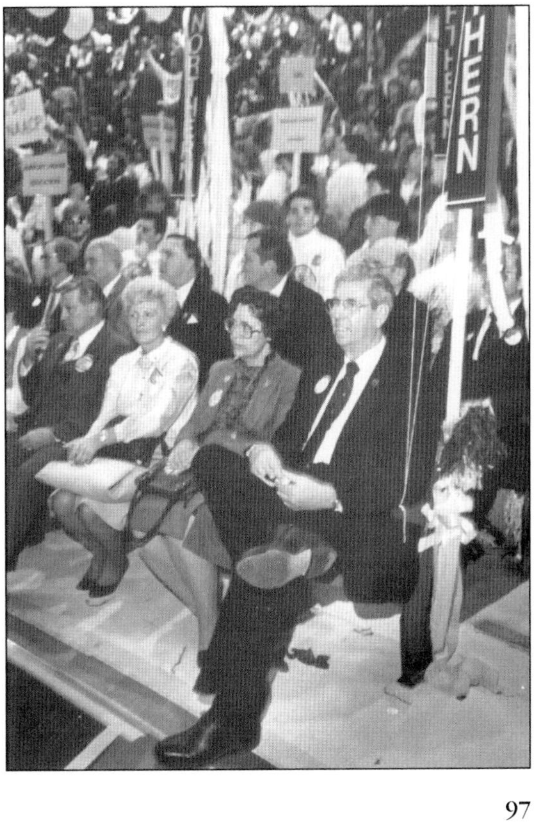

What at first glance appears to be a political nominating convention is actually a funding rally in Frankfort, Kentucky. Continued higher education budget cuts throughout the 1980s culminated in this 1988 rally. Every state institution sent representatives in the form of students, faculty, administrators, and even a few bands. The Northern contingent consisted of several hundred representatives including faculty, students, and university president Leon Boothe.

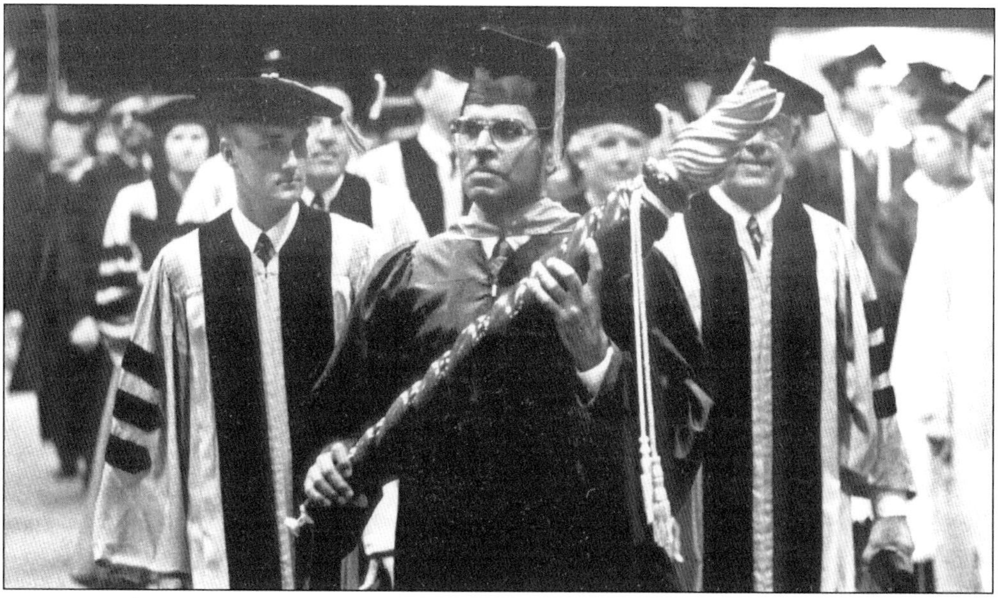

A newer tradition at NKU is the university mace. Used as a symbol of integrity and scholarship, it is carried by the university's grand marshal in the formal procession at commencement. The mace is carved mahogany with a walnut stain. The spiral design is meant to symbolize growth and movement toward higher achievement. The mace is topped with a flame covered in gold leaf, which symbolizes light and learning. The flame was inspired by the lamp of learning, which graces the university's official seal. The mace also features gold and white braided cords, NKU's school colors. In the photograph below, local artist Jack True is hard at work carving the mace.

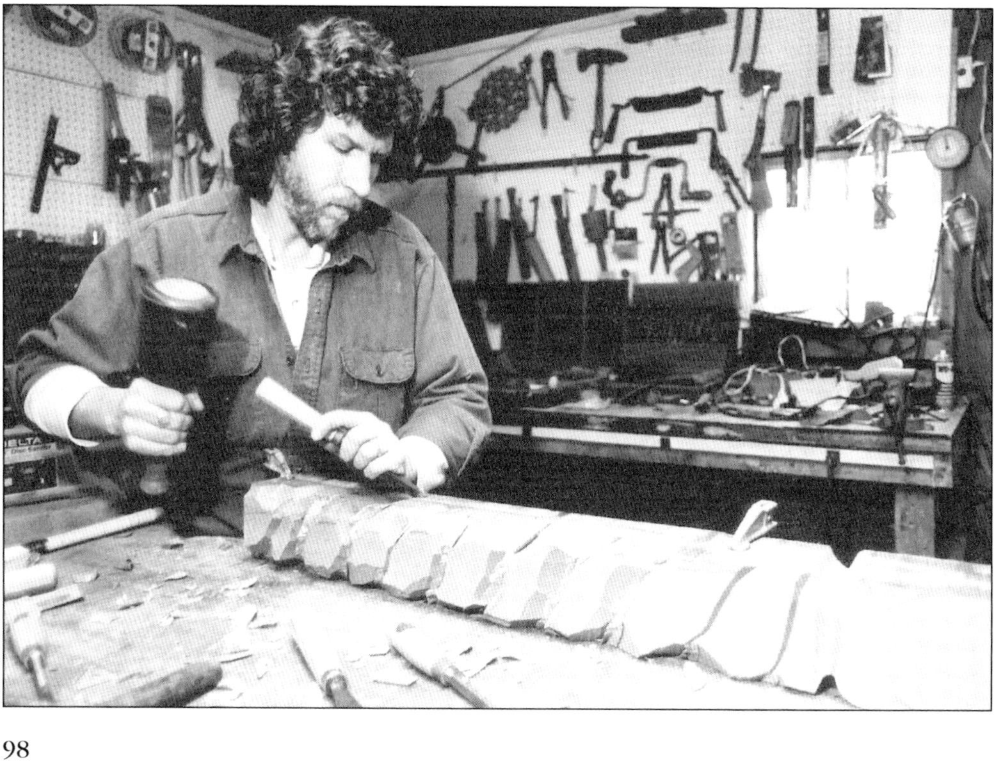

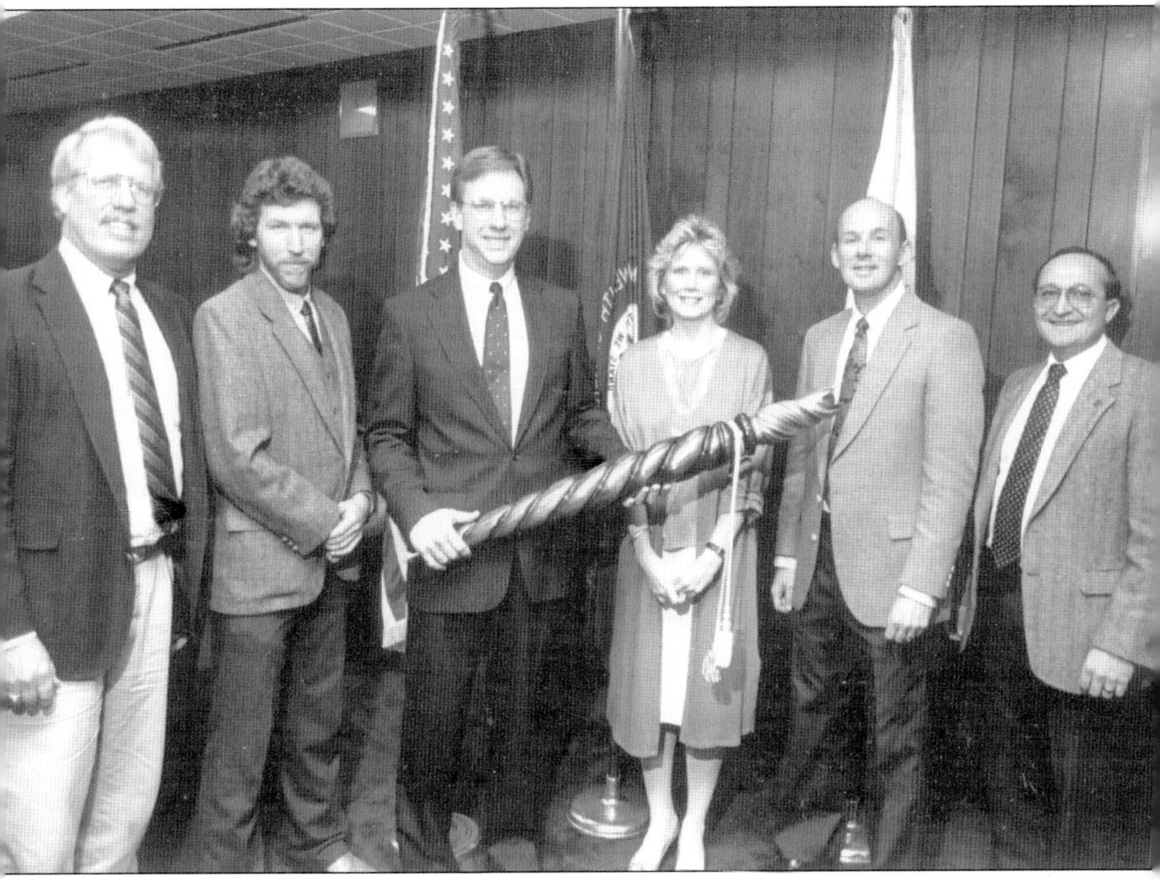

Shown here is the presentation of the university mace by the NKU Foundation, which commissioned the piece as a gift to the university. Attendees included, from left to right, David Thomson, an associate professor in communications; sculptor Jack True; Vice President and Provost David Jorns; student Kari Messner, who designed the mace; James Thomas, president of the faculty senate; and James Alford, executive director of the foundation.

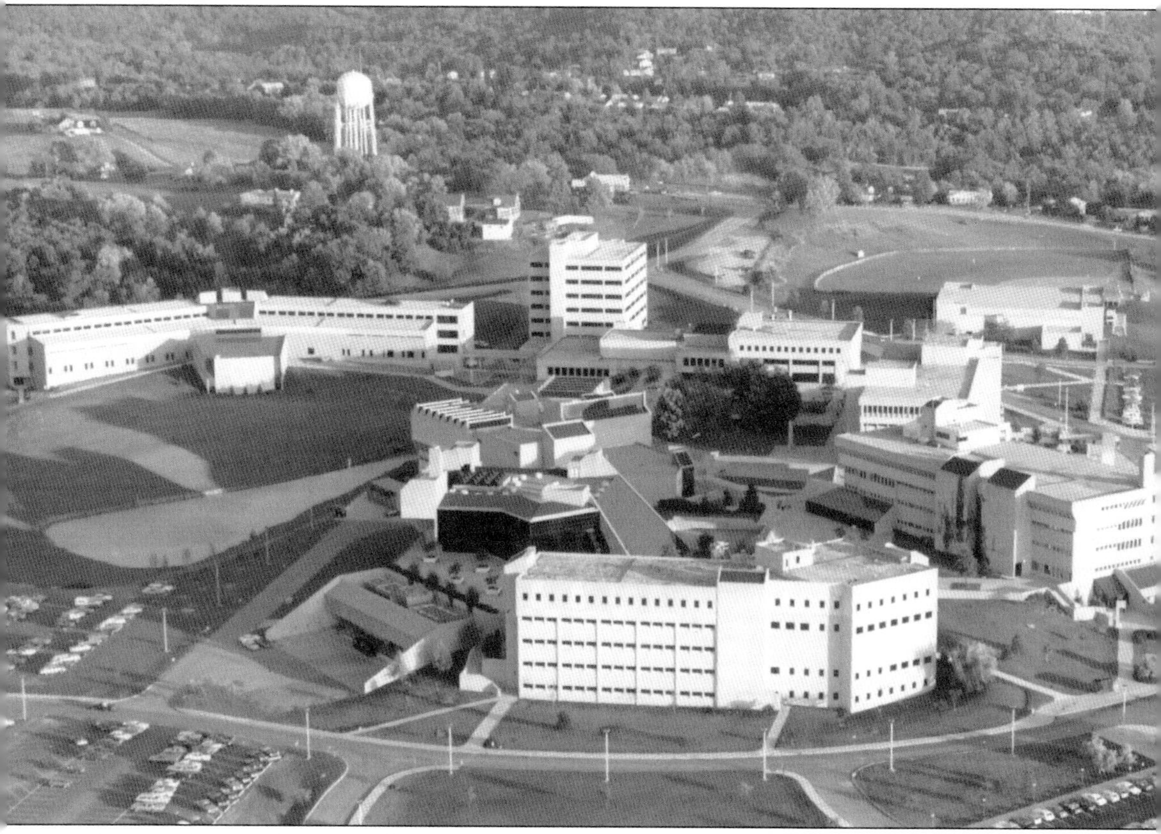

An aerial view of campus shows just how much a campus can grow in about 20 years. For the first decade, enrollment figures jumped higher than expected every year. New, tougher admissions standards, implemented to ensure student success, were expected to have the side effect of temporarily decreasing enrollment. This didn't happen. Enrollment slowed, but it continued to climb. NKU continues to be one of the two fastest-growing universities in the state of Kentucky.

Five

The Moreland and Votruba Era
A New Century in Northern Kentucky

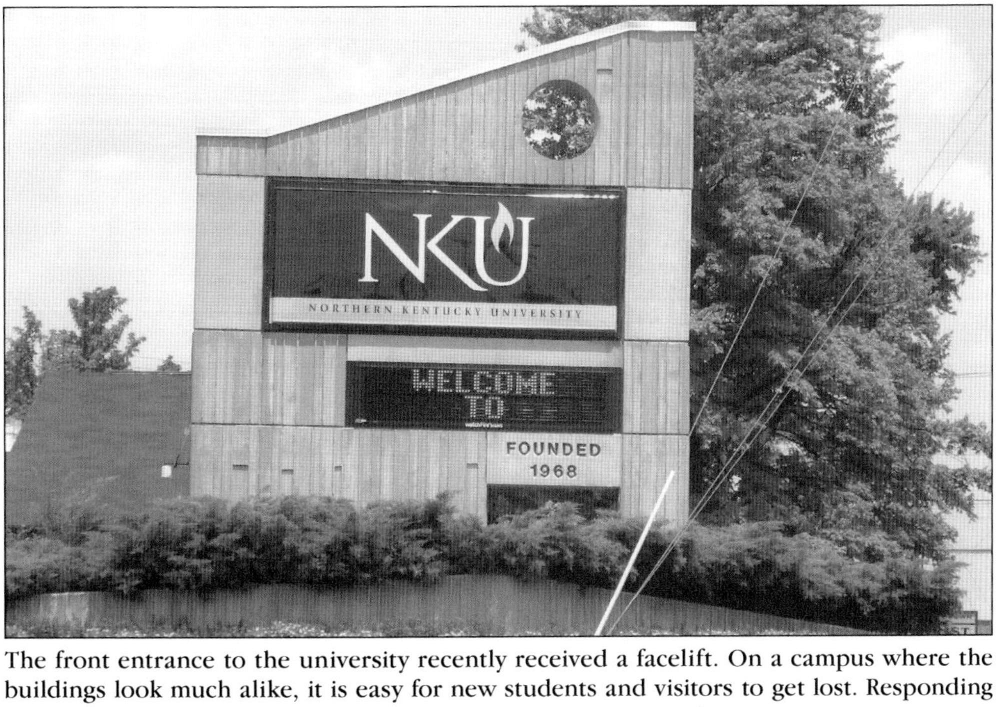

The front entrance to the university recently received a facelift. On a campus where the buildings look much alike, it is easy for new students and visitors to get lost. Responding to the cries for more and better signage, the university began placing signs at intersections around campus in the spring of 2006. These signs list the different buildings with directional arrows. As part of this project, part of the front entrance sign was also replaced.

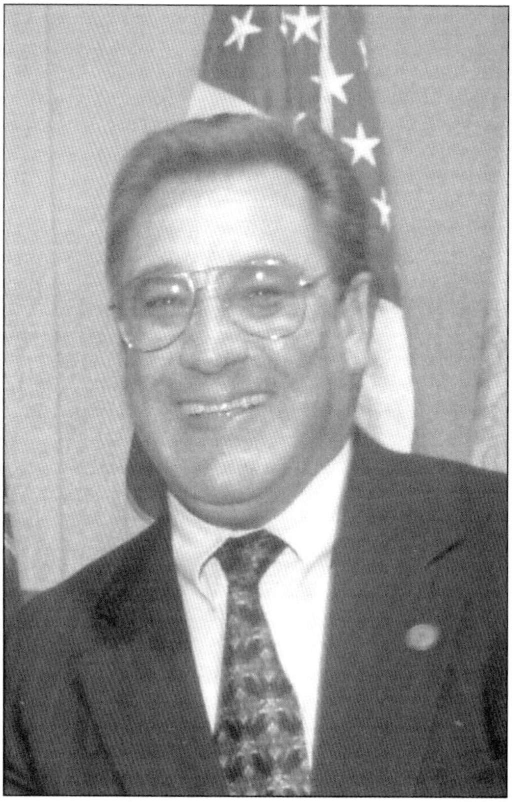

Jack Moreland was selected to serve as interim university president until the board of regents could choose a permanent replacement for Boothe. He was a well-known figure in local public education, having served previously as the superintendent for the public school system of nearby Dayton, Kentucky. Moreland is best remembered for his technology initiatives. During the year that he served as president (1996–1997), he started a drive to "put a computer on every desk." He also ramped up the campus e-mail system, for the first time making e-mail available to every member of the campus community. As seen in the photograph below, he also pioneered cooperative partnerships with local corporations. This ribbon-cutting ceremony opened the new Delta Air Lines call center. The center exclusively hired NKU students to operate the phones, making reservations for airline passengers, which provided much-needed jobs for students.

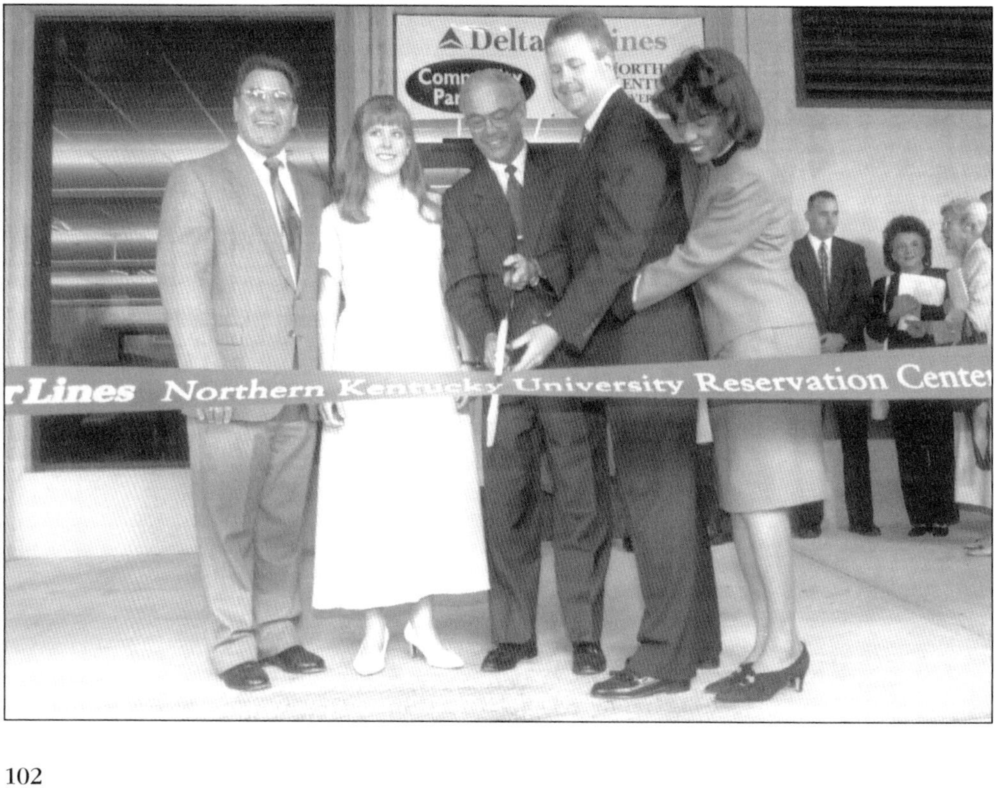

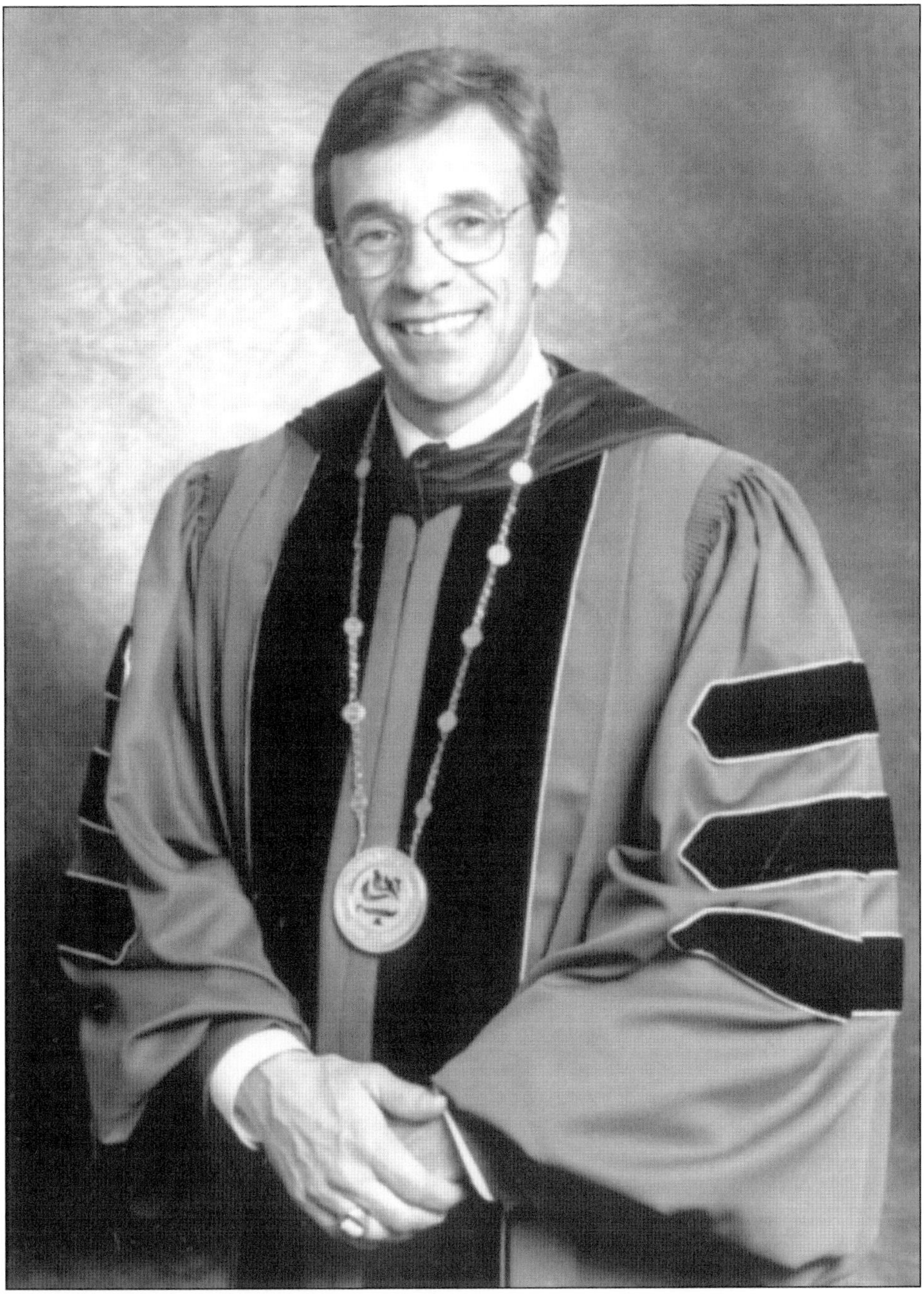

Dr. James Votruba became the fourth president of Northern Kentucky University on August 1, 1997, following the resignation of Dr. Leon Boothe. He had previously been a vice provost at Michigan State University. He has also held positions at Binghamton University, the University of Illinois at Urbana-Champaign, and Drake University. With degrees in political science, sociology, and higher education administration, Votruba represents a bit of a departure from NKU's tendency to hire historians for the presidential post. Votruba is shown here in his commencement robes wearing the Presidential Medallion, which is passed on to each president at his inauguration ceremony.

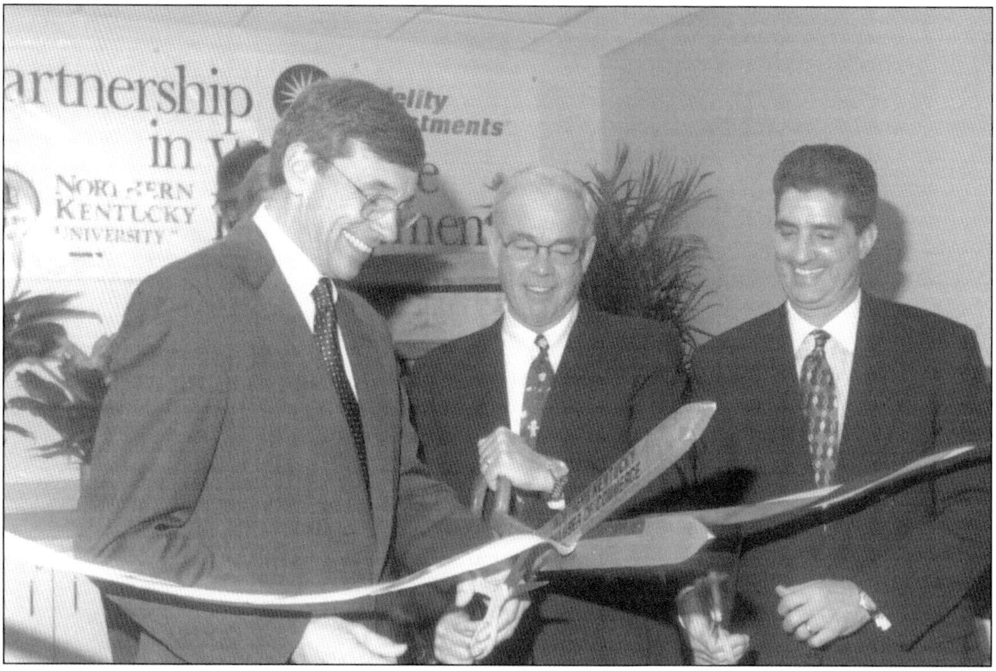

When cutbacks forced Delta Air Lines to close its call center on campus, many NKU students lost jobs. University president Jim Votruba followed in Moreland's footsteps and found a new corporation interested in partnering with the campus. Here Votruba cuts the ribbon at the official opening of a new call center for Fidelity Investments.

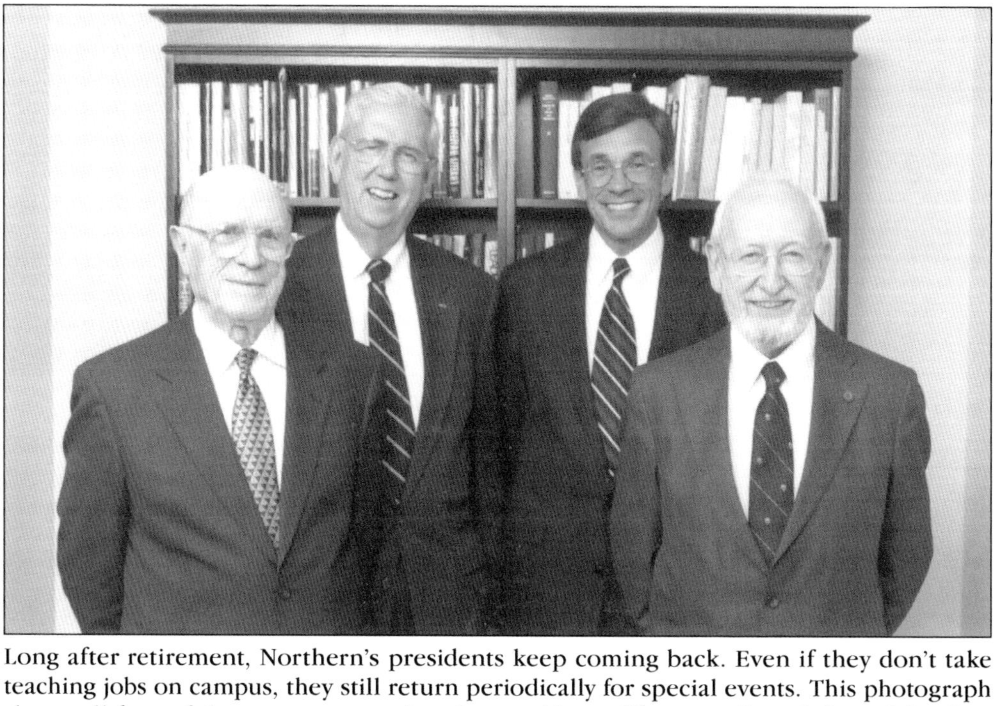

Long after retirement, Northern's presidents keep coming back. Even if they don't take teaching jobs on campus, they still return periodically for special events. This photograph shows all four of the permanent university presidents. They are, from left to right, Drs. A. D. Albright, Leon Boothe, James Votruba, and W. Frank Steely.

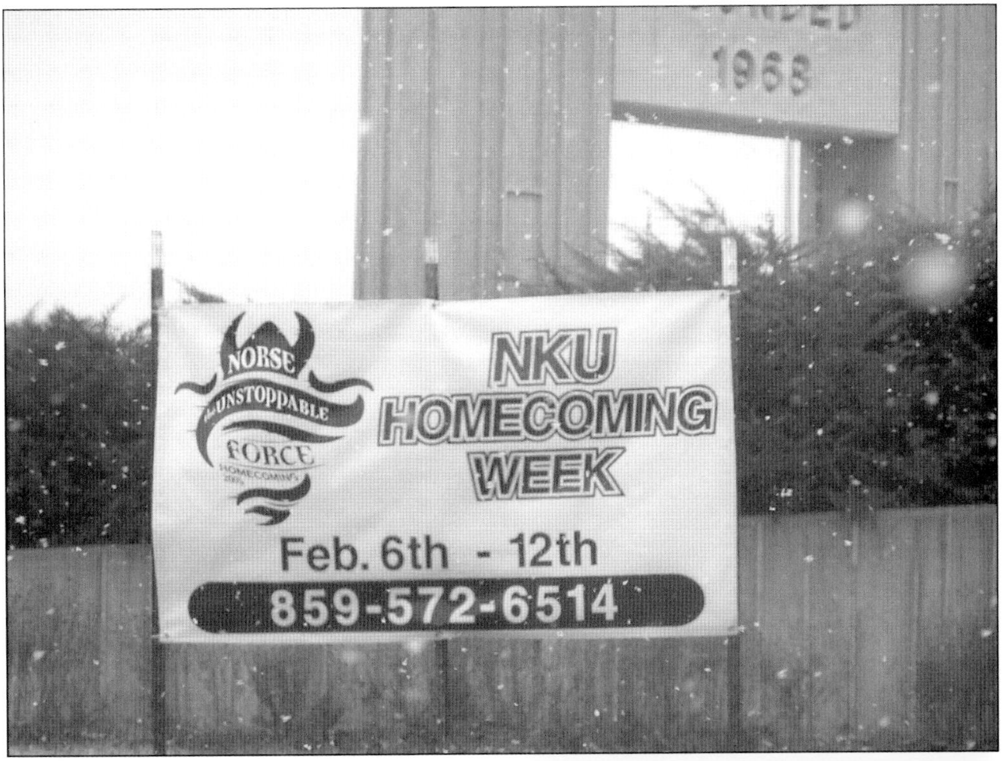

Homecoming remains a popular event at NKU. Though many schools have their homecoming in the autumn, NKU's is held in the early spring. This can sometimes be trying with the uncertain Northern Kentucky weather. Numerous alumni and students turn out for a weekend of events, even if it snows as it did in 2005. The homecoming king, queen, and court are crowned during halftime at the annual homecoming game. In the photograph at right, the 2001 homecoming queen, Jennifer Surgalski, is being crowned by the previous year's queen, Kara Clark. Both are members of the Delta Gamma sorority. Competition among the students in the Greek system for homecoming king and queen is fierce.

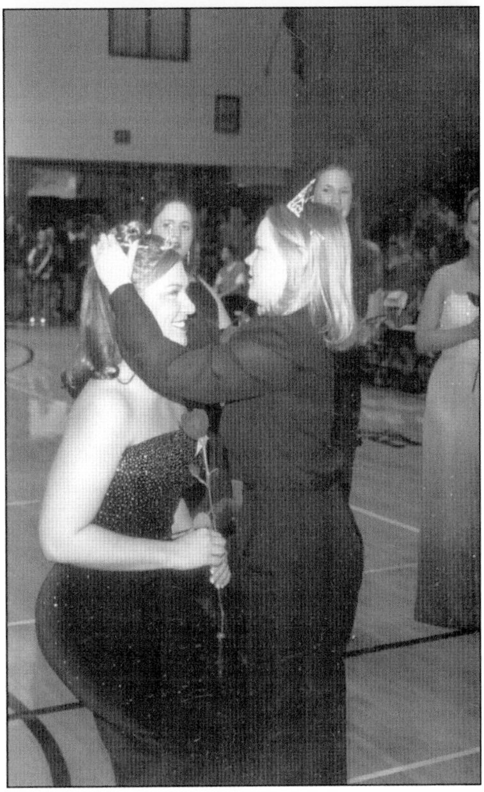

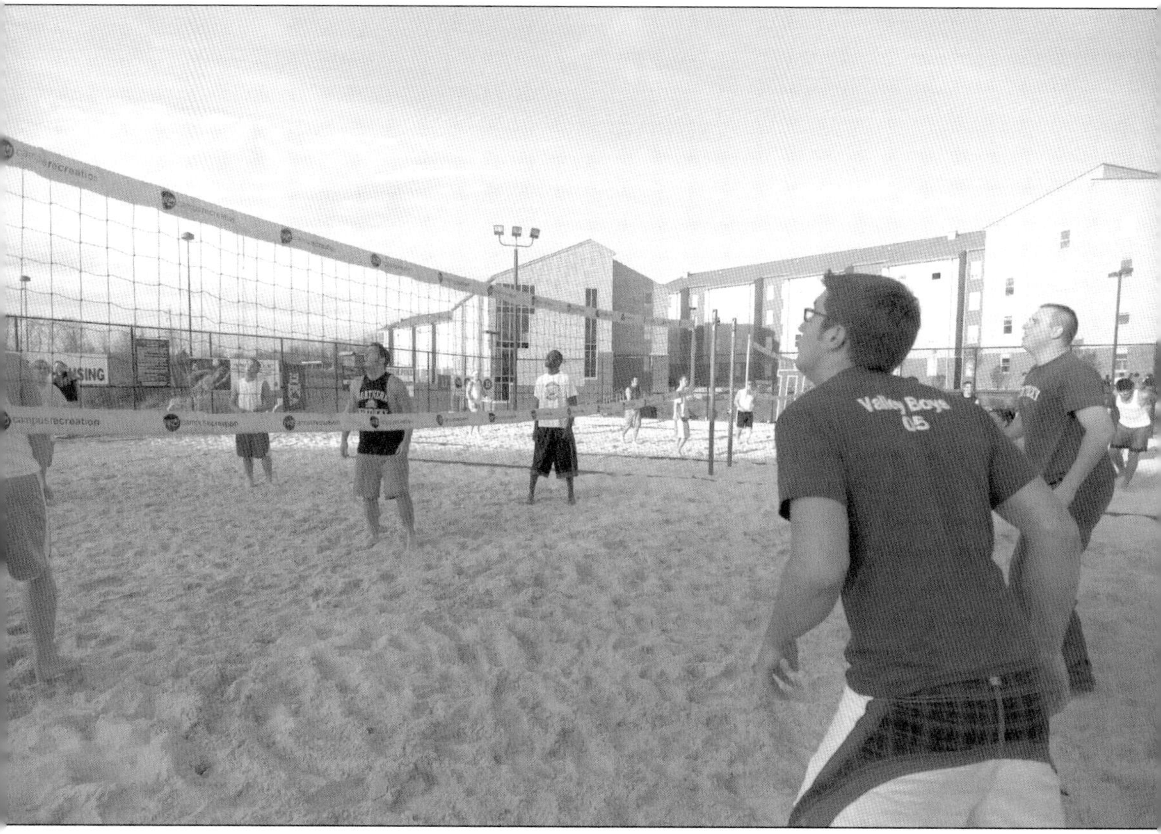

The annual Rites of Spring continues on campus, still scheduled between the spring thaw and semester final exams. In recent years, activities have been expanded to include newer sports such as beach volleyball, being played here at a sand court near the residence halls.

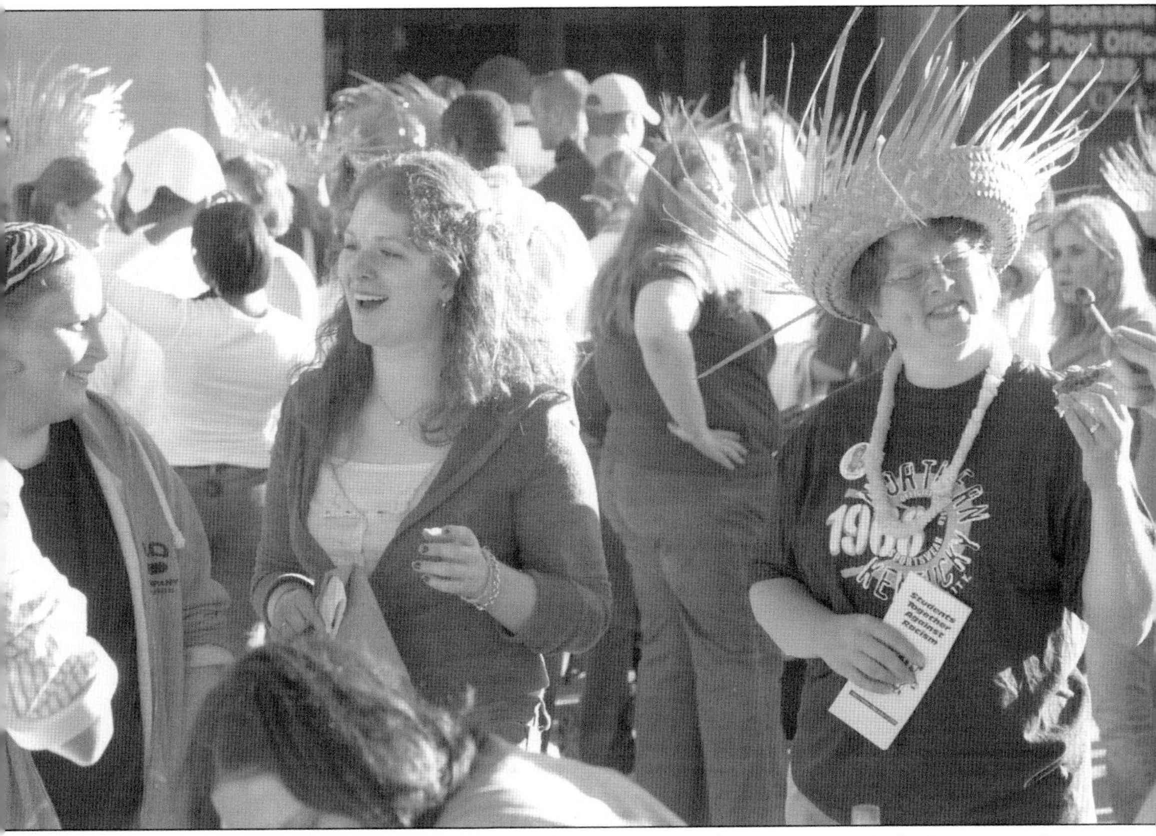

The first week of classes each fall is full of Welcome Week activities to help integrate the new students to campus. The week culminates with FreshFusion, a carnival-themed party on the main plaza. More than 2,000 students usually attend, many coming as part of their University 101 orientation class, providing an ice breaker to allow students in the class to get to know each other. More than 100 student organizations set up booths to distribute information and answer questions about campus activities. Complete with cotton candy, dunking booths, and live music, FreshFusion provides the students with a chance to unwind after a long, sometimes confusing first week.

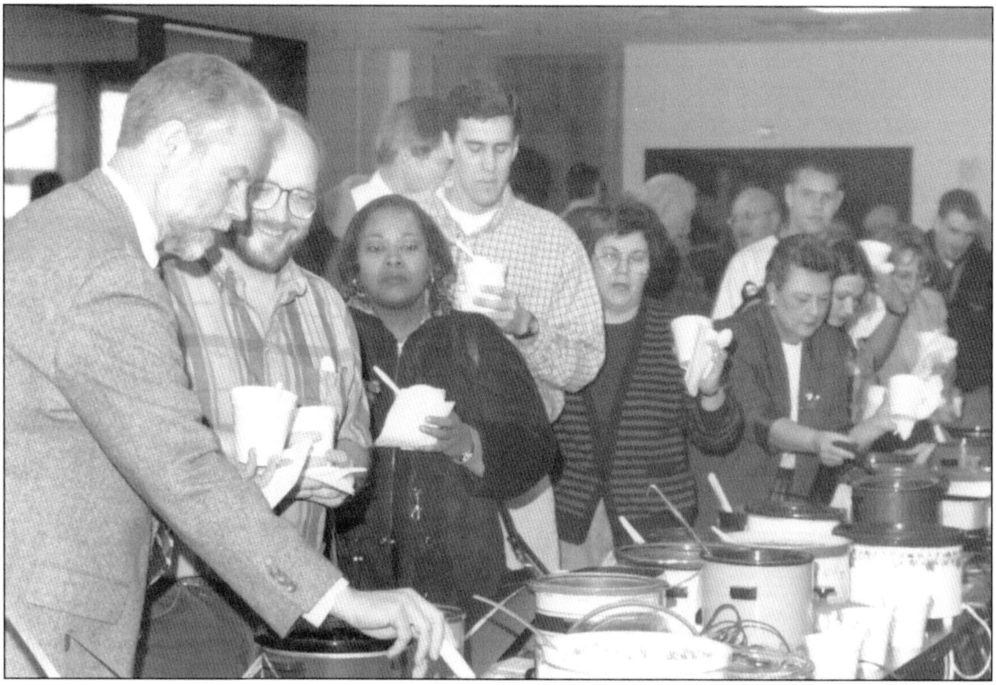

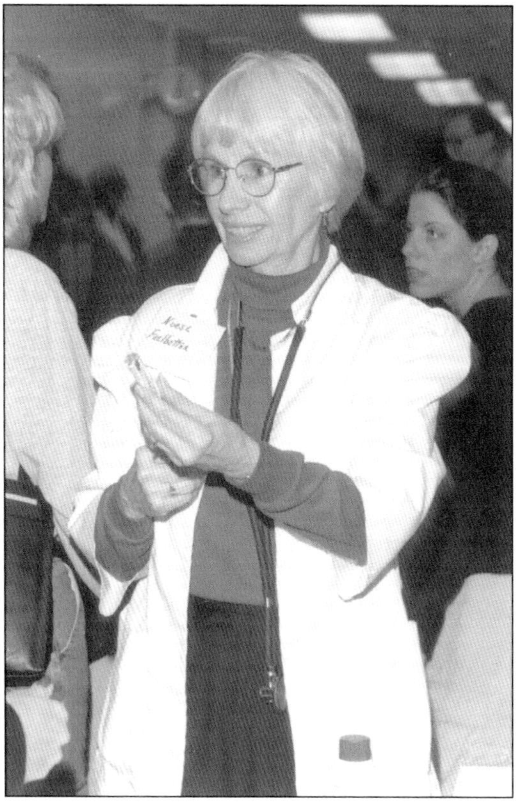

Another long-running NKU tradition is the annual Chili Cook-Off. Hosted by Staff Congress, the event is a fund-raiser for the NKU Benevolent Fund. The fund is available to help NKU faculty and staff who have suffered a major illness or other catastrophic event. Faculty and staff enter their favorite chili recipes. After the judging is completed, the chili is available for the rest of the campus community, who pay for the hot lunch. Antacids are needed by some when the chili is extra spicy. In the photograph at left, "Nurse Feelbetter" offers Rolaids to some of the diners.

Several sports on campus sometimes receive little recognition. One of these is cheerleading. The Norse cheerleaders aim to succeed, even when the fanfare is small. In 2006, the Norse squad won the Universal Cheerleading Association's national title for small coed squads in NCAA Division II—an achievement that did receive widespread coverage by the Northern Kentucky press. Another sport overshadowed by basketball is softball. The softball team plays at a consistently high level. Currently it holds the NCAA record for all divisions for most consecutive wins in a season with 55 victories.

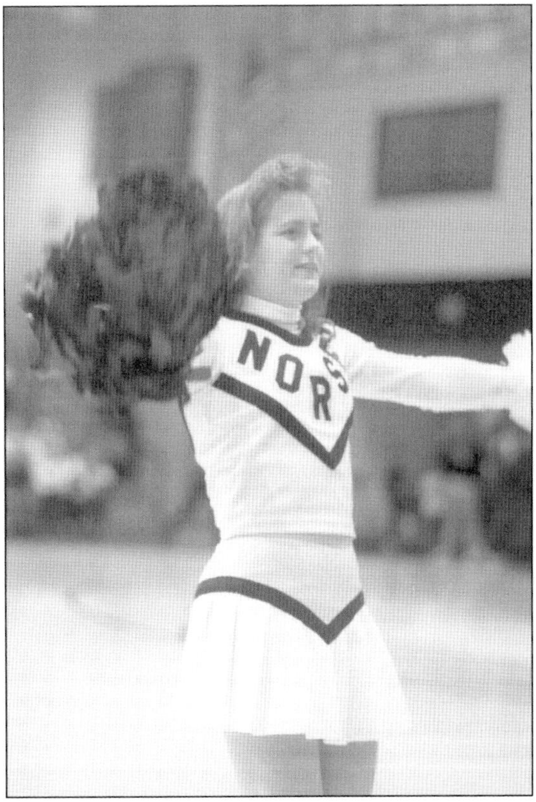

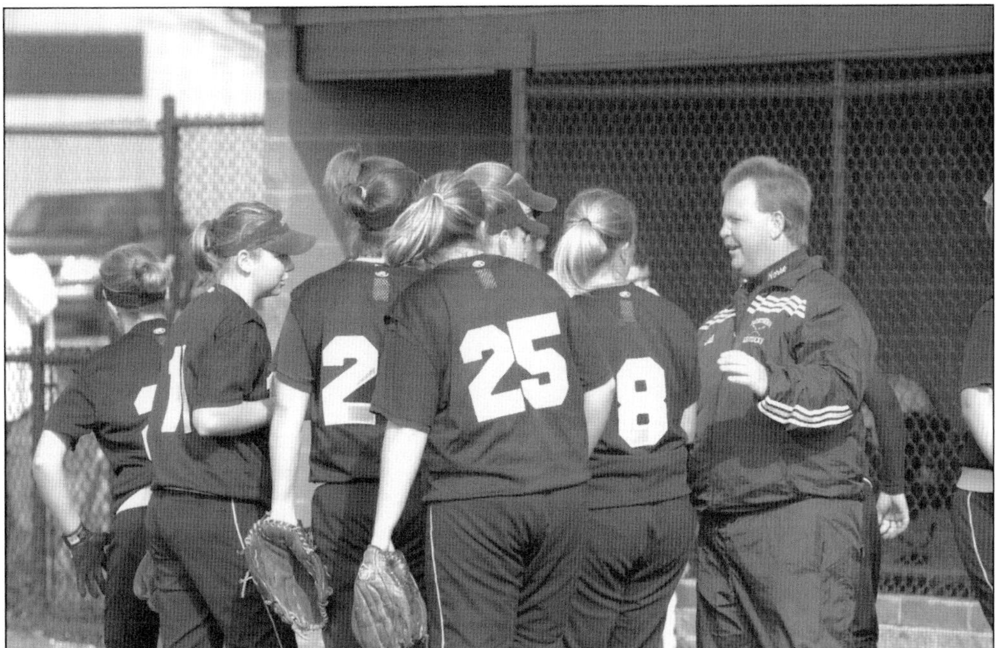

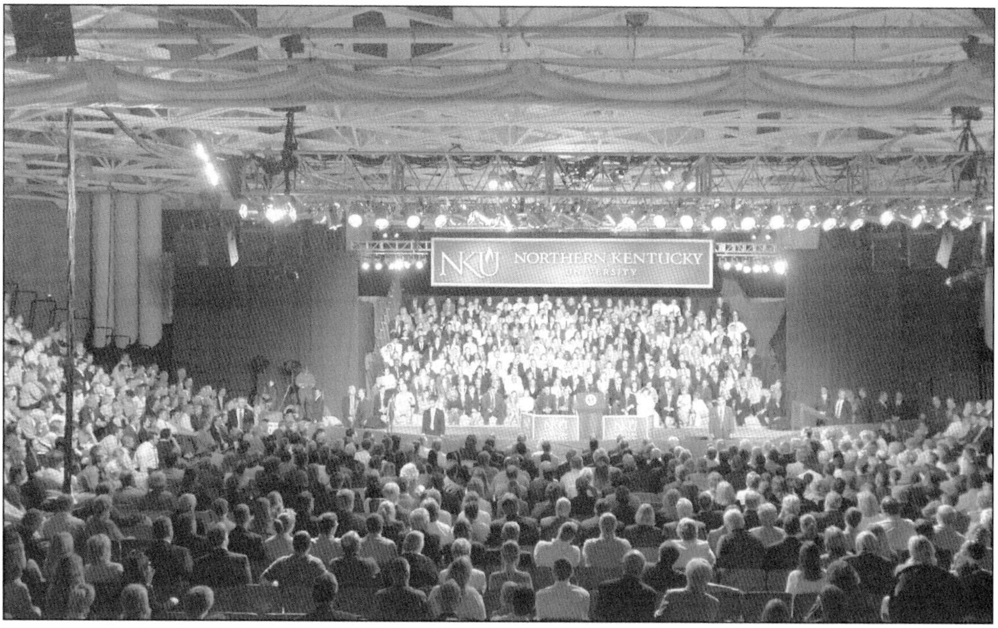

The most recent dignitary to visit Northern Kentucky University was Pres. George W. Bush, who appeared on campus for a speech in spring 2006. Regents Hall, sometimes joked about as "the most dismal high school gym in the region," was dressed up to a high polish for the occasion of Bush's visit. The first president to visit NKU's campus was Gerald Ford, shown in the photograph below shaking hands with the university president, Dr. A. D. Albright. While Bush may have been the second to visit, he holds the distinction of being the first sitting president to come to NKU. His visit was a remarkable event in the history of a young and growing university.

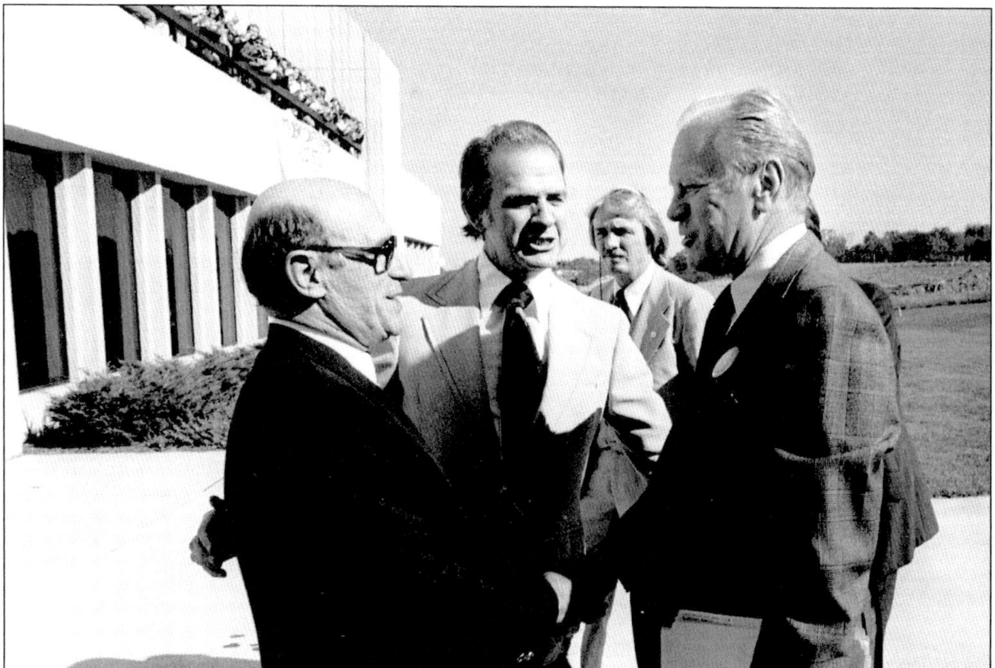

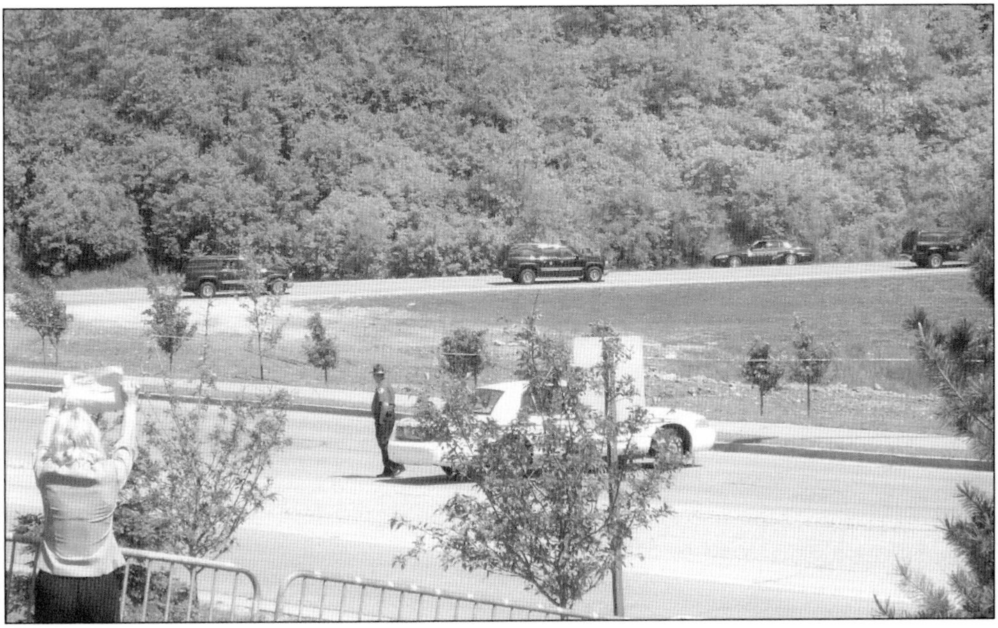

When Pres. George W. Bush came to campus to give a speech in Regents Hall in May 2006, security was especially tight. The Secret Service manned rooftops and swept one end of campus with specially trained dogs. Many roads and highways in Northern Kentucky were shut down for his motorcade, which can be seen entering campus in the photograph above. Nearly every law enforcement vehicle in the region was used to clear and close the roads, including county, municipality, and campus police cars. Bush's arrival brought out a number of protestors demanding everything from protection for immigrant workers to gay rights and an end to the war in Iraq.

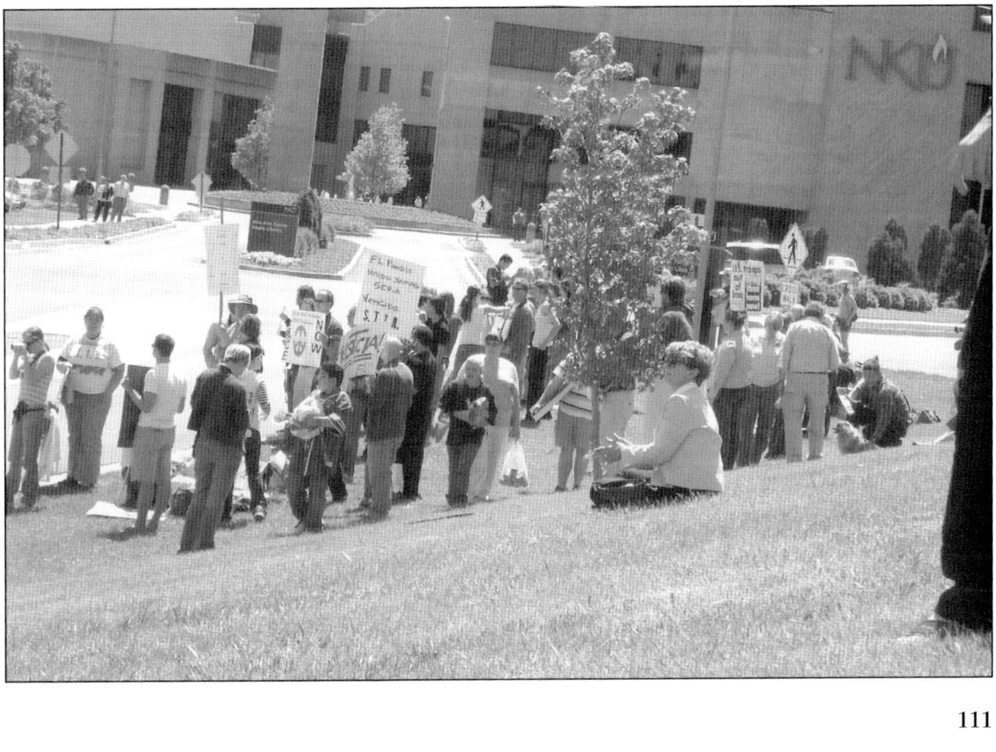

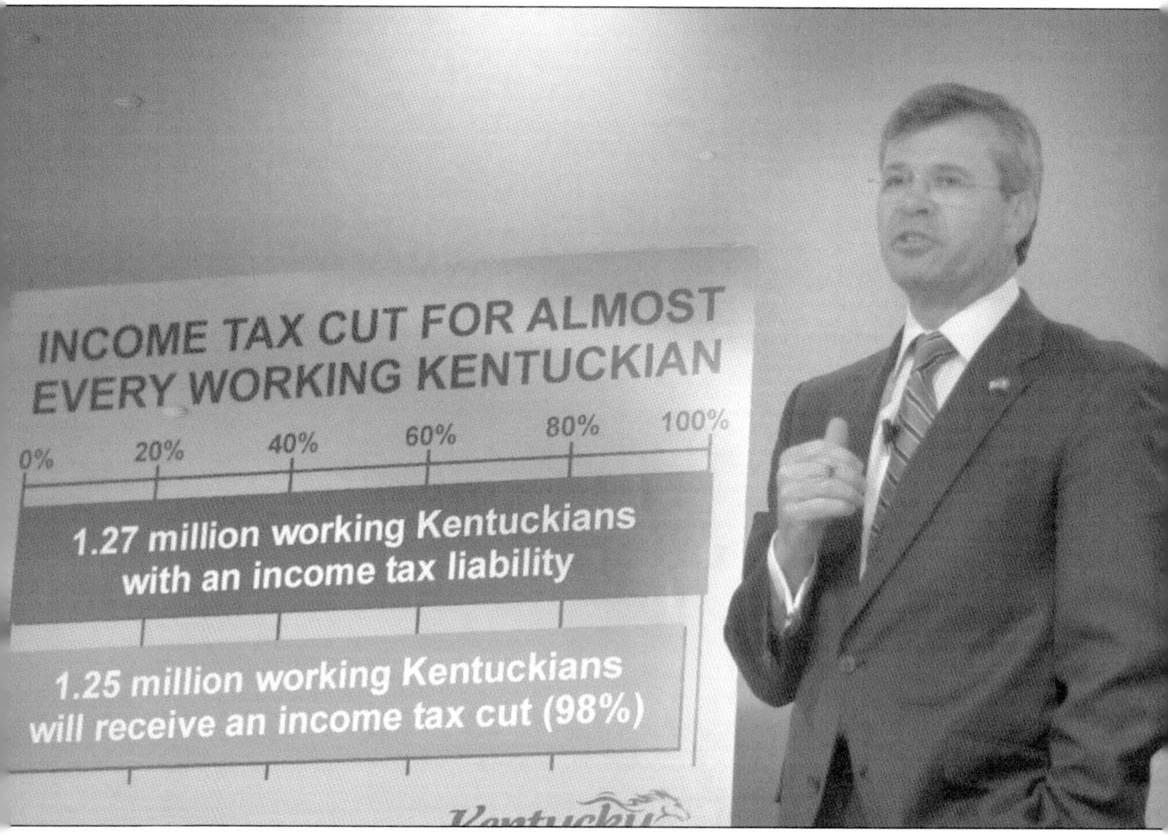

Current Kentucky governor Ernie Fletcher is a frequent visitor to the NKU campus. In addition to the number of recent groundbreaking ceremonies, Governor Fletcher often uses the university as a site for town meetings or to launch new initiatives, allowing local voters to ask questions on the proposals.

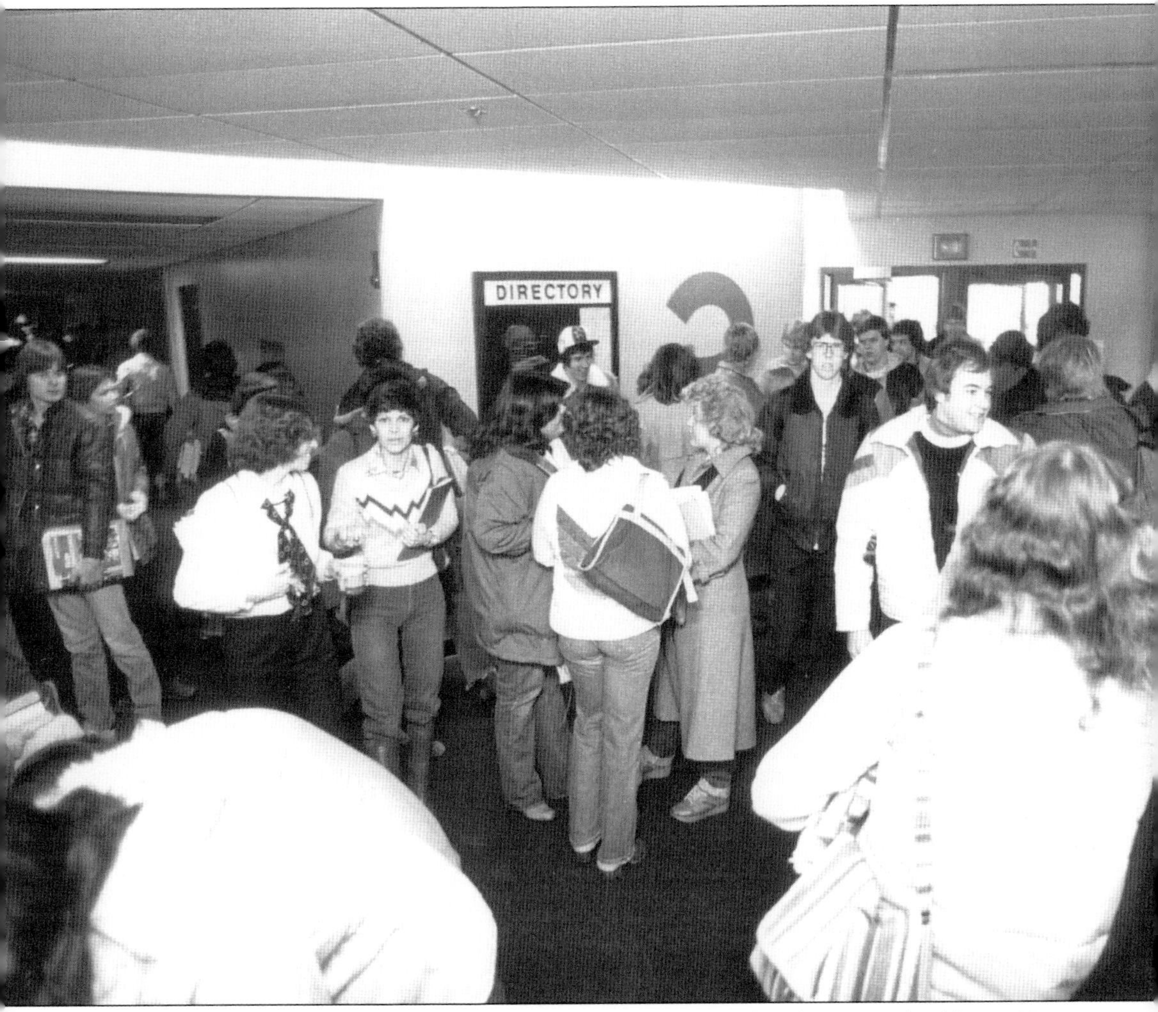

As enrollment continues to surge, space is at a premium in the classroom buildings. New admission standards were imposed recently in an effort to ensure that every student admitted to the university has the best chance to succeed. These tougher admission standards were expected to decrease enrollment as a side effect, at least in the short term. Instead enrollment slowed a bit but continued to increase each semester. The scene above is fairly typical of class change during the day in the overcrowded buildings.

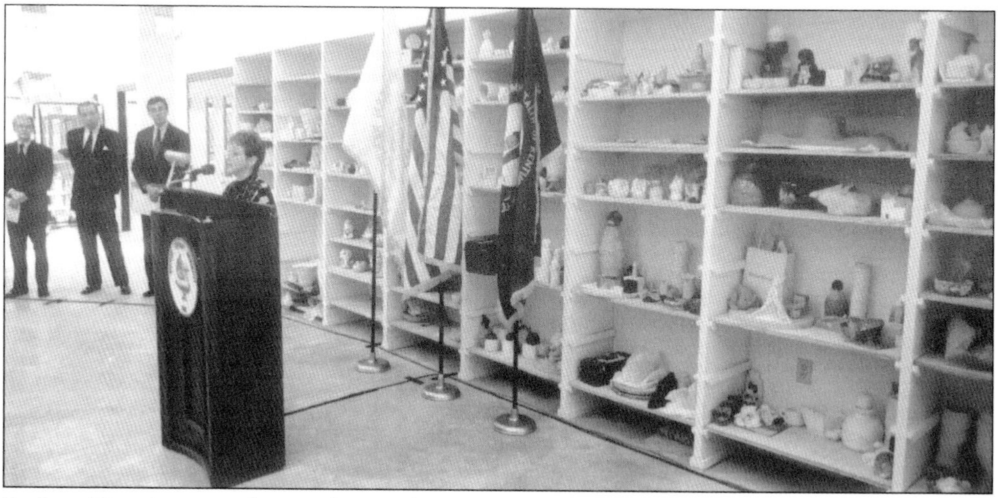

Barbara Houghton, professor of art and at that time department chair, speaks at the dedication ceremony for the new ceramics building. Opened in August 1997, the new facility features indoor and outdoor kilns as well as two large classrooms for different types of work. The facility is a far cry from the Keene Complex barn, where ceramics started out in 1972.

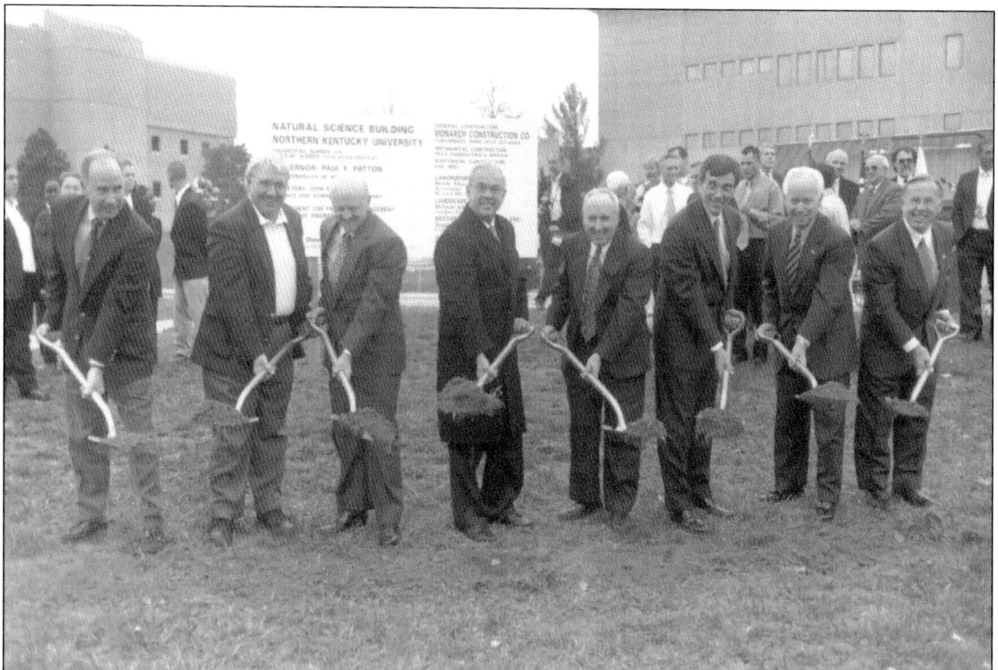

The groundbreaking for the new Dorothy Westerman Herrmann Natural Science Center in the summer of 1999 featured a number of state and local legislators as well as current university president James Votruba. The natural science center was completed in 2002, allowing the science departments to move out of their cramped and antiquated quarters in the old science building.

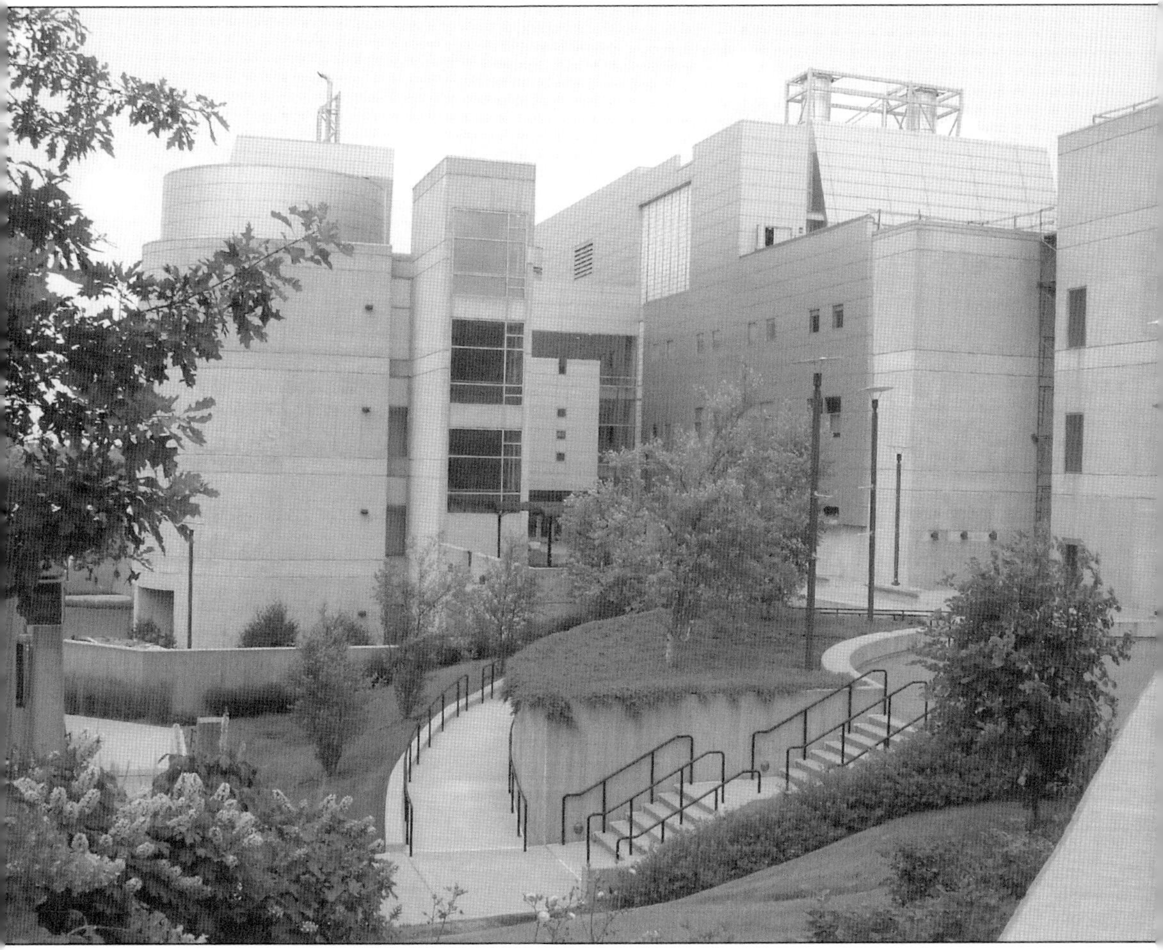

The addition of the new science center helped to ease the problem of overcrowding, as the space emptied out in the old building could be renovated to house other classes and departments. The old science building was called "Old Science" for a year in order to distinguish it from the new building. It was later renamed Founder's Hall in honor of those who persevered to build the university. The new science center opened to classes in the fall of 2002, with the official dedication on September 20. It is currently undergoing some renovation work in one corner in order to add a new state-of-the-art planetarium.

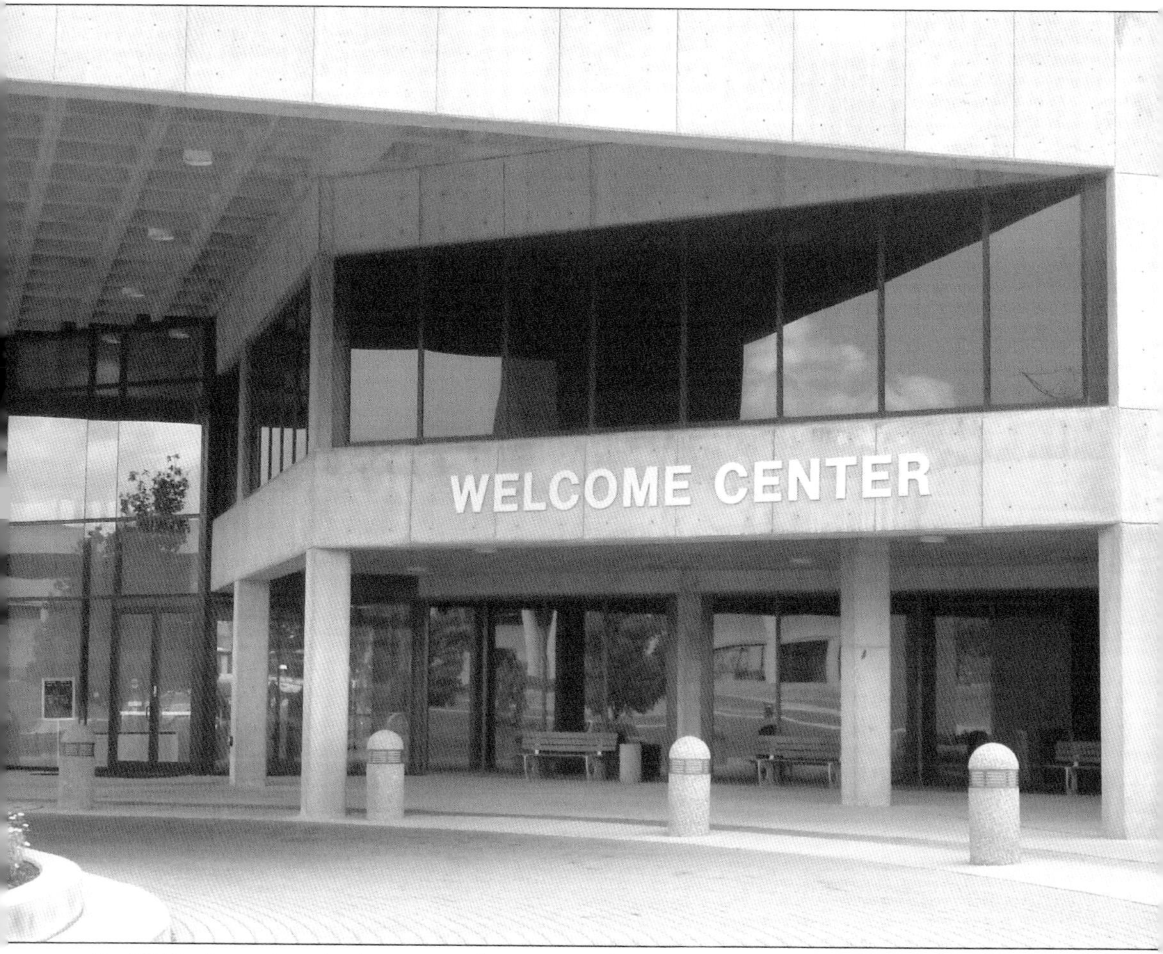

In 2002, the university began work on a much-needed Welcome Center. As the campus grows, so do the number of visitors looking for parking passes, directions, and a place to ask questions. The logical place to put such an office was at the end of the circular drive near the visitor parking area. There was just one problem: Steely Library already occupied this spot. The solution was to trim a little space out of the end of the library. Doing so also solved a problem for the library. Until the Welcome Center construction, the only public entrance to the building was off the main plaza on the library's third floor. The steps leading from the first floor–level parking up to the plaza were daunting for many library patrons. A first floor door was clearly needed. The Welcome Center gave the building a first floor entrance at last. A short corridor now takes patrons through the Welcome Center into the library.

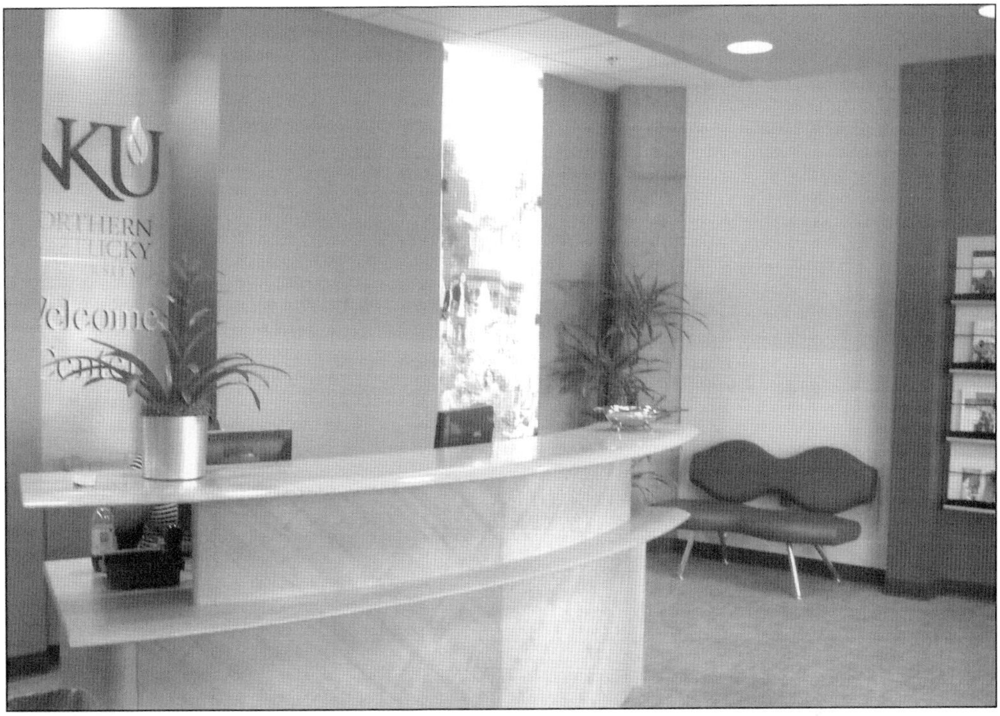

The Welcome Center provides a warm, friendly environment. The front desk is manned throughout the day by staff members who direct visitors looking for buildings or campus events. Campus tours, scheduled visits, and new-student orientation activities also run out of this office, which is operated by the Office of Admissions.

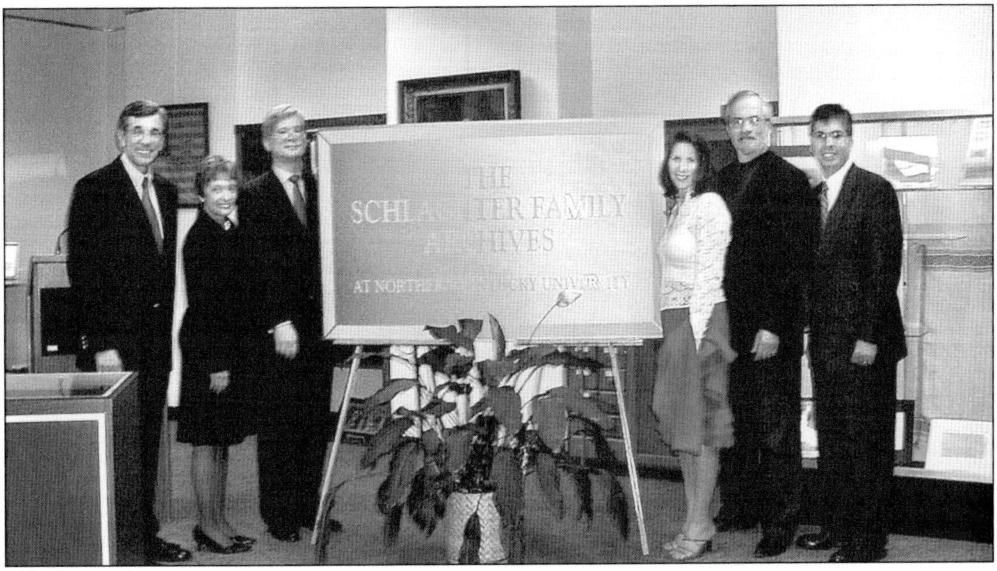

Much of the renovation work for special collections are archives was funded by Mark and Rosemary Schlachter and Oakley and Eva G. Farris. The dedication event celebrating the Schlachters' gift was held on November 6, 2004, in the special collections reading room. Pictured from left to right are Pres. James Votruba, Provost Gail Wells, Assistant Provost Arne Almquist, Rosemary Schlachter, Mark Schlachter, and development officer Andrew Wilson.

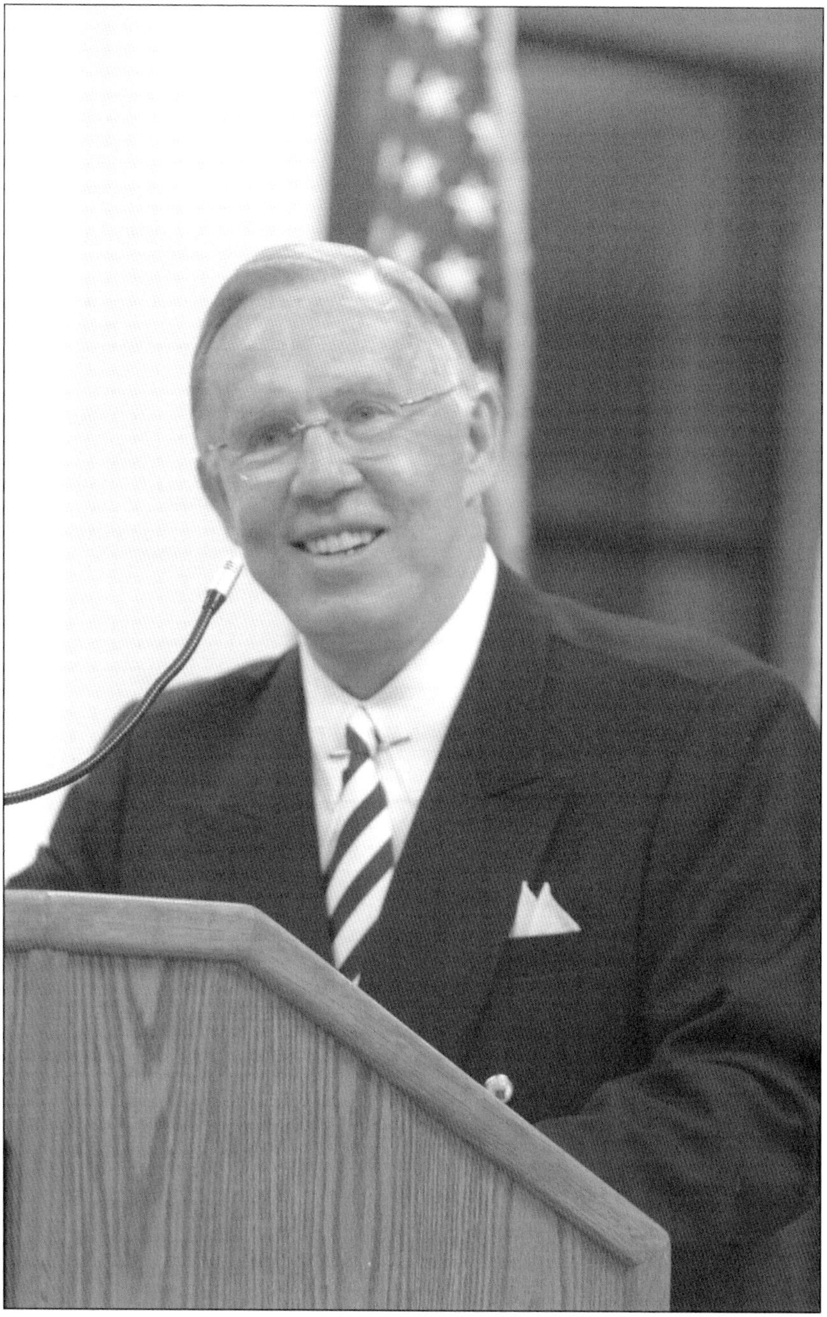

With all the new attention focused on the special collections and archives department, larger collections of material are being donated to the institution. In December 2004, retiring congressional representative Ken Lucas donated his political papers to the university. Lucas was a member of the university's board of regents in the 1980s and served the region in Congress for many years. The donation added to the growing body of political papers housed at NKU and served to draw even greater attention, resulting in new collections of military history and other materials being donated to the archives. The Ken Lucas collection may grow in the future, as Lucas has decided to come out of retirement and run for election in 2006.

In 2004, Northern Kentucky University expanded with the addition of a second branch campus. Located in Grant County, the new center is housed in a preexisting building. The move was accomplished just in time for the beginning of fall classes, with the formal dedication ceremony at right taking place on September 8. The step was a formal recognition that the Northern Kentucky region is no longer exclusively made up of the northernmost three counties of the state. The definition of the region continues to expand to enclose the next "tier" of counties to the south. With this change, NKU's regional focus also expands as it strives to fulfill its mission to bring higher education to all Northern Kentucky residents. In 2003, NKU also expanded into the realm of corporate education, opening the Metropolitan Education and Training Services, or METS, Center below. The high-tech conference center is located close to the local international airport.

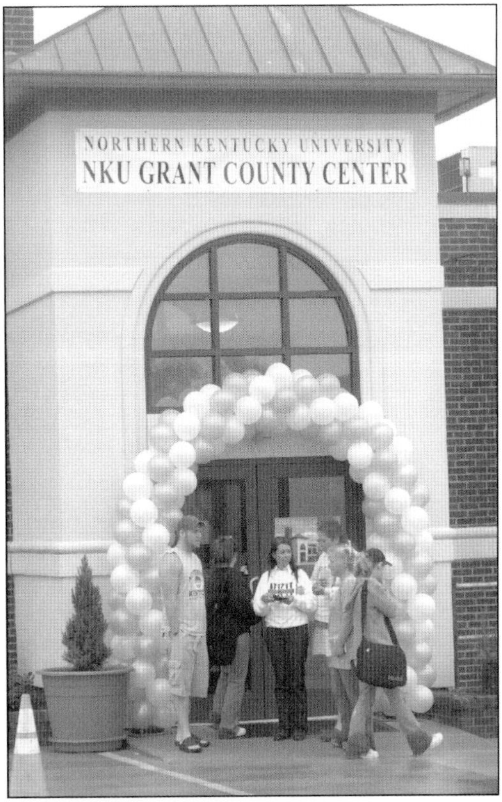

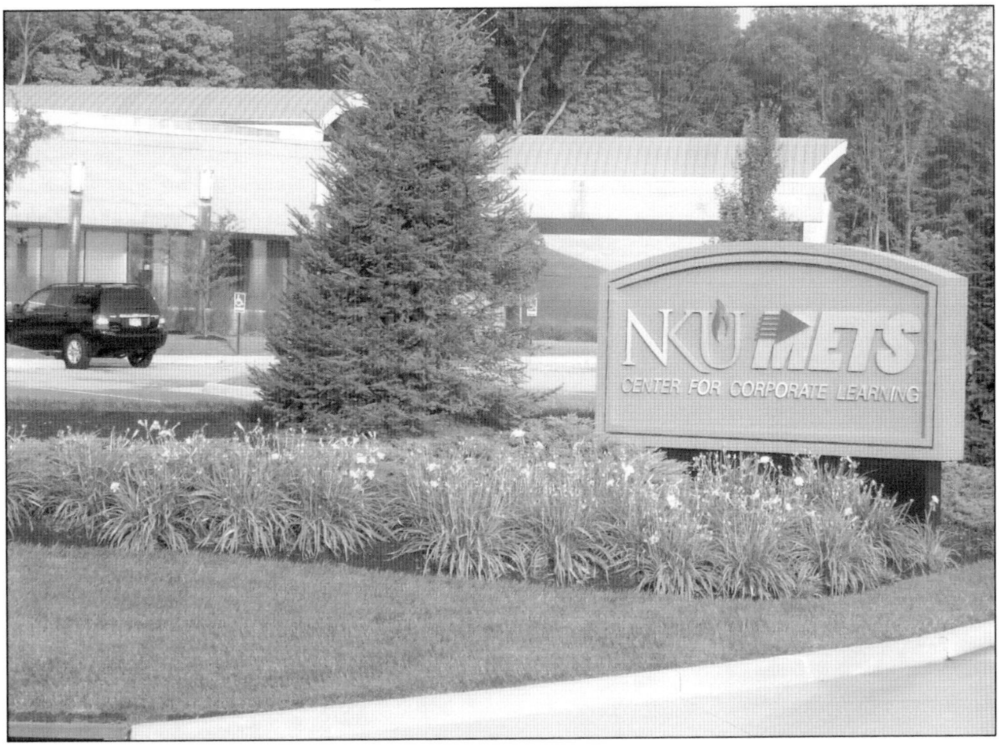

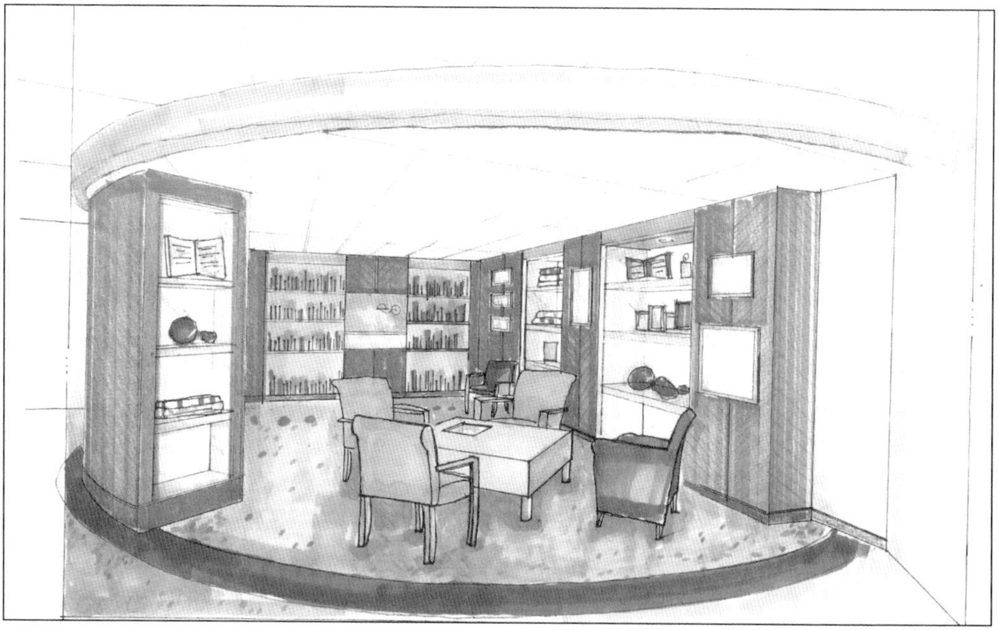

The special collections department within the Steely Library holds a wealth of documents, photographs, artifacts, and other material pertaining to the history of the Northern Kentucky region, as well as being the home of the university archives. One of the many renovation projects underway on campus is in special collections. This first phase of the project is a redesign of the research room addressing the needs of the department to care for and exhibit the cultural treasures it holds and the needs of the researchers who come to use the materials. The room will include better lighting, new exhibit space, and new furnishings. The room will reopen to the public in the fall of 2006.

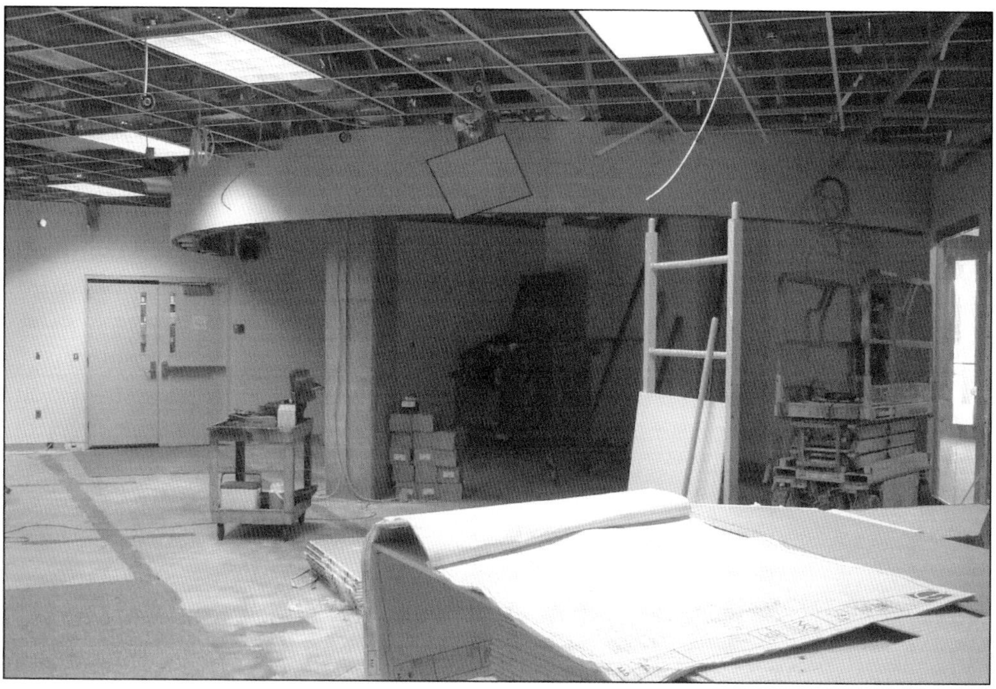

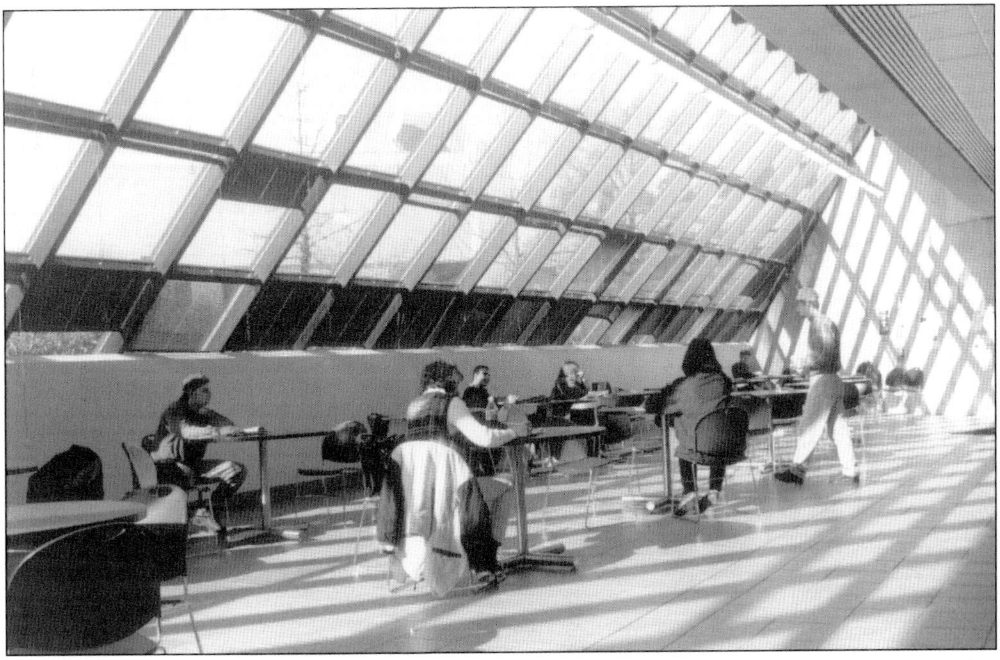

The library loggia, the front lobby and study area in Steely library, has always been a popular destination due to the extended hours it remains open for study. Originally the loggia was a rather barren place. In recent years, campus foodservice opened a Starbuck's-style coffee bar, making it a hot spot for the campus coffee drinkers. The library applied for and received several grants that allowed for the furnishings to be updated. The grant money also paid for a number of computers that are available to students even when the library is closed. The most recent additions have been chairs designed to accommodate laptops. Wi-Fi access to the campus networks has also been made available.

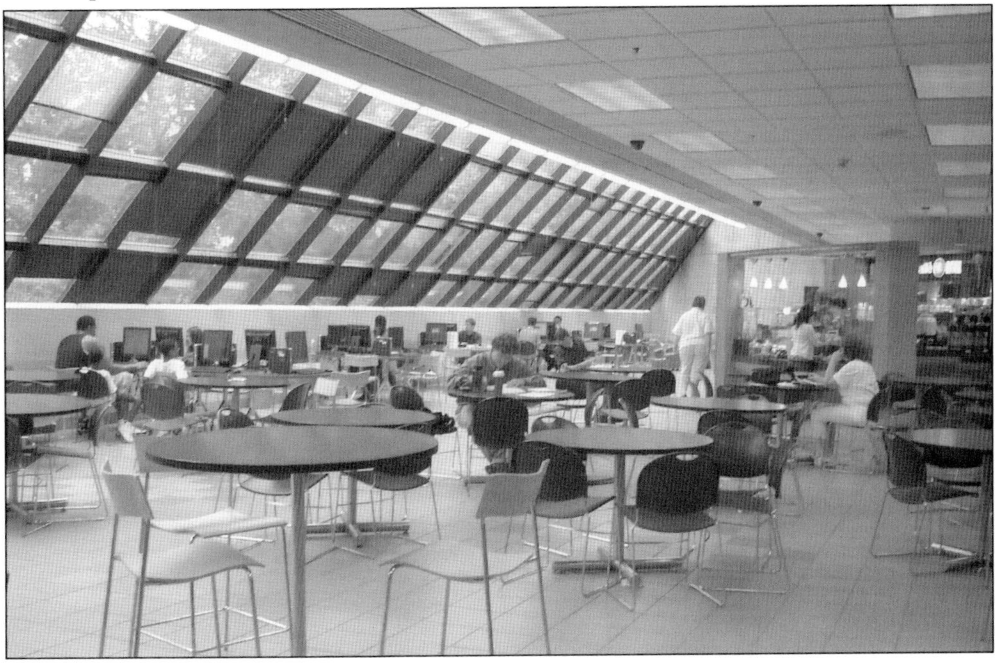

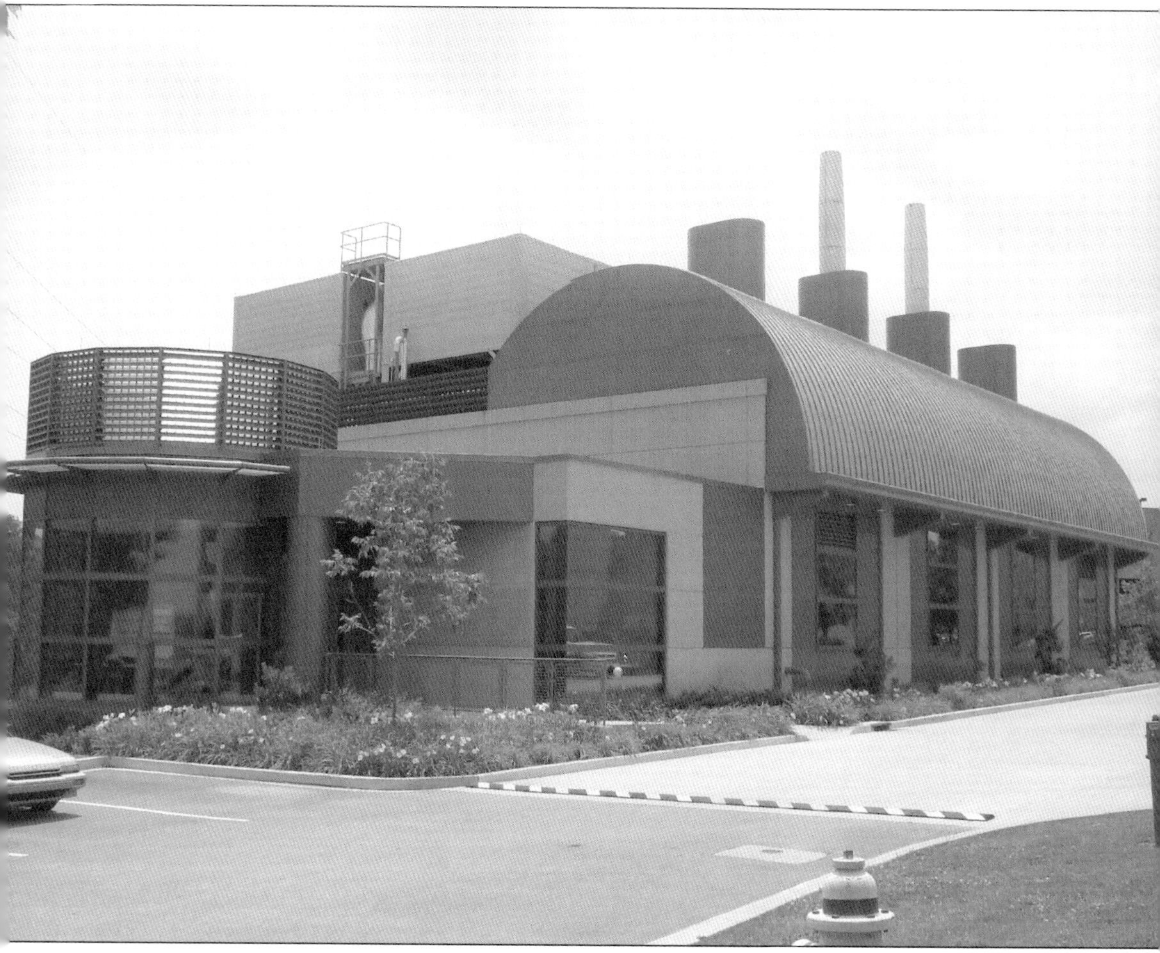

Other construction projects that have recently been completed include a new building to house physical facilities and the campus steam plant. The new location behind the Applied Science and Technology Center moves the plant away from the center of campus. The old space will be renovated for use by other departments on campus. Some of the space will probably be given to the adjoining Steely Library, while much of it will probably be used for fine arts. Current proposals include additional art gallery space and a performance area more suitable for senior recitals and other small events than the two-tier Greaves Concert Hall.

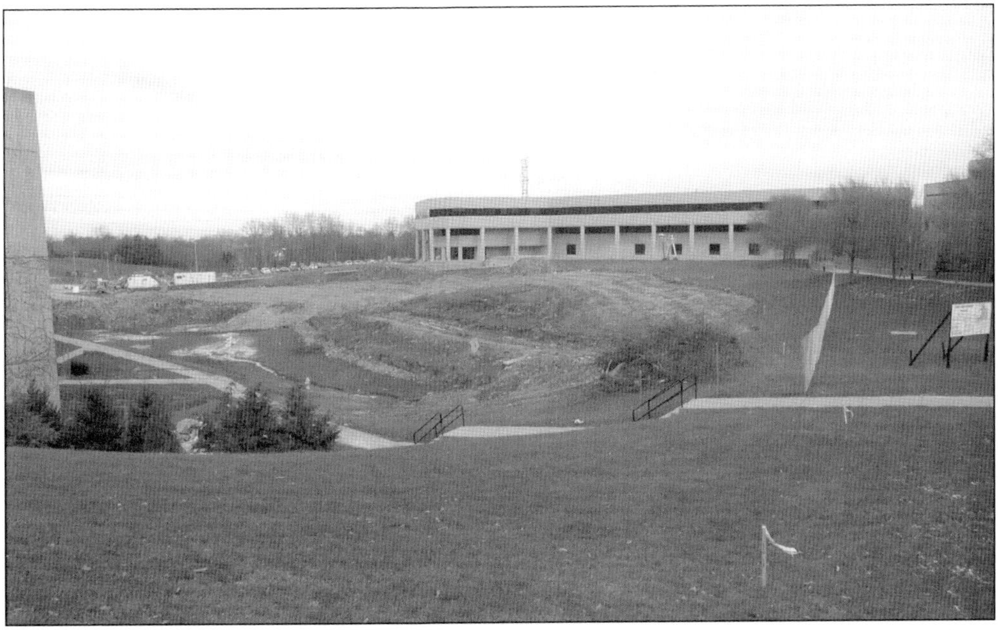

After receiving various campus beautification grants, the decision was made to do something about Lake Inferior. The lake was still in the form of the original farm pond that had predated the main campus. The wildlife that called the lake home was relocated, and the lake was drained. Construction crews labored through winter storms and spring rains to widen and divide the lake, creating two levels with a bridge across the center. The most striking feature of the new design is the waterfall under the bridge, one of two waterfalls on the new lake. With a new look, the lake needed a new name. Voting recently took place on several names that were submitted. These include "Lake Legacy," "Lake Odin," and "Norse Lake." The winning name, Loch Norse, was officially bestowed at the September 6, 2006, dedication ceremony.

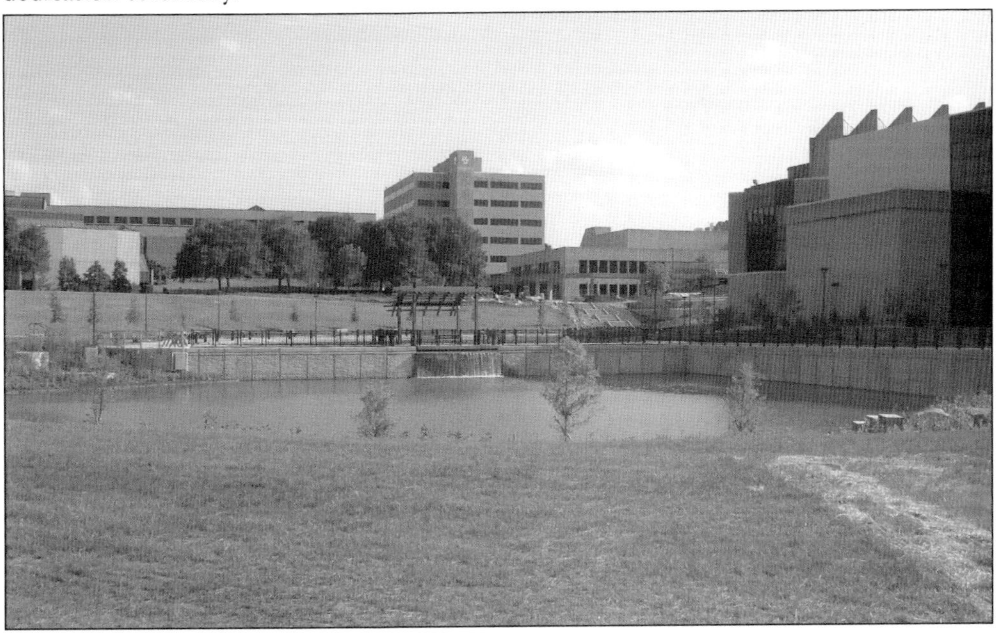

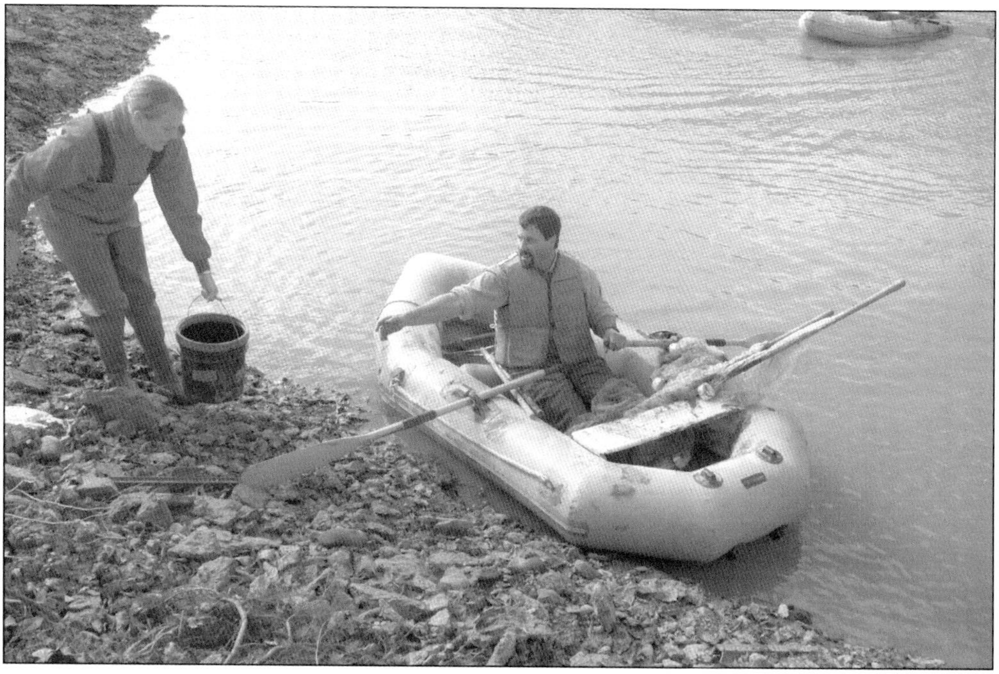

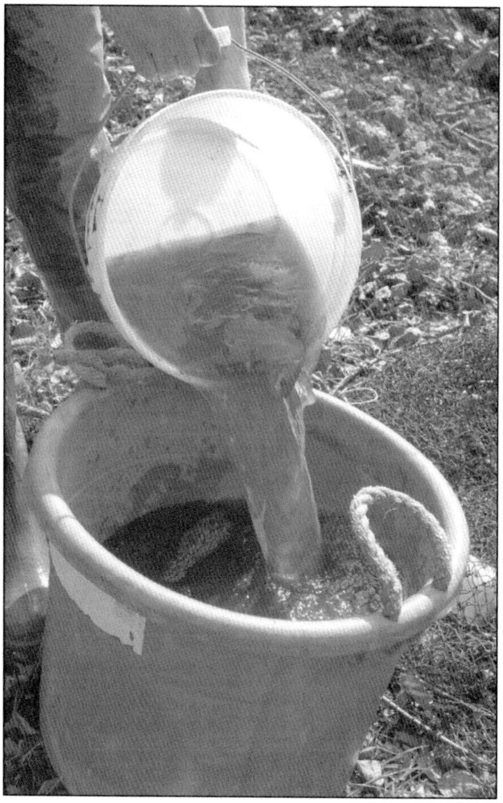

Moving the wildlife that lived in and around the lake was a time-consuming task. The ducks and geese were rounded up and taken to a local farm. The fish in the lake were another matter altogether. Teams of biology students were given the job of capturing the fish. They waited until the lake was nearly empty before setting out in rubber rafts. Above, a student in a raft hands up a bucket of lake water and fish. These buckets were emptied into larger containers, as can be seen in the photograph at left. Living in such a sheltered environment, some of the fish had grown quite large. The fish were transported to Doe Run Lake in neighboring Kenton County.

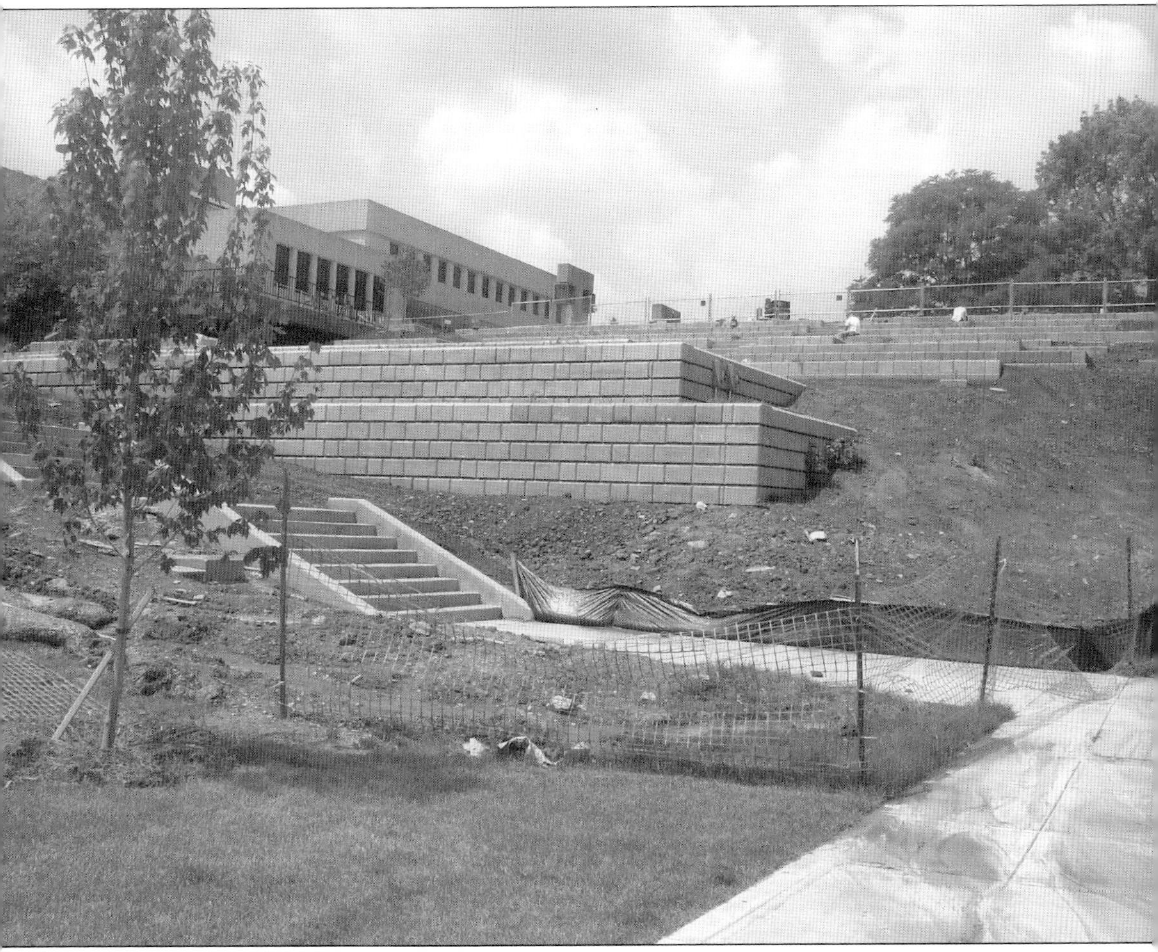

The lake dedication was on hold until the new outdoor amphitheater could be completed. The amphitheater is located between the Fine Arts Center and the University Center, where the ground slopes sharply away from the main plaza down to the shore of the lake. The construction crews have been delayed many times by weather and other problems, but progress can be seen as the structure approaches completion in this photograph.

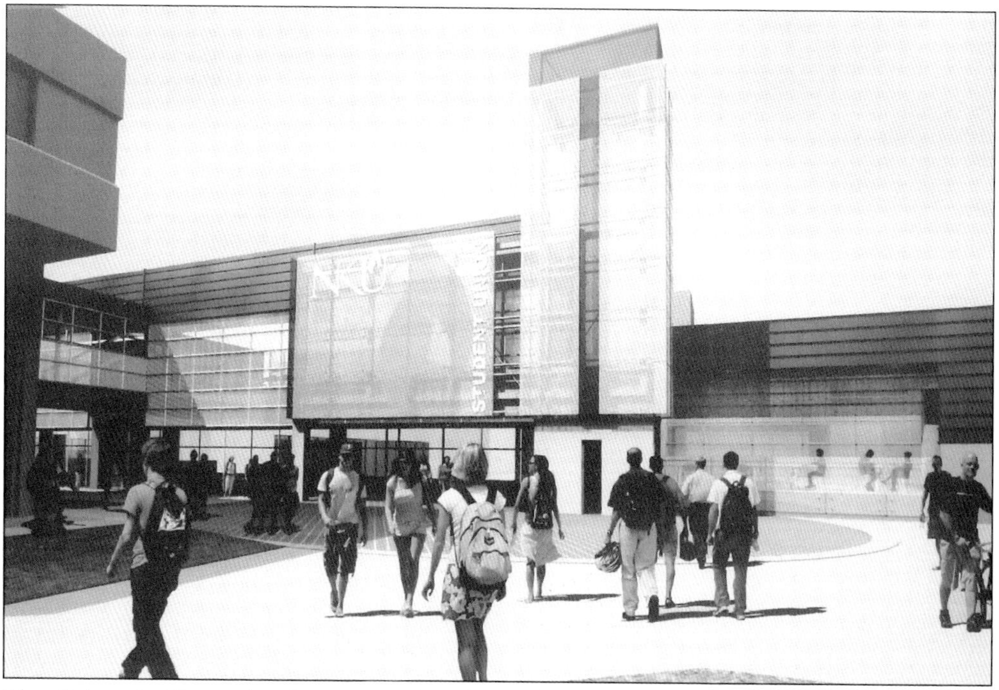

The University Center has long served as the student union for NKU's campus. It houses a food court, the campus bookstore, the television lounge, student activities offices, and the campus post office. As the university has grown, so has the need for larger, more modern facilities. On February 15, 2006, ground was broken for a new student center that would accomplish this goal. Located between Nunn Hall and the A. D. Albright Health Center, on the site of what used to be Parking Lot A, crews are hard at work preparing the site for the new construction. This location is just off the main plaza, and will keep the student union near the middle of campus.

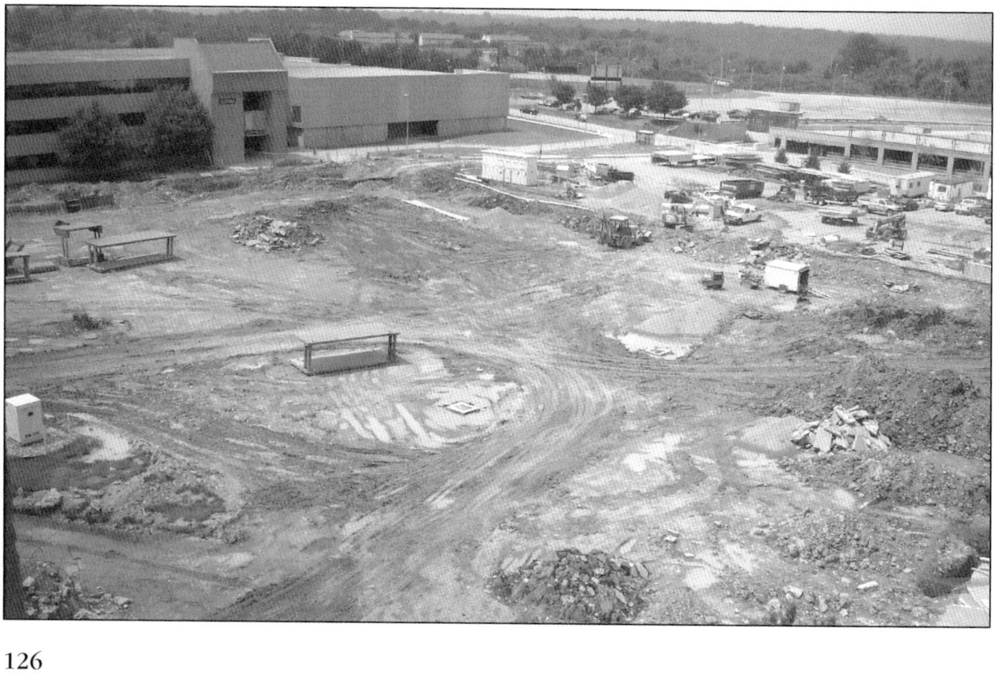

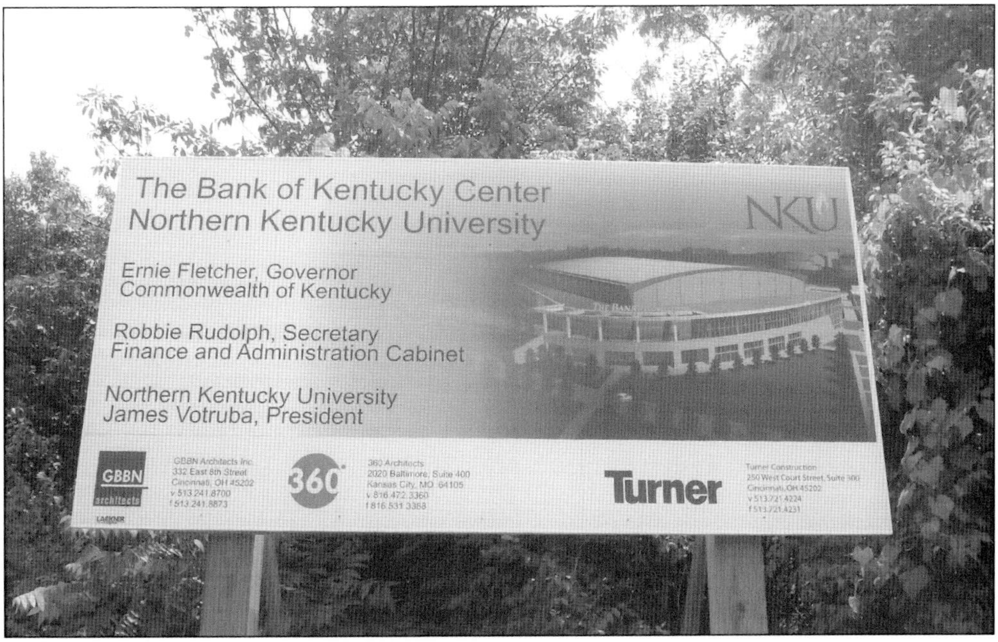

The most recent campus groundbreaking took place on May 20, 2006. The VIPs assembled to symbolically turn earth for the Bank of Kentucky Center, the new campus arena. The $6.1-million building will replace the aging and overcrowded Regents Hall as the site for the ever-popular Norse basketball games as well as campus events such as commencement. The site for the arena is a wooded hillside on Nunn Drive along the border the campus shares with the community of Highland Heights, Kentucky. A new parking garage will also be built for the facility. The garage will be located on the campus side of the arena, providing a buffer between the new building and the rest of campus. This is an important consideration as the arena is expected to host outside events such as music concerts in addition to campus functions.

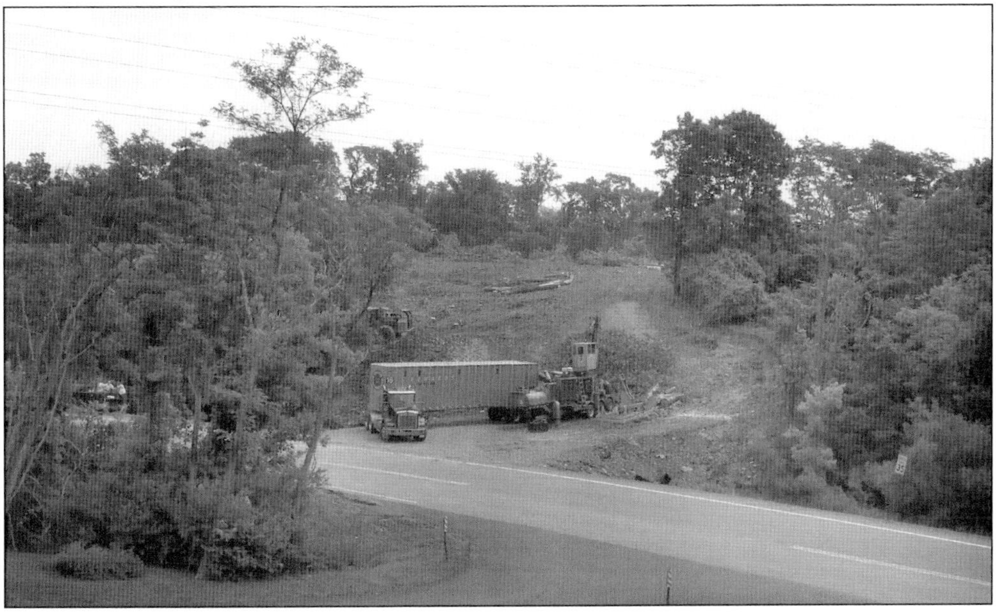

ACROSS AMERICA, PEOPLE ARE DISCOVERING SOMETHING WONDERFUL. *THEIR HERITAGE.*

Arcadia Publishing is the leading local history publisher in the United States. With more than 3,000 titles in print and hundreds of new titles released every year, Arcadia has extensive specialized experience chronicling the history of communities and celebrating America's hidden stories, bringing to life the people, places, and events from the past. To discover the history of other communities across the nation, please visit:

www.arcadiapublishing.com

Customized search tools allow you to find regional history books about the town where you grew up, the cities where your friends and family live, the town where your parents met, or even that retirement spot you've been dreaming about.

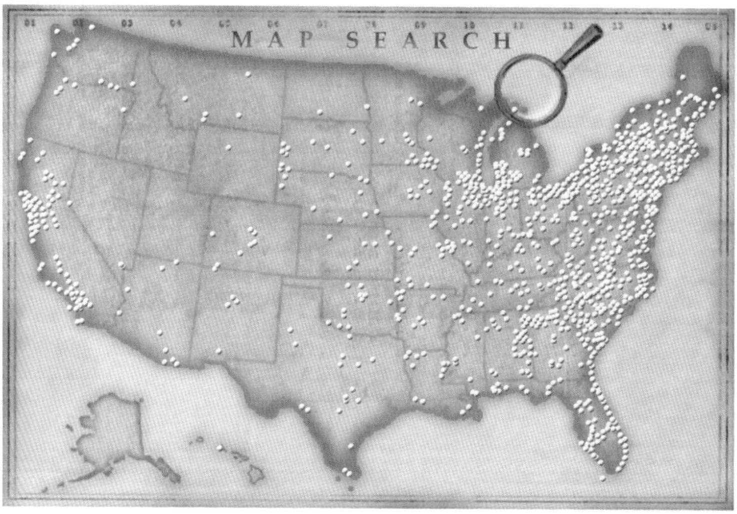